ACHIEVING EPIC BUSINESS RESULTS

RESULTS

with *STRATEGIC PROJECT MANAGEMENT*

Michael M. Bissonette

RTConfidence

ISBN: 978-1-7353999-0-4

PMI® (Project Management Institute, Inc.):
A Guide to the Project Management Body of Knowledge (PMBOK® Guide) – Fifth Edition, 2013;
A Guide to the Project Management Body of Knowledge (PMBOK® Guide) – Sixth Edition, 2017;
Practice Standard for Project Risk Management, 2009;
The Standard for Program Management – Third Edition, 2013;
Project Risk Management: A Practical Implementation Approach, by Michael M. Bissonette, 2016.
Copyright and all rights reserved. Material from these publications have been reproduced with the permission of PMI.
14 Campus Blvd.
Newtown Square, PA 19073
www.pmi.org

Front cover image: iStock by Getty Images
Credit: metamorworks

Cover design by Custom Software Solutions, Inc.

Printed by Lulu Press, Inc.
www.lulu.com

Publisher: RTConfidence, Inc.
5270 California Ave. #200
Irvine, CA 92617
www.RTConfidence.com

Table of Contents

ACKNOWLEDGEMENTS

The content of this book has developed over a long period of time. It was not conceived of or written in a vacuum or based on a single experience, thought, or idea. It was inspired by a lifetime of events and personal interactions – by over 40 years of actual practice – by requests to conduct organizational training sessions at companies where I've worked – by further requests to give talks on Project Management at PMI® (Project Management Institute) chapter meetings – by years of teaching the subject for Clarkson University at the post-graduate level – by my previous book published by PMI® Inc. – by my work as a volunteer to help individuals and Start-up Companies grow – by my work as a consultant and to help established organizations transform their business practices – by the work that my company, RTConfidence, Inc. performs to develop cost-effective Portfolio and Project Management Software Tools – by my passion to help others succeed – and by the great support and encouragement I have received from my family (especially my wife, Laura). These experiences and activities, along with a deep faith in God (and His guiding light) have led me down this path and has enabled this publication to emerge.

Some people who I want to give specific mention to for their specific support, review and help with this book's content are: Parvaneh Alavi, Thomas Cocotis, Steve Clark, Kelly Flint, Ace Lowder, Allen Lowder, David Maeschen, John Newton, and Craig Trivelpiece.

Finally, I want to dedicate this book to my wonderful parents, Martin (deceased) and Billie Jean Bissonette.

Special Recognition to *Thomas Cocotis*
(Agile Coach, PMI-ACP, A-CSM, A-CSPO, CAL I, ICP-ACC)

Mr. Cocotis provided valuable insights relative to the Agile and Scrum processes – from both practical application and scholarly standpoints. His review, contributions and editing of the content in Chapter 7 on the ***Product Development Processes*** is greatly appreciated.

PREFACE

What is the "right" way to set up and manage Projects? Is there a "single approach" that works for successfully managing ALL Projects? If there was, wouldn't we all know it by now? We would, but we do not know it because there is no such "animal". The Project Management Institute (PMI®) has endeavored to establish World-Wide Standards to help us figure this out, but even with all the credentialed individuals (e.g. Project Management Professionals, or PMP®s) in the world, organizations still struggle to consistently succeed at developing new Products, Services and Results to the satisfaction of Organizational Leaders and the market. What are we missing? I believe that to a degree, we are not strategic enough. Thus, the impetus behind the creation of this book.

It seems to be a cliché, but we all know that organizations that consistently "do more with less" win. How do we get costs down? How do we produce more (and better) business offerings in less time and effort than anyone else? And how can we do this without killing the morale of our workforce? If you (as an Organizational Leader) could figure this out, wouldn't you want to? My contention is that it is not only about knowing the Project Management processes, Tools & Techniques, and how to execute them well. It involves much more, and fortuitously (as I see it) it all starts at the top of the organization, and if initiated at the top, it is much more likely to gain traction and "stick".

I have been in the corporate world for over 4 decades now. Been in several different industries. Worked my way up the "corporate ladder". Wrote a textbook published by PMI®, and have been teaching a post-graduate course on Strategic Project Management for several years. I have learned much, and I have endeavored to pass this knowledge on to others. I also have many stories to tell, and my students tend to appreciate them. I am frequently told by past students that the stories and their underlining concepts made a positive impact on their work performance. This feedback, and my innate passion to help others succeed, has compelled me to write this book on Strategic Project Management, and to do so in first-person to better share the rationale behind a very logical and persuasive framework for organizational success. The word "**Epic**" comes from my son, who has always been quite the "gamer" – it is defined as "**extending beyond the usual or ordinary**" (Merriam-Webster, 2019). I know that the concepts espoused in this book do indeed work, for I have seen it first-hand. Thus, "**Achieving Epic Business Results with Strategic Project Management**" works, but it takes more than just the knowledge, understanding, and appropriate tools – it takes a willing "mind-set" that is permeated throughout the organization as well. This is where the "strategic" piece comes into play.

At different times in my career I considered successful Project performance to be primarily due to some single profound focus area (e.g. Risk Management, Requirements Management, the "Cost of Change", Leadership, Planning and Maintaining a Balanced Plan, etc.). I have come to recognize that it is all about the complimentary interaction of these various concepts, each of which is a chapter topic. Since these concepts do interact with each other, there is a fair amount of cross-referencing. It is the "strategic" path undertaken by the organization which effectively under-pins the individual efforts of good Program or Project Managers and Teams. This necessitates a healthy combination of individual capabilities coupled with the appropriate level of Organizational Governance. Both are therefore aptly addressed.

I have also recognized that the "technical" language associated with Project Management concepts tends to get confusing at times and can make a book like this difficult to read. Many of the nouns referred to can also be verbs (e.g. project, schedule, cost, resources, etc.), and we tend to group two or more words together into a phrase to describe specific items of interest. So, I capitalize those groupings (like how acronyms are basically called out), and sometimes use quotation marks to emphasis certain key words/phrases. This helps me communicate my thoughts better and will hopefully enable readers to comprehend the messages with greater ease. I truly believe that the concepts and suggestions are all logical and sensible, and together they can be combined to help you **Achieve Epic Business Results with Strategic Project Management.**

About the Author

Mike Bissonette has worked in several industries and in various positions throughout his career. Went from "Rocket Scientist" to Technical Lead, and eventually did what he had aspired to do – became a respected Program Manager within the Aerospace and Defense industry. He was one of the early users of Integrated Master Scheduling software – which ran on large "mainframe" computers, using "punch-card" decks that were batch-processed overnight. He was also one of the early users of Monte Carlo Modelling & Simulation for SRA (Schedule Risk Analysis). He "cut his teeth" on Earned Value Management when it was called Cost/Schedule Control System Criteria, and on Six Sigma when it was a little less formal/rigorous and referred to as Total Quality Management. He ended up becoming a successful Program/Project Manager and occasional organizational training asset. Eventually the Aerospace and Defense company that he worked for (an eventual Lockheed Martin acquisition) moved across country and he opted to enter the Consumer Electronics industry.

At Western Digital Mike become a "change agent". He arrived at a time when the company was struggling (the Hard Disk Drive industry was a "dog-eat-dog" competitive environment) and by the time he left, had run and transformed several Functional Departments (e.g. New Product Introduction, System Engineering, Program Management Office, World-Wide Quality, Product Management, and Electronics Procurement), established the iterative/incremental Hard Disk Drive Product Development Process that became the industry standard and helped enable Western Digital to become and remain an industry leader – one of only two remaining "power-houses" in that industry at the time of this publication. He was then recruited to run and transform a division of an innovative company that focused on Clean Technology and Aerospace and Defense – AeroVironment.

Mike became an Officer of AeroVironment, Inc. where he led the company into the nascent, and highly competitive Electric Vehicle

Charging industry, becoming the preferred supplier of EVSE (Electric Vehicle Supply Equipment) for several familiar companies in the Automotive industry, and championed organizational and IT Infrastructure changes to enable growth and business success.

Mike is a best-selling published Author (wrote ***Project Risk Management: A Practical Implementation Approach***, published by PMI®, Inc. ©2016), an Adjunct Professor within Clarkson University's Master of Science in Engineering Management curriculum teaching "Strategic Project Management", and a Founder of RTConfidence, Inc. – a company that develops SaaS (Software as a Service) products for Portfolio, Program and Project Management, and provides various business consulting and training services. He is an EIR (Expert in Residence) at the UC Irvine's Applied Innovation Center, where he helps Start-up Companies. And he is a VIP (Volunteer in Probation) who visits, and mentors (on behalf of the Catholic Church) young men incarcerated at detention facilities.

Mike holds a BSEE from Clarkson University, an MSEE from CSU, Long Beach, an MBA from UC Irvine, and a PfMP® (Portfolio Management Professional) certification through PMI®.

Mike has also been an active contributor to PMI's Global Standard publications: *The Guide to the Project Manager Body of Knowledge (PMBOK® Guide)* Sixth Edition (PMI Inc., ©2017), and *The Standard for Portfolio Management* Fourth Edition (PMI Inc., ©2017).

INTRODUCTION

There is no doubt that the basic "block and tackling" (or tactics) associated with Project Management are important for ensuring that Project Teams perform as well as they can. But as with most successful businesses, tactical execution is not, in and of itself, the only important part of the job – the over-arching strategy underpinning those tactics is the essential ingredient for organization-wide, consistent success. That said, what exactly is this *Strategic Project Management* that I allude to, and how does it differ from *Project Management*? And why is it so important in enabling organizations to *Achieve Epic Business Results*? This book explains.

Let us start from the top. Business leaders strive to continually improve on "what works well, and what does not" within their organizations – they realize that this typically leads to more productive and profitable outcomes. We normally want to **Achieve Epic Business Results** (i.e. performance that extends beyond the ordinary) on our most important financial metrics. Bottom-line, business leaders want their organizations to prosper, and stakeholders (including the people both within and outside the organization) all want to reap the rewards. To achieve "Epic-level" results, you must first have a good understanding of what it means to be successful – then establish and execute effective strategies and "game-plans" to make it happen. Success can be defined in many ways, but there are several indicators/measures which tend to corroborate whether a business organization is indeed successful. One measure might be performance-based objective evidence that the Vision and Mission Statements are being satisfied. Another might be how the Stock Price is performing. Some other generally accepted indicators are:

- Customer Satisfaction and Loyalty
- Recognition for Products with "Best-in-Class" Quality
- Being a Preferred Supplier
- Recognition for Best Value Offerings
- Being a Popular Investment Choice

ACHIEVING EPIC BUSINESS RESULTS

- Being Recognized as a Good Place to Work
- Recognized for Top Performing Products
- Producing the Highest Sales, Revenues and/or Margins within the industry

Whatever measurements are used to gauge success, there is usually a clear expectation that to achieve acceptable results, a solid Business Strategy and Operating Plan, coupled with solid leadership and high-output workforce performance is needed within On-Going Operations by the various Functional Groups and Projects undertaken in support of Strategic Initiatives. This Book focuses on the latter – i.e. the coordinated activities that work best for achieving "Epic-level" results on strategically important Projects conducted to elevate the organization's value proposition. And since ALL Projects should be intimately aligned to Business Strategies and Initiatives, they should ALL be appropriately managed to achieve the kind of results needed (and expected) to bolster organizational business success and improve stakeholder wealth.

A common complaint that I have heard at various companies is "Our innovation and performance are stifled by the bureaucratic procedures and requirements imposed by **management**." This may or may not be true. So, where do you draw the line between being too lax (i.e. exerting few or no controls) and too rigid/bureaucratic (i.e. exerting too much control) relative to Project Team Governance? On one extreme, employees tend to like working at their own pace and not having to deal with management interference/intervention or deadlines. On the other hand, Organizational Managers are typically expected to develop winning strategies and meet critical business commitments – and they do not usually have the latitude or luxury to avoid or ignore stakeholder expectations. I call that ideal middle ground the place where **Strategic Project Management** practices come into play. My experiences have caused me to realize that we can **Achieve Epic Business Results with Strategic Project Management.** So, let's investigate "why" and "how".

Years ago, I began teaching a post-graduate college course entitled "Strategic Project Management" – a core course for earning an MS-EM (Master of Science in Engineering Management) degree. This MS-EM curriculum is designed for full-time professionals endeavoring to advance their careers and is basically an alternative to pursuing and obtaining an MBA (Master's in Business Administration) degree. Thus, the students are not necessarily taking this course to become expert Project Managers, but rather, to become more capable and better prepared Organizational Managers and executives. Not being an academic, I created a syllabus based on what I believed to be the fundamental "strategic" concepts that managers should understand and apply to ensure Projects under their purview are well planned and executed. If so, they improve internal capabilities, strengthen competitiveness, and ultimately produce better business results. I drew upon decades of relevant experience in leading the development of a myriad of successful Products and Services within several industries, working in many different roles. I started out by endeavoring to articulate the most rational working definition of Strategic Project Management I could find. Unfortunately, I did not find a suitable definition published anywhere, so I derived one by first considering the meaning of "Strategic Management" and expanding upon that definition to define "Strategic Project Management."

Strategic Management

"The formulation and implementation of the major goals and initiatives taken by a company's top management on behalf of owners, based on consideration of resources and an assessment of the internal and external environments in which the organization competes. It provides overall direction to the enterprise and involves specifying the organization's objectives, developing policies and plans designed to achieve these objectives, and then allocating resources to implement the plans. It is not static in nature: the models often include a feedback loop to monitor execution and inform the next round of planning." (Wikipedia, 2018)

ACHIEVING EPIC BUSINESS RESULTS

I cannot argue with that definition of Strategic Management for it makes perfect sense from my experience. Inserting the word "Project", the following definition for "Strategic Project Management" emerges:

Strategic Project Management

The formation and implementation of over-arching Project Management guidelines and initiatives taken by an organization's management on behalf of Project Stakeholders, based on resources and an assessment of tools, techniques and competencies considered "Best Practices" for Projects being implemented to meet Organizational Strategic Goals and Objectives. It provides overall direction to the enterprise and involves specifying the organization's Project Management objectives, developing policies and plans designed to achieve these objectives, and then allocating resources to implement the plans. It is often not static in nature, for it includes a feedback loop to monitor execution, develop and enact systemic change and inform subsequent Projects.

I believe that the above definition is "spot on". Fundamentally, "**Strategic** Project Management" is not "**Advanced** Project Management", but something more over-arching and expansive – more than how to simply manage a Project better, but how to successfully manage all Projects enterprise-wide, consistently with confidence and with results that meet or exceed stakeholder expectations. Doing so in an optimal way necessitates recognition of "management's" role in the process, as well as understanding of the tools, techniques, and competencies necessary to optimize Project Team performance capabilities. Couple this technical understanding with the general objective/goal to get the most production out of the organization's resources (i.e. continually "do more with less"), in the most positive way relative to employee satisfaction and development, and you have an incredibly powerful "formula-for-success". From an experiential standpoint, I know this works. Many of my past students have taken it upon themselves to champion this mindset within their organizations, to the bests of their abilities. This has led me to the realization that I should introduce others to the over-arching benefits of Strategic Project Management concepts and the underlying principles which enable organizations to **Achieve Epic Business Results**. Thus, the genesis of this book.

My objective is to provide readers with sensible insights into proven processes that work and do so with anecdotal examples to drive the key points home. An added advantage to this Strategic Project Management approach is that when practiced in a cohesive way, everybody (Executives, Functional/Organizational Managers, Project Managers, and Team Members) all have their needs met – which is hard to criticize.

As one might infer from this book's chapter titles, over the years I have concluded that flawless, productive Project Management is all about various "key concepts" – as listed, per chapter. Interestingly, I have expanded this conclusion to recognize that true <u>Strategic</u> Project Management is essentially all about the symbiotic interaction of these various key concepts. Thus, the content of this book is fundamentally high level, but each chapter is written to convey a stand-alone logical concept or principle that can be readily digested and implemented. Readers should be able to see the inter-relationships between these concepts – and if not all of them, at least some. Further, experienced Organizational Managers should be able to "connect the dots" and see the holistic benefits that the aggregate can produce – in particular, from an organizational performance stand-point, to ensure the type of results needed to achieve or exceed Organizational Strategic Business Goals and Objectives.

This text does not only contain descriptions of key concepts, but also examples to effectively articulate their benefits – all drawn from many years of practical experiences and revelations I have arrived at from an innate determination to continually learn from mistakes and improve. I am passionate about this subject, in part because the conclusions are logical (i.e. not based on esoteric "silver bullet" methodologies), and I have seen and experienced the benefits that can result from the practical application of these important principles.

ACHIEVING EPIC BUSINESS RESULTS

Although the chapters are placed in an order that seems most appropriate (and logical) for the flow of information, they are meant (as mentioned earlier) to be stand-alone as well – so feel free to skip around. My ultimate hope is that Organizational Leaders and managers who read this book (especially those who endeavor to make positive changes within their enterprises) may see the benefit of (and implement) changes which align with this philosophy. Even if the reading of this book leads to only one small positive change to your organization's performance, I will consider this publication a major success. That said, I firmly believe that organizations who follow this holistic approach in its entirety will prosper the most, for these concepts do inter-relate and support each other, and like a well-oiled machine, when all parts are running smoothly the output is maximized – and that enables us to achieve those Epic Business Results we are all seeking.

I also provide 5 Questions at the end of each chapter for your consideration. They enable you to evaluate and keep tabs on how well you believe your organization embraces the key Strategic Project Management concepts conveyed in that chapter. Obviously, this is a somewhat imprecise assessment, and resulting scores do not mean a lot in-and-of themselves. The idea here is to provide a general assessment tool that can be used to baseline your operations, and to periodically reassess – as a way of measuring your organization's progress in practicing **Strategic Project Management**.

Best of fortunes to you all! I am confident that Strategic Project Management works and encourage you to consider these underlying ideas. At a high level, Achieving Epic Business Results on all Projects undertaken should: maximize overall business performance; provide growth; and ensure the type of success epitomized by the success factors noted at the beginning of this introductory chapter.

CHAPTER 1

IT'S *MANAGING*

REQUIREMENTS

Requirements Management is one of the most strategic of Project Management activities, and it is the higher levels of management within organizations who are primarily responsible for making these decisions, not necessarily the Project Managers. Ideally, every activity conducted within an organization (i.e. every Project and On-Going Operation) should tie directly to (and satisfy) one or more of the organization's Strategic Goals and Objectives. Projects are considered temporary endeavors of any kind, and their completion culminates in Products, Services or Results which either bolster business directly, or enable On-Going Operations to perform more efficiently – this ultimately provides greater overall value to the organization's stakeholders and customer base. Thus, Projects should be well aligned with Organizational Initiatives established to meet its Goals and Objectives. And since Market Dynamics and Organizational Capabilities tend to change over time, managing "requirements changes" over time is an on-going iterative activity which should expediently ripple down to all other work performed in the organization. That rippling affect is facilitated by what I call the "connective tissue" and refer to as Portfolio

ACHIEVING EPIC BUSINESS RESULTS

Management. To provide context, please refer to Figure 1, which depicts various generic organizational activities and their inter-relationships. The larger lighter shaded ovals represent major organizational activities, and the smaller darker ovals denote the interactions between the activities they overlap. The large rounded-rectangular-shaped area represents the over-arching organizational On-Going Operations which both benefit from, and support, the other activities – and provide the organization's value propositions.

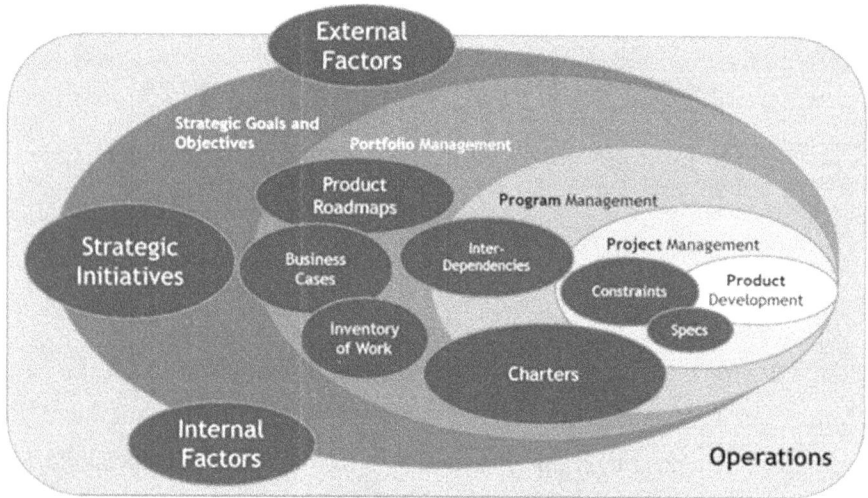

Figure 1. Organizational Requirements and Change Activity Interactions

PORTFOLIO MANAGEMENT MAKES THE CONNECTION

The main message inferred from Figure 1 is that, from an organizational stand-point (assuming a sizeable enterprise), the strategically important requirements are typically filtered down through the organization via some sort of "middle-management conduit" – referred to here as Portfolio Management. Whether the organization calls this "Portfolio" Management or something else (e.g. Business Unit Management, Division or Segment or Group Management, etc.) it exists in part to ensure alignment of all Project activities to Organizational Goals and Objectives. Portfolio Management also enables the organization to manage near- and long-term priorities at the highest levels, while managing the separate initiatives in smaller, more manageable groupings. Thus, Portfolios are commonly identified as separate stand-alone elements of the overall Organizational Structure. This decomposition of work facilitates separate business and financial goal-setting and enables objective performance visibility and management accountability – a common practice in large organizations. Portfolio Management also provides more detailed control over resource capabilities (i.e. specific technical abilities), capacity (i.e. amount of each technical ability) and their time-phased allocation.

Portfolio Governance and Unique Best Practices

Have you ever worked in an organization where a strong-willed influential manager insisted upon doing everything the same way whether it was best to do so or not – for it is what worked in the past for that individual, thus it must be the only right way to get everything done? I have, and it can be quite frustrating, especially if you are passionate about performing the best you can, and know that there is a better, more effective and/or efficient methodology to use.

> I remember when CAD (Computer Aided Design) first surfaced. Almost all the more experienced Mechanical Design Engineers still insisted that it was better to use the drafting board. Many would never change. Eventually, over time, everybody got on board the CAD train. It was clearly more efficient, and even though you would hear an occasional scream from an engineer who just lost the last 4 hours of work, once those bugs and issues were resolved there were no more excuses to fall back on to avoid the inevitable.

> More to the point of Strategic Project Management, I received a huge personal jolt when I made a job/industry change from working in Aerospace and Defense (my entire early career) to Consumer Electronics. The differences were "mind-blowing" to me, and it made me realize why some very capable Aerospace and Defense cohorts of mine struggled so much when they switched industries. A key part of my new job was to establish a better, more appropriate Product Development Process, for the company had been struggling to

compete and knew that they had to either get better or would not survive. Fortunately, I elected to first immerse myself into a couple Projects to understand why we did what we did. Bottom-line, the Consumer Electronics industry requirements necessitated a faster-paced and inherently riskier Product Development Process versus that of the Aerospace and Defense industry. Consumer Electronics focused on "time-to-market", not on meeting deterministic contract commitment dates, as in Aerospace and Defense. More on these specific processes in Chapter 7 (Product Development Process). Suffice it to say, after about two years of immersion I figured things out and established a Product Development Process that eventually became the industry standard – placing the company I worked for in a "market leadership" position. And, yes, the process did not look anything like that which I was accustomed to when in the Aerospace and Defense industry – but it turned out to be a "best practice" within that Consumer Electronics segment. More on "Best Practices" in Chapter 8.

The above experience taught me plenty. Specifically, it afforded me a better understanding of the world of Strategic Project Management – in particular, both the common "threads" associated with Project Management in any industry, and those activities which are unique to the market, industry and/or organization. These differences are essentially dictated by the Project Profile (also referred to in Chapter 8), internal and external expectations (i.e. requirements), and organizational capabilities and preferences. This experience also gave me a better appreciation for Organizational Governance – specifically, the inherent value of Standardized Procedures, applicable Tools & Techniques, and Project Management competencies relative to managing complex/risky Projects in different markets, industries and/or organizations.

I do not consider myself a bureaucrat, for I abhor wasting time, energy, and money. But instead, I understand the value of a certain level of systemic process control to ensure consistency and adherence to established "Best Practices" (i.e. those methods or techniques that have consistently shown results superior to those achieved with other means and are used as benchmarks – Wikipedia). So, whether popular or not, I believe that there is a certain amount of "process" that makes sense (and enables growth), and thus, the need for some level of Portfolio Governance to ensure results that I consider to be in the "Epic" realm.

Holistic Organizational Change Management is Vital

Nobody working on a Project welcomes seemingly random requirements changes "mid-stream". A typical reaction from those impacted is: "Why is **management** jerking us around? Can't they make up their minds?" This is usually caused by a communication issue of some sort. The fact of the matter is, if the organization has a good Strategic Planning process, changes to Projects and On-Going Operations are inevitable and should be quickly acted upon (see Chapter 5: Cost of Change). If managed and communicated well, the organization clearly benefits.

Most large companies establish Annual Operating Plans (for the impending or current fiscal year) based on long- and short-term Strategic Planning Imperatives. The outcomes are typically high-level initiatives derived in support of Strategic Goals and Objectives. Furthermore, many companies (especially Public Companies) re-evaluate their Annual Operating Plans and Strategic Objectives on a quarterly basis (a Public Company shareholder expectation), if not monthly. All initiatives should be supported by the "inventory of work" (i.e. the entirety of Projects and On-Going Operations/Activities). The entire "strategic algorithmic solution" is normally iterated with consideration of several potential options. It is typically financially-based and is influenced by the changing status of both internal and external influencing factors. Figure 2 depicts this general process flow, leaving out all the iterative cycles that usually take place. Typically, the Portfolio Manager and his or her key personnel (especially those whose activities are potentially impacted by strategic changes in direction) will provide data and alternative solutions to factor into the analysis.

ACHIEVING EPIC BUSINESS RESULTS

Internal Factors
- Organizational Performance & Risk Tolerance
- Technological Advancements
- Strengths & Weaknesses
- Resource Capabilities & Capacity
- Organizational Assets

External Factors
- Market Dynamics
- Competitive Landscape
- Regulatory Environment
- Environmental Conditions
- Social-Political Concerns

Organizational Strategic Goals and Objectives
(Changes to Accommodate Evolution of Internal & External Factors to Enhance/Maximize Business Results)

Portfolio Definition and Alignment
(Changes to Continually Align Strategy, Initiatives, and Business Case and Charter with Organization Goals and Objectives)

Program Business Case and Charter Adjustments
(Changes to Enable More Efficient Planning and Execution of Prioritized Interdependent Work Items)

Project Business Case and Charter Adjustments
(Changes to Address Issues to Project Constraints which Necessitate the re-Balancing of: Scope, Cost, Schedule, Quality, Resources and Risks)

Figure 2. Generic Strategic Planning and Portfolio Management Process Flow

Given the nature and sensitivity of organizational strategies, there is usually a limit to what is communicated to the "employees at large". Strategic communications are typically restricted based on a "need-to-know". And as soon as changes to the plan are approved, it behooves the Organizational Managers to implement those changes expediently (see Chapter 5: Cost of Change). Unfortunately, sometimes the underlying rationale is not totally divulged to the entire employee population due to competitive sensitivities – this, in turn, leads to the type of questions noted at the beginning of this section.

Holistic Risk Management Makes a Big Difference

Project Risk Management is generally understood as a "good practice" but based on my experience some of the most beneficial Tools & Techniques are not well understood nor put into practice by all organizations. If they were, more organizations would be religiously using Modelling & Simulation techniques as a standard tool in their Project Management toolbox for assessing overall Project Cost and/or Schedule Risk. Please let me explain why I assert this.

I am occasionally requested to speak at local PMI® (Project Management Institute) chapter meetings. Most attendees are PMP®s (Project Management Professionals), and most are <u>practicing</u> PMP®s. Their certification attests to the fact that they know the processes espoused by the PMBOK® (Project Management Body of Knowledge) Guide, the global standard studied intently to pass the PMP® exam. And this knowledge includes a good understanding of Project Risk Management Tools & Techniques. I make it a point at the beginning of my presentations to always ask people in attendance to raise their hand if they use "Modelling & Simulation" techniques to manage overall Project Risks (the other alternative is the use of "Expert Judgement" which is much more subjective). I have yet to see a single hand go up after asking that question. I mention this, not to downplay the importance of the PMP® certification at all, but to highlight the data behind my assertion. I have nothing but respect for PMI®, and admiration for all those who are credentialed. Thus, assuming my data sample is representative of most the total population, it is safe to assume that most organizations rely on Expert Judgement when assessing overall Project Risk, and even though this methodology is categorized as a "quantitative" approach, it is a very "subjective quantitative" approach and I whole-heartedly believe that many organizations are generally "missing the boat" regarding the power and appropriateness of Modelling & Simulation approaches. I am a huge advocate of using SRA (Schedule Risk Analysis) tools on schedule-sensitive or TTM (Time-to-Market) driven Product Development Projects. More on this in Chapter 4 (Managing Risks).

Overall Project Risk Management aside, there are several other areas where Risk Management practices come into play relative to Strategic Project Management. Figure 3 is taken from my book on ***Project Risk Management: A Practical Implementation Approach*** and identifies these other areas that I am alluding to as concentric over-lapping ovals, underpinned by Portfolio Project Risk Management. The central process is the classical Project Risk Management Basics which includes the overall Project Risk Management process discussed above. Project Risk Management Basics are extensively covered in the eleventh chapter of the PMBOK® Guide, my book *Project Risk Management: A Practical Implementation Approach*, and Chapter 4 of this book (Managing Risks). We focus on the Portfolio piece in this chapter. Project Management Tools & Techniques are addressed in Chapter 8. Project Management Competencies are highlighted in Chapter 10. Stakeholder Risk Tolerances are addressed in the combination of Chapter 2 (Managing Expectations), Chapter 4 (Managing Risks), and Chapter 6 (Maintaining a Balanced Plan). Organizational Assets are discussed throughout this book. And the topic of Continuous Improvements is covered in Chapter 9 (Lessons Learned).

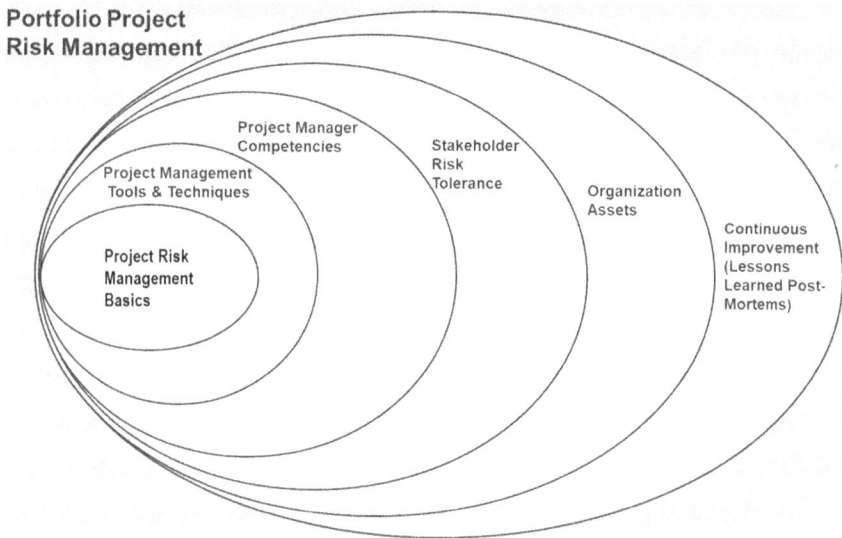

Portfolio Project Risk Management

Project Manager Competencies

Stakeholder Risk Tolerance

Project Management Tools & Techniques

Organization Assets

Continuous Improvement (Lessons Learned Post-Mortems)

Project Risk Management Basics

Figure 3. The Holistic Project Risk Management Big Picture. Project Risk Management (PMI, 2016, p. 4)

It should therefore be evident that Holistic Project Risk Management permeates through, and links with, all key topics associated with Strategic Project Management.

Up-to-date Business Cases Provide Change Justification

We close this section on Portfolio Management with a discussion about the key driving forces behind all organizational Projects – i.e. their corresponding Business Cases. A Project Business Case is a subset of the overall Portfolio Business Case which feeds into the organization's over-arching Business Strategy and Operating Plans. Thus, the Project Business Case (which serves as the guiding light behind the Project Charter) is one of the final pieces of "connective tissue" within Portfolio Management – that piece which justifies the Projects' existence. I believe that it is safe to say that most Projects are initiated with a justifiable Business Case regardless of how formal the process of establishing, documenting, and communicating the Business Case is.

Strategic Project Management calls for the continual updating of (or confirmation that there are no changes to) Business Case specifics. This would include Project cancellation when appropriate as well. The objective is to continually align the Projects with Organizational Strategic Goals and Objectives and change them when necessary to accommodate strategic Portfolio changes (e.g. adjustments to Product Roadmaps and/or Strategic Initiatives). Below is an example of the type of information that might be contained in a Project Business Case.

- Connection to Organizational Strategies, Goals & Objectives
    - Statement of Need (Business Problem or Opportunity)

- Market
    - Business Benefit (e.g. Volumes, Revenues)
    - Market Assessment (Total, Target, Addressable)
    - Product Expectations (Applications)
    - Competitive Assessment
    - Financial Model Assumptions
    - Challenges / Risks

- Project Requirements – Success Factors
    - Key Assumptions
    - Timing

- o Deliverables
- o Costs which Satisfy Business Model
- o Scalability

- Product Requirements
  - o Key Technical Attributes
  - o Product Versatility and Variants
  - o Quality
  - o Risks

The importance (i.e. benefits) of synchronizing Project Business Case changes to align with Strategic Goals and Objectives, as they are adjusted, is further elaborated upon in Chapter 5 (Cost of Change).

PROJECT INITIATION AND THE PROJECT CHARTER

Once a Project Business Case justification is approved (or when it is close to being approved) the job of organizing the top-level Project Requirements is initiated. This essentially entails turning the Business Case requirements into a Project Charter, but without the specific business and market-related financial information. Again, as in any of the general concepts espoused throughout this book, some people may say "We do not do that!", yet the fact remains that somehow Project Requirements are accumulated and communicated to give guidance/direction to those responsible for Project planning. Whether referred to as a "Project Charter" or not, is not of concern here. Providing this direction in writing is typically the safest, most communicative approach – a "good practice".

The following is a listing of items which might be contained in a Project Charter:

- Project Name
- Sponsor Name and Information
- Project Manager Information
- Key Team Members (e.g. Functional Leads, SMEs)
- Key Support Staff (e.g. Financial Analyst, Contracts Admin, etc.)

- Summary of the Business Opportunity (from Business Case)
- Statement of Work Narrative (high level)
- Customer Definition
- Key Performance & Product Acceptance Criteria
- Prioritized Project Objectives (i.e. Cost, Schedule, Quality, Scope)
- Project Funding and Budget
- Project Start Date, Duration and Scheduled Deliverables
- Major Project Milestones
- Critical Internal Resources (e.g. People, Facilities, Software, etc.)
- Critical External Resources (e.g. Sub-contractors, Suppliers, etc.)
- Key Assumptions (i.e. Items which take away Project Risks)
- Key Management Guidelines and Expectations
- Imposed Constraints, Challenges, Risks

I like restricting the breadth/detail contained within Project Charters. They should be concise and to-the-point but leave room for the Project Team to have some latitude for making appropriate trade-off decisions to get to a viable and reasonable Project Plan.

PRODUCT REQUIREMENTS REVIEWS ARE A WAY TO START

I was a "Systems" Engineer early in my career, and I have tended to continue acting like one throughout my life. What this means is, I look at Project Scope as a "transfer function". You have inputs (i.e. requirements) and outputs (i.e. validated deliverables). The "transfer function" is basically the Product Development Process executed to turn those inputs into the expected outputs per the remaining over-arching Project Constraints (Cost, Schedule, Resources and Risks). Grant it, sometimes, depending on which Product Development Process is considered the "Best Practice" for your type of development activity (refer to Chapter 7: Product Development Process), some of the requirements may not be definitively determined prior to Project Kick-Off. Regardless, it is typically considered a "good practice" to solidify as many requirements as possible/practical at the onset of the Project. A coordinated System (or

Product) Requirements Review (SRR) process helps. Figure 4 provides an example process flow.

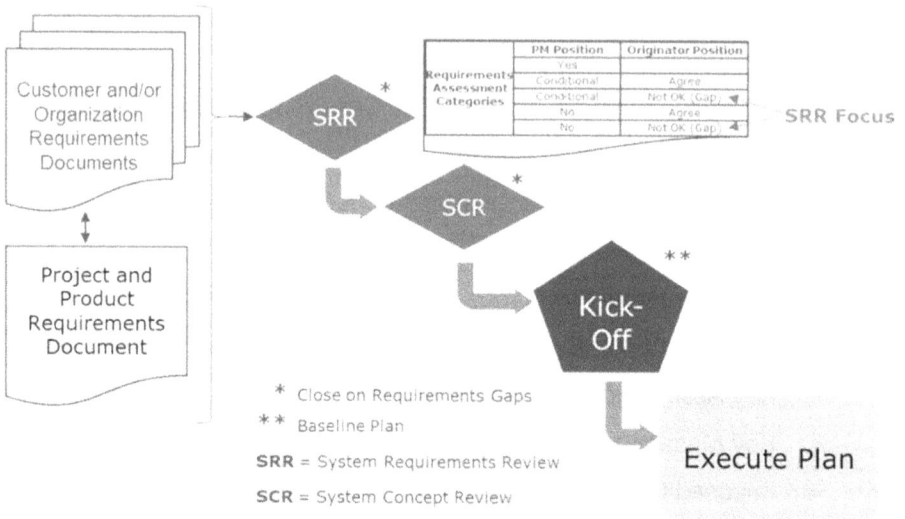

Figure 4. Example Systems Requirement Review Process

This above SRR process is commonly facilitated by use of a "Requirements Compliance" table or matrix. Basically, all Project and Product Requirements are individually listed in a configuration-controlled (i.e. date-stamped and/or uniquely identified alpha-numeric string, per each sequential update) document that specifies approval status and planned validation methodology. The most common validation methodologies are:

- Test (sample size, method, acceptance criteria, test data)
- Analysis (typically computer aided computations)
- Similarity (comparative assessment to a previous product)
- Inspection (witnessed visually via measurements, readings, etc.)

This type of process could vary considerably between similar Projects within an organization if not standardized by Organizational Governance procedures. Thus, the use of an SRR process is another good Strategic Project Management approach to consider.

It is important to also recognize that Project and Product Requirements are not immune from being changed over the course of the

Project Life Cycle. This is particularly the case in "Iterative" and "Agile" Product Development Processes (Chapter 7) which tend to anticipate and accommodate changing requirements throughout the Project Life Cycle. And although frowned upon, changes are also likely in "Waterfall" (or Predictive) Development Processes as well, when deemed necessary to deal with unexpected issues that surface throughout the Project Life Cycle. This topic is expanded upon within Chapter 5 (Cost of Change). Suffice it to say here, however, it behooves the organization to pro-actively establish processes that deal with how Project Requirements changes are managed and appropriately accommodated (e.g. requested, evaluated, and decided upon), based in part on levels of severity (i.e. how much of an impact the change could have on Project Objectives) which typically correspond to pre-determined organizational decision-making authority levels.

TASK HAND-SHAKES AND THE DEFINITION OF "COMPLETE"

One the most over-looked Project Requirements-related issues pertains to the definition of "complete" as it relates to "supplier-to-customer" task output expectations. If Projects are planned well and tasks are segregated by the Functional Groups performing them, "task outputs" tend to be the "task inputs" of subsequent tasks performed by other Functional Groups. The question is – was there a prior "hand-shake" agreement established between "supplier" and "customer" regarding the quality expectations of the "task outputs"? Seems simple, but I have seen and arbitrated many arguments due to mis-understandings in this area. I ultimately found that time spent in the planning process to avoid this type of issue was always worthwhile.

When either internal or external "customer" expectations are not satisfied due to undocumented definitions of "complete" the Project Plan is potentially jeopardized and usually unexpected recovery plans must be established and implemented. This can lead to compromises that impose additional Project Risk and/or Scope-of-Work (along with the corresponding Project Schedule and Cost impacts) to remedy the situation. Too many of these types of situations can totally derail a

Project. Good, experienced Project Managers tend to pro-actively prevent this. But most organizations have people with varying levels of experience and capability in Project Management positions. Thus, from a Strategic Project Management stand-point, the best way to avoid these task-to-task Product Development Process requirements issues is to establish a coordinated "hand-shake" process on all key Projects. This could be facilitated in any number of ways (e.g. when in the Aerospace and Defense industry we used WADs [Work Authorization Documents] which spelled out the "supplier-to-customer" task output expectations). When Project execution is highly scrutinized, the goal is to arrive at un-ambiguous "hand-shake" agreements that are well-documented and appropriately accounted for in the Project Plan.

FINAL NOTE ON IMPORTANCE OF MANAGING REQUIREMENTS

Think about this – if you change (e.g. add to) a Product Requirement, the typical rippling affect is: (A) you add Scope-of-Work to accommodate the Project Requirement change; (B) you add Resources to accommodate the added Scope; (C) you add Costs to accommodate the added Resources; (D) you may impact Schedule; and (E) you may also add Risk to the Project, especially if you try to simply absorb the Product Requirement change. All constraints associated with maintaining a Balanced Project Plan (refer to Chapter 6) are potentially impacted. Thus, it should obviously behoove us to monitor and manage Project Requirements diligently and transparently.

Is Your Organization Managing Projects Strategically?

Take the test, or at least see how your organization stacks up. An inventory of the key Strategic Project Management concepts espoused by this book can be kept, Chapter by Chapter. There is no established reference of good or bad, but you can see where your organization currently is, and use this tool to monitor progress. Each question starts with the phrase: To what extent does your organization......

1. periodically ensure that **All Projects** are aligned with and support current **Strategic Goals and Objectives?**

1	2	3	4	5
O	O	O	O	O
Never	Rarely	Sometimes	Most of the Time	Always

2. recognize that **Project Management Best Practices** can vary for different **Project Types?**

1	2	3	4	5
O	O	O	O	O
Never	Rarely	Sometimes	Most of the Time	Always

3. consider **Project Risk Management** something that should be treated **Holistically?**

1	2	3	4	5
O	O	O	O	O
Never	Rarely	Sometimes	Most of the Time	Always

4. govern directed **Project Changes** via **Charters** driven by up-to-date **Business Cases?**

1	2	3	4	5
O	O	O	O	O
Never	Rarely	Sometimes	Most of the Time	Always

5. control **All Project-Related Requirements** in organized, consistent, and transparent ways?

1	2	3	4	5
O	O	O	O	O
Never	Rarely	Sometimes	Most of the Time	Always

CHAPTER 2

IT'S *MANAGING EXPECTATIONS*

In an ideal corporate world, all management expectations are honorable, and good/effective systems/processes are in place to manage them. Further, people are aware that conflicting expectations exist, yet the solutions/compromises that are arrived at are those deemed most supportive of overall Organizational Goals and Objectives. In this scenario, discussions and decisions are open and transparent. And whether the decision is in favor of your group or not, at the end of the process you "climb on board", accept it, and support it. This ideal situation is predicated on the existence of several key enablers:

- Organizational conflicts are considered healthy
- Escalation is non-threatening
- Decision-making authorities are well-understood and respected
- Project Stakeholders are appropriately and acceptably engaged
- Good Processes are in place to enable "win-win" outcomes
- There is a high level of trust and integrity within the organization

ACHIEVING EPIC BUSINESS RESULTS

We discuss the first five bullet points in the subsequent sub-sections. The latter point pretty much speaks for itself.

ORGANIZATIONAL CONFLICTS CAN BE HEALTHY

Here is the scenario I have seen much too often:

> The Project Team is requested to launch a new or derivative Product by a market-driven date "or else", and the Project Team knows that doing so requires "all the stars to align". The Product is complex enough to require dependence on multiple outside sources (i.e. suppliers or contractors) for several critical sub-systems, components, and services. The requirements are loaded up to enable the "Best-in-Class" competitive positioning and include every Product feature and specification deemed necessary to satisfy ALL potential markets and customers – including several SKUs (Stock Keeping Units) that are unique enough to necessitate separate design and qualification efforts. Internal resources are limited. Product cost targets necessitate multiple suppliers for each component to maximize negotiation leverage. The Manufacturing and Quality Assurance groups insist upon a low maintenance Product launch (e.g. high end-to-end Yields, low level of Final Quality Audit fall-out, and "Best-in-Class" Product Field Failure Rates, etc.). And to keep with past practices, Product Marketing says ALL Product Requirements are "priority 1". Further, nobody in the management ranks understands the Risk Matrix, nor do they care – their directive is to "Just make it happen!"

The above might seem a little extreme, but I have personally witnessed this in a couple organizations I have worked for. Some managers might believe that this above situation is "healthy" and/or warranted. Yet the Project Team Members basically become the scape-goats and "whipping boys/girls" for the rest of the organization. The only "saving grace" is that those individuals and their managers were often well compensated. Unfortunately, in the above scenario, many stakeholders seemed to recognize that these requirements were indeed onerous, and some Organizational Managers were more concerned about ensuring that their group's specific performance expectations were met at all costs (to basically keep their jobs secure), so they became adept at deflecting blame. The people who are always in the front of the firing line are the Project Managers. This is an extreme example of a company that does not practice sound Strategic Project Management, and unfortunately, a company where those sitting in powerful positions do not necessarily want to practice it. These types of people may complain and pontificate about the need for change but are indeed more concerned that doing so would materially compromise their group's power and/or competitive advantage – and thus, they become resistant to change. This is somewhat endemic of the "Why fix something that isn't broken!" mentality. Sometimes this internal situation is not recognized or understood by the highest-level Organizational Leaders (those in the C-Suite). Organizations like these do tend to eventually change, however, and usually do so because of business issues, moral issues, and/or changes in the management ranks.

The reason I start off with this scenario is two-fold:

1. to articulate an admittedly extreme case of where an organization can end up if it is not at least somewhat committed to Strategic Project Management; and

2. to use this as a Case Study for highlighting some of the key inherent conflicts which can exist between competing organizational (i.e. management) expectations.

One organization I worked at (which had many of those above characteristics) was a multi-national (i.e. geographically dispersed), multi-billion-dollar enterprise organized into multiple Business Units (i.e. Portfolios) with a mix of Matrix Structures – mostly "weak" Matrix Structures (please refer to Figure 5) where Project Managers were held accountable but given very little actual authority. It should be obvious that this is not your most "healthy" situation.

Project Characteristics \ Organization Structure	Functional	Matrix			Projectized
		Weak Matrix	Balanced Matrix	Strong Matrix	
Project Manager's Authority	Little or None	Low	Low to Moderate	Moderate to High	High to Almost Total
Resource Availability	Little or None	Low	Low to Moderate	Moderate to High	High to Almost Total
Who manages the project budget	Functional Manager	Functional Manager	Mixed	Project Manager	Project Manager
Project Manager's Role	Part-time	Part-time	Full-time	Full-time	Full-time
Project Management Administrative Staff	Part-time	Part-time	Part-time	Full-time	Full-time

Figure 5. General Characteristics of Various Organizational Structures.
PMBOK® Guide - Fifth Edition (PMI, 2013b, p. 22)

I would go as far as saying that the high-level executives in organizations like the one that I just described may not be fully aware of the "political games" being played and the impact it has at the working-level employees. The "tell-tale" signs might be visible, but they are either hidden, ignored, or rationalized away.

The following sub-sections delve into some of the more common inherent organizational conflicts.

Every Project Conflict is Solvable with Risk Absorption

Yes, if unlimited risk absorption is allowed on a Project, all other requirements can be (theoretically) met. However, this obviously should never be allowed, for it usually provides a false sense of security, leading to unrealistic expectations, and ultimately an "ugly surprise". It is basically a situation where Organizational Managers and Project Managers "stick their heads in the sand" and ignore the issues until they can no longer keep them "under wraps". The problem can be due to several causes, such as:

- Some Organizational Leaders either do not require a formal Risk Management Plan, or only require that the Project Teams document/communicate risks at the onset of the Project, and possibly at the key phase "exit" and/or "entrance" reviews, but not continuously throughout the Project Life Cycle.

- Some Project Managers do not understand how to effectively manage risks.

- Even when Risk Register and Matrix tools (discussed in Chapter 4: Managing Risks) are diligently used by a Project Manager and Project Team, the Organizational Managers typically cannot gauge what the information really means from an overall Project Risk stand-point – and this is totally understandable, for those tools do not provide that direct/specific information.

- Although tried and proven Modelling & Simulation techniques (discussed in Chapter 4: Managing Risks) are available to enable Project Teams to determine overall Project Cost and Schedule Risks from a "% Confidence" stand-point (versus simply using "Expert Judgement"), most Project Teams do not use them. There are some good reasons for this, including the fact that most of the existing available tools (e.g. Schedule Risk Analysis tools, etc.) are difficult and frustrating to use without a sizable support staff.

- Risk Tolerance guidelines are typically not understood, established, or provided to Project Teams by the organization's leaders via Governance Guidelines. Thus, risk absorption is basically allowed to get out-of-control, jeopardizing Project Objectives, and thus, Organizational Strategic Objectives.

More about the above in Chapter 4 (Managing Risks), where Tools & Techniques which prevent the above are presented.

When Issues Arise, we Avoid non-Risk Absorption Changes

If you (as a Project Manager) want to avoid conflict, you tend to absorb more and more Project Risk on a regular basis. We seem to be talking a lot about risks here. So, this should be indicative of what our priorities should be. Here is my version (from my experience) of the typical Project change process. When an issue occurs during the Project Life Cycle, the following steps are typically considered and taken, in this order (overtly or inadvertently):

1. "Absorb" the Risk. We see from the prior section how detrimental this can become. My experience shows that most Consumer Product development Projects are driven by the "served" market, and Market Dynamics tends to dictate a need to adjust our Project Plan to accommodate seemingly never-ending customer preference changes. This is, in general, a good thing to do. But our management stakeholders do not like allowing other Project Constraints (i.e. Scope, Schedule, Cost, Product Quality/Requirements) to change as a result – for that might imply that the Project Team (or their Functional Group) is "out-of-control". Bottom-line, Project Stakeholders usually place a tremendous amount of pressure on the Project Team to absorb risks versus changing the other Project Constraints – and these stakeholders tend to be at a higher level, very influential and better (or more effective) negotiators than Project Managers. So, you can guess what usually happens. Yes, risks tend to be absorbed without consideration of making other pro-active changes to the Project Plan.

2. Change the Durations and/or Costs of Future Tasks/Activities. If there is anything a Project Manager understands best, it is that when an issue surfaces, he or she is expected to figure out how to get back on track, or consequently receive unwelcome "management" help. So, when an issue materializes due to Project Team performance, or human error, or poor original estimates of effort needed, the remedial action that is commonly taken is to change the durations and/or costs of future tasks/activities to compensate. Many times, this can go un-noticed – which is likely assumed to be a "good thing" by the Project Team. But it is essentially the same as "absorbing risk" and tends to jeopardize ultimate chances of Project success. If done too frequently, there will likely be a time along the Project Life Cycle (e.g. at the half-way point) when a major surprise reconciliation must be conceded –

not usually a "good thing" – and consequentially, a reason why EVM (Earned Value Management) processes are sometimes imposed on long-term, expensive, and strategic-important Project endeavors (discussed further in Chapter 5: Cost of Change).

3. Eat into Reserves or Buffers. If your Project has been afforded the luxury of having an established Budget Reserve (Management and/or Contingency Reserve), it will likely be tapped into before engaging in any other "non-risk-absorption" trade-off actions. The same can be said for Schedule Buffer. This is an appropriate action to take if the Project Reserves and/or Buffers were established to deal specifically with risks associated with that type of materialized issue. If not, you guessed it, you are essentially "absorbing risk". In this latter scenario, you are depleting resources put aside for other purposes, but you normally considered this to be a better option to exercise than the pain and "aesthetics" associated with changing other Project Constraints.

4. Make a Change to One or More Other Project Constraint and Absorb Some Risk. We tend to fall back on risk absorption whenever we can. In this scenario, we take more than one action and do not fully absorb the risk – but do absorb some. One of the more common occurrences associated with this option is when a Product Requirement is changed or added, and another Product Requirement is either amended or deleted. Usually, the amount of scope associated with the different requirements being traded off is not equal. So, in the scenario where the additional Product Requirement takes more Project Scope to implement than the one it is traded-off against, some additional risk is absorbed as well – although it might never be overtly or officially recognized as added risk.

5. Make a Change to One or More of the Other Constraints. This is typically the last resort, for it is usually the most painful path to go down. Think of it as a "tug-of-war" between stakeholders having different priorities, for that is what it usually feels like, and the caution is, if gone unchecked or un-escalated, the "winner" is usually the best

negotiator – and that may not necessarily lead to the "best solution". Many alternative scenarios can be conceived of, and a few are specifically addressed in Chapter 6: Maintaining a Balanced Plan.

The above alternatives are not abnormal nor inappropriate, for we prefer to always take the "path of least resistance" when at all possible. The message, however, is clear:

Since we naturally tend to take the "path of least resistance" and "absorb risk" whenever possible, we (as Project Managers, Project Team Members and Organizational Managers) should understand the consequences and know our realistic "threshold of pain" (i.e. the Risk Tolerance Threshold). Project Risk Tolerance expectations should be overtly established by the organization (see Chapter 4: Managing Risks) – a key and essential element of Strategic Project Management.

What is admittedly left out of the above options is expecting Project Team Members to work over-time (uncompensated, if possible) to catch up. This is akin to adjusting Project Resources and is likely to be Option 3.b for many organizations. I am not opposed to "playing this card" on occasion, provided it is somewhat warranted and not a frequent occurrence. In this scenario, such a decision or request is better received by the individuals impacted if the other potential culprits within and outside the Project Team (especially "management") lead the way by example.

Other Inherent Organizational Conflicts

Although "internal politics" can certainly cause conflicts, I choose not to go down that path any further in this section. Rather, let us focus on the "healthy" inherent conflicts within Functional Groups which make up a Matrix Organization Structure. Some of the more obvious situations are provided below.

- Product Cost versus Product Quality. At a very high level, it should be obvious that Product Cost and Quality can conflict. Look at a comparison of a piece of equipment that is expected to be used on a battlefield (where lives are at stake if it does not work when needed) versus a similar piece of equipment (say a Portable Power Generator) used for residential home improvement Projects. The Product price paid for the latter is more market-sensitive and likely to be lower, for reliability and robustness requirements are typically less stringent, and this is acceptable to customers as long as the price is right. The quality and reliability of the former is paramount, and the Product price is not as high a priority. In Consumer or Commercial markets there tends to be a customer tolerance for occasional Product failure that factors into Product pricing decisions. The QA (Quality Assurance) organization is typically more concerned with Product quality and reliability (to improve operational metrics and prevent or greatly mitigate the need for customer "damage control" actions) and the Sales and Marketing organizations are typically more concerned about Product pricing and its impact to the company financials. The tolerance levels vary from organization to organization, and industry to industry, but this general conflict is typical in Matrix Organization Structures. The QA folks are rewarded for Product quality and reliability performance and the Sales and Marketing folks are rewarded for overall sales volume. These incentives do indeed drive behaviors, but also provide a "healthy check-and-balance".

- Time-to-Market versus Product Quality. I struggled mightily with the concept that we could launch a new Product knowing that a certain population would be returned due to "early life" or "infant mortality" failures. That happened when I was an Aerospace and Defense guy entering the Consumer Electronics world. I was accustomed to ensuring that deliverable Products had to always perform well and had to be robust to the nth degree. This is not the case in a highly competitive TTM (Time-to-Market) driven Consumer Electronics industry, but there is usually a limit to how poor the Product quality can indeed be – it is just that the boundary is a bit "blurry". On one hand, the "business-oriented" folks (normally the Sales, Marketing and

Finance personnel) want to reap the near-term benefits (i.e. market share and initial higher prices) typically bestowed on the TTM leader. On the other hand, the "quality-oriented" folks (i.e. Quality Assurance/Customer Satisfaction, Operations and Engineering) do not want to continually deal with poor yields, tons of scrap and rework, post-launch design changes and customer "damage control" due to dissatisfaction with end-user complaints and excessive Field Failure Rates. This type of conflict can be both professionally and personally taxing on an organization's workforce, but if handled appropriately, can be very rewarding as well.

- Project Cost versus Project Delivery Schedule. The most pronounced example of this is the notion of paying supplier expedite costs to improve delivery schedule. Suppliers tend to increase "standard" lead-times for Products that are in demand. This is in part justified, and a sceptic would say that this is also to gain more "expedite business" and boost Product margins whenever possible. Expediting feeds off the desire by Project Team Members to preserve as much schedule as possible, or to decrease Schedule Risk to the greatest extent possible. How far a Project Team goes to pay for "schedule compression" is certainly a function of how important Project Schedule is relative to Project Costs. Thus, a natural conflict typically exists between Project Team Members who are dependent on materials from out-side sources (i.e. suppliers of Goods and Services) and the Purchasing Group which is asked to obtain high-quality parts as quickly as possible, but within a set budget. In the latter scenario, Procurement Group managers are typically held to tight fiscal constraints and are motivated/incentivized to not exceed their budgets.

- Project Resources versus Schedule and Budget. Is the capability of the individuals (i.e. Project Human Resources) good enough to satisfy the budgetary and schedule commitments to complete the assigned tasks? Think about this. The cost and schedule estimates derived for a job must assume a certain level of skill, but is that consistent with the capability of the resource assigned? We attempt to use averages, but "outliers" tend to mess this up. An issue arises when resource capability varies significantly (i.e. is a lot less capable, technically). Sometimes there is a belief that you can replace an expert with a novice with only a slight impact, that may be okay (for novices typically command a lower cost basis or rate), and that can make up for the expected schedule hit – but this is not typically a safe assumption from my experience. The bottom-line is that Project Resource changes (due to their different skill levels) can certainly affect Project performance and/or add Project Risk. Thus, Resource Management is another important ingredient within Strategic Project Management.

ESCALATION CAN BE A GOOD THING

There are distinct pros and cons associated with Matrix Organizations. One of the biggest issues (cons) is that this structure can easily foster conflicting expectations and behavior differences between the various Functional Groups. And when you, as a Project Manager, must deal with these conflicts it can be over-whelming, and potentially explosive. This is, in part, the reason PMOs (Project Management Offices) are established – to enable objective intercession at a higher level. Conversely, one of the principal side-benefits (pros) of a Matrix Structure is that it can facilitate a productive escalation process where decisions can be more naturally elevated to higher levels of management for resolution, if necessary. Productized and Functional Structures do not typically experience as many of these issues but have their own difficulties to deal with (i.e. personal preferences and biases can rule over objectivity and/or functional autonomy -- which if gone unchecked, can lead to activities that are misaligned with Organizational Strategic Goals. Some keys aspects of "healthy" escalation are provided below.

Escalation Protocols are Important to Understand

I have never been in a company where "escalation protocols" are formally established and communicated. But I do know that, whether overtly stated or not, it is good to understand generally accepted "escalation protocols".

ACHIEVING EPIC BUSINESS RESULTS

And I do assert that since Matrix Structures tend to foster conflict (sometimes referred to as "healthy conflict") a certain amount of escalation is expected. As a division General Manager, I established this expectation. The alternative, lack of escalation, can also impose issues, as is noted below.

So, let us examine a conflict that could potentially surface within a Matrix Organization Structure and warrant escalation:

Issue: The Electrical Engineering Manager decides to take two key people off a Project for two weeks to help fix an issue on another Project, even though that other Project has lower priority. The Project Manager finds out and knows that if this happens his/her Project Schedule will be unduly jeopardized. The PM confronts the Functional Manager but is told that his/her Project would have to wait. How does the PM deal with this?

Options:

    a) Says okay (i.e. agrees), updates the Project Plan and communicates the issues at the next Monthly Review.

    b) Sends a scathing e-mail to the CEO, letting him/her know about the issues and potential repercussions.

    c) Informs the Functional Manager that he/she plans to immediately brief the PMO Director, and requests that the Functional Manager informs the Director of Engineering.

Option "c" is the obvious better choice. The PM is not doing his/her job if he/she proceeds with option "a", by accepting the disruption and reporting on it well after-the-fact (when opportunity was lost to potentially rectify the situation). Taking the option "b" route will most likely cause a major disruption within the organization, especially when the CEO calls his/her "direct reports" to find out more, and everyone is unaware (not necessarily good for the PM's career!). These are a bit exaggerated, but you should get the gist. The appropriate protocol is to try to resolve the issue amicably, and to let the other party know that you plan to escalate.

This might cause that person to re-consider or soften their stance a bit. But if not, at least you gave fair warning and got the ball rolling as soon as possible so that the Project disruption, if overturned, is minimized. If the decision handed down because of the escalation is to accept the Functional Manager's decision, then in an ideal world the PM would be given a commensurate Project extension and budget adjustment (or in contract terms, an "equitable adjustment").

Over-Escalation is Typically Frowned Upon

I have seen situations where a PM escalated almost everything that did not go his way, even to the point where impact assessments and resolution options were not even considered. Sometimes this situation leads to Functional Managers feeling forced and obligated to attend most of the Project Team meetings to act as full-time intercessors. This is an example of excessive over-escalation and is indicative of different types of employee issues – dysfunction, passive-aggressiveness, or incompetence. It might mean that the PM is not ready for that level of responsibility and either more mentoring or a personnel change is warranted. There needs to be a healthy balance to cultivate a positive work environment.

Lack of Escalation Leads to "Best Negotiator Wins"

Just like over-escalation can be an "early warning indicator" of potential organizational issues, lack of escalation within a Matrix Organization can be as well. Perfect collaboration within an organization that was established to foster a "healthy" degree of conflict means some individuals (or Functional Groups) are probably acquiescing too often. This usually means that "the best negotiators are winning", and suboptimal decisions are possibly being made too frequently. This may be a sign that there could be organizational dysfunction or frustration within the ranks, potentially leading to personnel conflicts and/or morale issues. Another sign could be that there are too many "surprises" that surface, and too much "finger pointing" taking place. Usually, if the acquiescing party fails in meeting expectations, that person's organization is blamed for the ensuing problems. Here is an example:

The Project Manager hears about some proposed Product changes (e.g. addition of a feature and a couple new Product SKUs [Stock Keeping Units]) that the Product Manager decides are necessary to gain additional business from a new potential customer. Engineering leads are requested to evaluate the impact, and a meeting ensues to decide on the course of action. The Product Manager (typically being more marketing-centric) makes a convincing argument that the executive team will overlook any potential Project Schedule delay if the Project Business Case numbers are exceeded, and these changes will enable that. The request is that the Project Team perform the added effort and absorb the schedule risk. The PM and team agree. Toward the end of the Project the PM must declare a six-week Product launch delay – due primarily to those accepted changes. As a result, a key customer decides to cancel their Product Qualification (meaning no production business from them and a less favorable Project Business Case outlook). Senior executives are upset and want answers. Team tensions rise between the various members. Natural self-preservation instincts kick in, and the "blame game" begins. Relationships are jeopardized, and negative management perceptions are born.   Healthy escalation could have prevented this, whereby a higher-level discussion could have taken the decision off the Project Team's shoulders – nobody would have been surprised, and the Project crisis would have been averted.

STAKEHOLDER EXPECTATIONS – THE BIG PICTURE

As we have progressed through this chapter, we have discussed situations involving several different Project Stakeholders – individuals and groups. This community can be vast. It is important to understand the over-arching influence that the various stakeholders possess and how to effectively address their expectations. Figure 6 provides insight into the potential breadth of this Stakeholder Community. The Project Sponsor can be one person, several people, or an organization – and can be directly involved (e.g. Executive, Product Marketing Manager, or Point of

Contact for a Contracting Agency, if applicable) or indirectly involved (e.g. Sales Team and Customer Support personnel). Sellers are basically the Supply Base and out-side Consultants/Contractors. Functional Managers (in a Matrix Organization Structure) are typically those who own the key resources that support the Projects. And Operations Management are typical those who receive the Project outputs (Goods, Services or Results), generate/produce the customer offerings, and deliver or deploy those offerings.

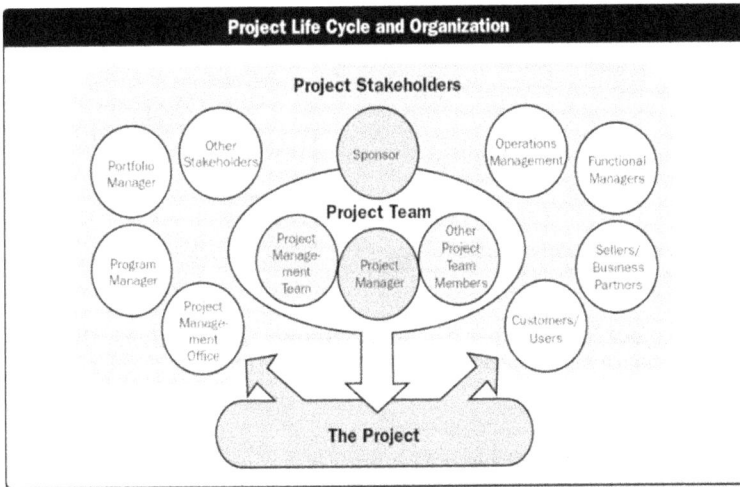

Figure 6. The Project Stakeholder Community. PMBOK® Guide - Fifth Edition (PMI, 2013b, p. 31)

The Stakeholder Analysis

Those in the Project Stakeholder Community are not all equal. They tend to have differing amounts/levels of "interest" and "power" and can therefore be separated into different general "buckets". The left-hand chart in Figure 7 is taken from *The Standard for Program Management* (PMI, 2013b) and the right-hand side provides an illustrative example of the different stakeholder characteristics and how individuals within those groupings might be managed by the Project Manager and Team. The side benefit of performing this type of analysis is that it provides insight into stakeholder expectations, whether overtly stated or not. It answers the basic questions regarding: (1) how and when do you communicate to the various stakeholder individuals/groups; (2) whose opinion do you give priority to regarding "change" decisions; and (3) who should you keep abreast of concerns, issues or changes as they surface? This can help prevent unnecessary and avoidable surprises. The matrix on the left is the template and that on the right is an example of how it might be filled out.

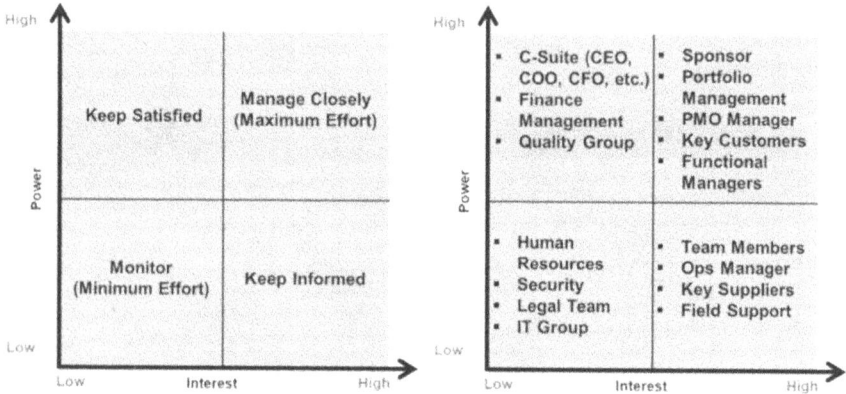

Figure 7. Project Stakeholder Analyses: General and Notional Example. The Standard for Program Management – Third Edition (PMI, 2013a, p. 47)

No Surprises, Please!

The "kiss of death" for a Project Manager is a major "surprise" regarding an issue that could have been easily avoided if some prior communication, discussion and/or escalation had been pursued. People tend to get upset when surprised with bad news. It is never a good feeling when you get bombarded with questions that you struggle to answer and know that you "messed up" and have no real defense. That "deer in the head-lights" look is never becoming, nor does it exude anything other than lack of confidence and/or competence. The key is to avoid surprises altogether. Sometimes we tend to try to "sweep" potential issues "under the rug" and hope they will somehow go away. Sometimes they are eventually discovered and come back to bite us. A "good practice" is to be completely up-front and forthright about concerns and issues – even if we are implored by others (maybe "partners in crime") to not be. Below are some "surprise scenarios" to avoid – and to prevent via Strategic Project Management:

- Assumption that was Not Officially Agreed to. I have cancelled an entire business pursuit due to finding out that it was predicated on a poor Assumption. After inheriting a new group and being requested by my boss to probe into the Business Case behind a very large R&D (Research and Development) Project, I found out that the entire business hinged on winning a single large contract, whereby the Business Development Manager estimated we had only a 10% probability of winning. The contract was very large and thus made the Business Case look good (even at 10%), but nobody else in the organization knew that the contract was that large, and our chances of winning were so low. This was a major surprise to everyone, but the Business Development Manager was sure that he had conveyed the details to the management team and was given approval to proceed, yet nobody in the "decision loop" knew about the underlying Business Case assumptions, nor were they documented – thus resulting in a major surprise, and an apt Project cancellation.

- Taking or giving unintentional direction. While walking around in one of the facilities within my organization, I put on my "engineering hat" and mentioned to a Project Manager (who led a very innovative Product Development effort) that it would be even better if we could design the Product to be assembled in the field (i.e. where it was to be erected). At the next Project Review meeting I was informed that the Project could not meet the original Baseline Cost and Schedule commitments due to the changes being made to assemble it on-site versus in the factory. I was able to at least get the Project back on track, for I did not intend for the Project Manager to proceed without having an official review of the impact and receiving a more official "go-ahead" decision. This was a lesson learned by me, and an example of a situation that could have been completely avoided if a structured Change Control process were in place.

- Weaving a False Story to a Critical Customer. After being re-assigned to take on a new internal position, I found out that my new group had intentionally misled a key customer about the cause of a significant issue with a Product that we were supplying them. I attended a meeting where the group was trying to figure out how to further "spin" the story, and I ended up deciding that we had to "come clean" with that customer – much to the chagrin of everyone else involved. As it turned out, this customer appreciated the honesty and decided to continue to do business with us, but our sponsor within that company was obviously upset about the situation, and a bit surprised. It took a while to mend this relationship, but everyone involved ended up feeling relieved. During this process I found out that this sponsor was very confused about the reports he had been receiving (his team was very astute) and was contemplating (before my intervention) moving their business elsewhere due to a lack of trust in our ability to resolve issues. In this case, a major business crisis was averted.

- <u>Not pre-Briefing Project Sponsors Regarding Issues</u>. There are far too many situations when I was either on the delivering or receiving end of a situation where a key Project Stakeholder in the "Manage Closely (Maximum Effort)" Category was "blind-sided" (i.e. surprised) by bad news. Either they heard about it from their boss before their own people gave them a "heads-up" or similarly, heard about a major issue in a Project status update presentation "in front of the world" before having been briefed and given the opportunity to help determine the remedial course of action to take – always an awkward situation. I have not done this (as deliverer) in a while – I tend to try to learn from, and not repeat, certain mistakes. When I am on the receiving end of this type of situation it always prompts an impromptu mentoring session.

  I emphasis the importance of pre-briefings in the post-graduate course I teach on Strategic Project Management – I consider it an essential piece of knowledge for someone having a desire to move up in their career.

- Speaking Unofficially on Behalf of Your Boss. Project Managers and Project Team Leads are constantly put in positions where they are being asked to make decisions or take a stance on controversial topics "on the spot". Usually there is a tacit understanding that certain decisions cannot be made without the consent of your supervisor. When all is said and done, within these positions, we are all representing our bosses and should not make decisions contrary to their desires. Doing so could be detrimental to our jobs. Understanding your supervisor's position and decision-making expectations is thus essential. From a manager's perspective, these expectations should be well-communicated.

Have an Action Plan

One of the first instructions I give people who report directly to me is to "never complain without providing a viable solution." Akin to that is, "never present a concern or issue without an action plan." Generally, it is unwise to present a problem pre-maturely (i.e. without a good understanding of the issue; having a set of alternative solutions to potentially address the issue; and providing a recommended course of action). Sometimes people "jump the gun" to avoid (or mitigate the impact of) a later surprise, but it usually only makes things worse. If you do not have a "plan of action" you will likely be "helped" with putting one together, and this kind of "help" is typically not good and/or pleasant to receive.

Some general rules that I espouse relative to how a Project Manager should handle last minute surprises or bad news are:

- Always inform the key Project Stakeholders that an issue has potentially surfaced ("potentially", because sometimes these are "false alarms"). That you and the team are digging into the details and will provide a debriefing soon.

- If the news was received just prior to a status update meeting, attempt to inform the key Project Stakeholders before the meeting and let the attendees know that you and your team have been recently made aware of a potential issue, and details will be forthcoming as soon as a thorough assessment is made.

- Try not to provide much information during a large gathering (i.e. meeting), especially if the news is fresh and you have not fully assessed the situation.

- Resist the temptation to speculate, even when under pressure to do so. This can mislead and create inappropriate/wrong expectations – it is not worth the risk.

WHO HAS DECISION-MAKING AUTHORITY?

One of the most basic Project Stakeholder expectations is that all decisions (relative to "material" changes to a Project's Constraints) are handled in an appropriate and acceptable manner. This means that the right people are, or were, involved and informed. Typically, organizations define approval authorities and limits for decisions by individuals in various roles. Company Policies and Procedures tend to address decision-making authorities at the highest management levels. Organizational Governance Procedures may give further direction to lower levels of management as well. Sometimes these procedural directives are intentionally left a bit vague to not unduly "tie the hands" of employees and create too much of a bureaucratic environment, stifling the ability to make expedient decisions (refer to Chapter 5: Cost of Change).

Some useful management tools and processes that can facilitate decision-making are provided below, along with some behavioral considerations that should be understood and effectively handled.

The RACI Matrix is a Good Tool

Do all the people in your organization truly understand their Roles and Responsibilities? This can be a bit of a "loaded" question. Sometimes it becomes obvious that some individuals do not completely understand their Roles and Responsibilities, or that there is some confusion between people about their responsibilities and authority levels – resulting in arguments and potentially leading to organizational dysfunction. I have used the RACI (Responsible, Accountable, Consulted, Informed) Matrix on several occasions to expose and prevent these types of issues. The most beneficial time to utilize such a tool is when organizational growth leads to a management decision to re-organize into a Matrix Structure, and Roles and Responsibilities appropriately change. The development of a RACI Matrix is ideal in this situation. Before explaining why this is so, we should first discuss the tool.

An example of a notional RACI Matrix is provided in Figure 8, below. This matrix was constructed to ensure that the organization was aligned on decision-making and communication responsibilities associated with key Project Management activities, in an organization with a Matrix Structure. This RACI Matrix, after being completed, ensures that each Functional Management discipline (or group) agrees to their responsibilities and understands the corresponding responsibilities of others. It establishes clear expectations. The individual "responsible" for evaluating options and providing recommendations is denoted with an "R" for that activity. Ideally, there should only be one "R" for each activity – one person with "the X on their forehead". [Note: the below matrix shows more than one "R" in some rows. This is a "short-cut" for not having to replicate rows for each of the potential "R's"]. It is not uncommon in a Matrix Organization Structure to have two individuals (or positions) with the shared decision-making, or approval authority. These "approvers" are therefore accountable and are denoted with and "A" in that activity row. Many people like having only one "A" per item/row. To do this you need to decompose and separate the specific responsibilities for some of the more involved items to better delineate the authorities of each "A". Typically, decisions are facilitated by obtaining information and facts from others. In addition, decisions might directly impact activities performed by other functional organizations. These individuals must therefore be "consulted" to ensure decisions are appropriately considering all requisite interests – and are denoted with a "C" in the matrix. It is incumbent upon the "R" individual to ensure that inputs are solicited from (and provided by) these "consultants". There are other stakeholders who expect to be only "informed" about key Project decisions – those are denoted with an "I".

PROJECT RESPONSIBILITY / DECISION MATRIX -- Example

Project Activities	Customer(s), if applicable	Sr. Functional Management	Sponsor (e.g., Marketing)	PM	Legal / Contracts	Finance	Technical (e.g., Eng. Lead)	Operations Lead	Procurement Lead	Quality Lead	HR	Safety	IT	Security
1. Project Governance														
1.1. Changes to Project Objectives:														
1.1.1. Deliverables (Specs & Rqmts.)	A	C	A	R	C	I	C	I	I	I				
1.1.2. Major Milestones	A	C	A	R	C	I	C	C	C	C				
1.1.3. Budget Adjustments	A	C	A	R	C	C	C	C	C	C				
1.1.4. Scope of Work	A	C	A	R	C	I	C	I	I	I				
1.1.5. Priorities	A	C	A	R	C	I	I	I	I	I				
1.2. Changes to PMP:														
1.2.1. Interim Milestones	I	I	I	A		I	R	R	R	R				
1.2.2. Cost Account Budgets		A	A	R	C	C	C	C	C	C				
1.2.3. Scheduled Activity		I	I	A		I	R	R	R	R	I	I	I	I
1.2.4. Detailed Technical/Quality Specs		I	A	R	I		I	C	C	C	C			
1.2.5. Development Process		C	I	A		I		R	R	R	R			
1.2.6. PM Tools & Techniques	A	C	A	R	C	C	I	I	I	I	I		C	
1.2.7. Risk Management Plan	A	C	A	R	I	C	C	C	C	C	C	C	C	C
1.2.8. Quality Management Plan	A	A	A	A	C	I	C	C	C	R				
1.2.9. HR Management Plan	I	A	I	R		I	C	C	C	C	C		I	I
1.2.10. Supplier Management Plan	I	A	I	A	I	I	C	C	R	C	I			

Legend	
R	Responsible - the person who is assigned to do the work
A	Accountable - the person(s) who make the final decision and has ultimate ownership
C	Consulted - the person(s) who must be consulted before a decision or action is taken
I	Informed - the person(s) who must be informed of a decision or that an action has been taken

Figure 8. Example RACI Matrix. Project Risk Management (PMI, 2016, p.166)

I have found that the real benefit of a RACI Matrix is the process of constructing it. This process typically exposes gaps, over-laps and mis-understandings. Discussions can be quite animated, to say the least. Sometimes disagreements need to be escalated to achieve a resolution. The key is that, from a Strategic Project Management stand-point, expectations can be discussed up-front to avoid unnecessary confrontations, delays and/or inappropriate or "unhealthy" decisions later. Another benefit is that the appropriate organizational "checks-and-balances" can be amicably established to mitigate organizational "bullying" or biased behavior which can exist when Individuals or groups feel left out of decisions regarding items they have a vested interest in (e.g. a

Mechanical Engineering manager finding out about a Product Requirement change that was decided upon without their input, adding Project Scope and Costs which were not factored into the decision, which they are now expected to "absorb").

What the RACI Matrix Does Not Provide

The RACI Matrix provides a good general frame-work for decision-making, with respect to roles, responsibilities, and decision-making expectations. But the tool does not ensure that "good decisions" are always arrived at. It is impossible to make the "right decisions" all the time, but it is not impossible to make "good decisions" all the time. "Good decisions" are not always going to be the "right decisions", for situations change, and the future is not able to be precisely foreseen. So, what is a "good decision"? My "acid test" regarding decision-making is that regardless of the ultimate outcome, did the decision-maker(s):

1. Factor in ALL the Available Data;
2. Evaluate ALL the most Viable Options; and
3. Make the Best Decision possible at that time?

Basically, the above conditions help determine whether the decision was justified and defendable. For when our decisions turn out to be wrong, we occasionally need to be prepared to defend them and show that we were diligent and not remiss in our assessment – that our decision was rational and justifiable at the time when it was made.

Not a Democracy -- "No Voting"

I am not an advocate of Project Stakeholder voting to make key Project decisions, especially change-related decisions. Dependence on "majority rules" voting can greatly diminish the Project Manager's role and in my opinion should be avoided. But I also believe in careful consideration of all viable options and complete transparency. The Project Manager is expected to "juggle" all Project Requirements, and to act as an "Honest Broker" to ensure that the "best decisions" (from the Project's standpoint) are made. If this person does not make or recommend rational decisions, then a personnel change might be warranted. Allowing the Project Team to vote on decisions is a way of potentially abdicating, especially if the Project Manager is not in agreement with the majority. Project Managers need to be 100% behind their decisions/recommendations and cannot (and should not be allowed to) push blame onto the Project Team when those decisions "back-fire".

When a tough decision must be made, the Project Manager should assemble the right Project Stakeholders, collect all the pertinent information, solicit all the opinions/options, analyze (and debate if necessary) the pros and cons associated with the options, appropriately consider Project priorities, and ultimately determine his/her decision or recommendation. Depending on the severity of the situation which needs to be reconciled, the Project Manager should consider openly communicating any major dissenting positions as a show of transparency and to enable escalation options by dissenters.

Given the inherent conflicts within Matrix Organizations, based on earlier discussions in this chapter, escalation should be expected at times. In my opinion, I'd rather see issues escalated than to see Project Managers concede to the "best negotiators" or "vailed threats".

Delegation is Not Abdication

The last section touched on the notion of abdication – basically, the act of failing to accept accountability for one's duties and/or responsibilities. Delegation, on the other hand, is "assignment of any responsibility or authority to another person (normally from a manager to a subordinate) to carry out specific activities.... However, the person who delegated the work remains accountable for the outcome of the delegated work." (Wikipedia, 2018). The key difference is relative to that last sentence.

To effectively delegate, the "manager" needs to trust that the "delegate" (or subordinate) will carry out the work (including making acceptable decisions relative to that work, if necessary) per the "manager's" expectations. This is a very good deal when all goes well, for managers typically delegate to reduce some of their personal work-load, and thus, they typically become more productive. Effective delegation essentially supports organizational growth – the "divide and conquer" mentality which good leaders embrace and exploit. When all does not go well, issues can surface and in extreme cases "heads can roll" – meaning, jobs could be at stake. In these situations, good/responsible leaders do not abdicate, but accept the consequences. The temptation to abdicate must be resisted, for this action is usually more negatively received (by Organizational Leaders) than hearing about the resulting issues – I, unfortunately, know this from personal experience.

If you have ever struggled with delegation, join the club. It was one of the most difficult transitions for me to make as a young leader. For the longest time I was of the mind-set that "if I needed (or wanted) the job done right I had to do it myself". This was manageable to a degree, until my responsibilities expanded, and I **had** to delegate to maintain sanity and survive in my position. I ended up settling on the following ground-rules which seemed to have served me best:

- Do not treat all subordinates equally relative to delegation. Since effective delegation requires trust (to get the job done and make acceptable decisions when required), this is a condition that certainly must be individually determined and earned.

    o Every potential delegate behaves differently and has different strengths and weaknesses. Realize this and account for it.

    o Start with less-consequential duties or responsibilities and work up from there, keeping a good accounting of results.

- Establish the right expectations.

    o Clearly articulate your expectations relative to preferences.

    o Make sure you are very clear on decision-making authority. Agree on the boundaries relative to situations that:

        ▪ are "fair game" to make autonomous decisions;

        ▪ must be elevated to you to handle completely; and

        ▪ require your pre-review, and concurrence.

WIN-WIN PROCESSES FOR DEALING WITH EXPECTATIONS

Strategic Project Management is much more than "tactical" Project Management – it calls for the organization to extract the highest performance from Project Teams and provide the best and most professional work environment. As such, I cannot over-stress the importance of establishing processes which are good for all involved. They should be beneficial, fair, and equitable to the extent possible. Expectations should be well-understood to avoid unnecessary conflicts. Clear Governance Guidelines, and establishment of a collaborative cultural environment, are two of the most important factors.

Organizational Governance Sets the Stage

Strategic direction is the natural outcome of Organization Governance. Holes or gaps in that direction are typically filled somehow. Why leave those addendums to chance? It can breed inconsistencies, wasted effort, unnecessary conflict, sub-optimal decisions and/or complacency. On the opposite end of the spectrum, too much bureaucracy can stifle creativity, over-burden the workforce, and/or lead to unproductive passive-aggressive legalism. A solid set of productive Governance Policies, Procedures and Standards centered around the satisfaction of organizational expectations, is thus well-worth pursuing. A brief mention of some Governance items which have not been previously discussed within this chapter are provided below.

- Project Status Update Content and Phase Review Content. Project Managers tend to like their independence – I did. I always knew the best way to organize and present my Project Status Update Review information. Had my own definitions of Red/Yellow/Green ratings. I knew the content that made sense to communicate. I did not like to have to conform to a standard. The problem with this is it is very hard and frustrating for managers/reviewers to "re-calibrate" for each Project due to the different definitions of Red/Yellow/Green ratings. Plus, there should be a specific set of data that is consistently reported on (like the 6 key Project Constraints – Product Quality/Requirements,

Project Cost, Schedule, Scope, Resources, and Risks) to ensure all important issues are surfaced. Phase Reviews have similar issues. The DoD solved this by establishing Military Standards to follow, which have been improved upon over time. Simple, consistent content guidelines, with latitude given for inclusion of other information, if desired, is "the ticket". Some ideas are provided in Chapter 5: Cost of Change.

- Product Development Processes. Within some industries, a standard Product Development Process, or Product Life Cycle as it is sometimes referred to, is established to promote development process consistency and to ensure that past mistakes are not repeated. This primarily applies to the continual development of improved derivative Products or Services over time. Much more about this topic in Chapter 7: Product Development Process.

- Project Management Tools & Techniques. Since there is a correlation between the Project Management Tools & Techniques employed and Project success rates, it is incumbent upon the organization to know what the "Best Practices" are, and where appropriate, direct their usage by the Project Teams – and ensure that all users are adequately trained to use them. More about this topic in Chapter 8: Employing Best Practices.

- WBSs (Work Breakdown Structures) and Data Recording. The WBS can be a very powerful tool, if constructed properly for enabling your organization to improve Project Estimating skills, and to facilitate transparency and accountability. One approach is to establish an ERP (Enterprise Resource Planning) database structure that is used consistently by all Project Teams. More about this topic in Chapter 3: Planning.

A Collaborative Environment Sends a Great Message

Win-win outcomes are ideal in most situations – not just in "deal-making" negotiations but also in how managers and employees interact. Mutually beneficial (and shared) expectations tend to manifest a more collaborative, positive work environment. People, in general, want to be productive and appreciated for they efforts. And appreciation is usually more than just getting a pay-check – although that is indeed important as well. We also want to be fairly treated. Most managers that I know like to think that they are always fair and equitable – even when it is pointed out (with specific examples) that they are not. I once had a boss who whole-heartedly believed he was being appropriately fair when he insisted on commitments for "both" mutually exclusive outcomes – e.g. expecting a new Product to be successfully launched in 12 months AND costing no more than $1.5M, even though my team and I were adamant that it would take $2M. If I said, "I could realistically provide a higher cost Product with fewer features for that budget", he would just tell me that he wanted "both" and that was the end of the discussion. When I ended up needing more funds I would be chastised and figured that I had to just "suck-it-up". This same person never wanted any Organizational Business Segment to actually meet its annual commitments – always wanted to point out that "you have never met any of your annual commitments" to shame us. One year my organization did meet every commitment, and I had to advise him of this whenever he made that comment – this tended to irk him for he never wanted to think that he might have left anything "on the table", and if you did meet all the annual commitments, he assumed that he did. This approach did not breed a win-win culture, and it was difficult to resist the urge to "ripple this down" to my subordinates, but I managed to resist.

Unfortunately, I do not believe that the above scenario is that uncommon. In fact, this same kind of situation is somewhat commonplace (from my experience) when it comes to negotiating Project Team commitments – and many of the executives and managers involved are not likely to be either aware of it or inclined to admit it. The six key Project Constraints/Expectations (i.e. Project Cost, Project Schedule, Project Scope, Project Resources, Project Risks and Product Quality) that we discuss in Chapter 3 (Planning) are negotiated as a group and become the essential drivers behind the Project Plan. When we "balance" a Project

Plan, the one Project Constraint that is typically the least understood and most variable is Project Risk. Chapter 4 (Managing Risks) discusses Project Risks in more detail but suffice it to say here that many Project Stakeholders do not really understand Project Risks, nor do they really accept them for what they represent – potential causes of unsuccessful Project performance. I have heard executives say, "Just make the risks go away", and they say this without agreeing to accept commensurate changes to any of the other Project Constraints – a key topic for Chapter 6 (Maintaining a Balanced Plan). Bottom-line, when Project Risks are not understood and/or accepted, the Project Team (whether realizing it or not) is not being given a "win-win deal", and unfair expectations have been established.

A couple questions to ponder:

- Are we (as managers) maximizing our own personal job performance metrics to ensure that we are recognized as the "best performers" and reaping the most personal rewards possible?

- Or are we doing our best to ensure that the organization (as a whole) performs to its peak potential so that all who are part of it prosper?

It takes a degree of selflessness to do the latter, but if we can, we are not only being great leaders and followers, but fostering a collaborative environment that can satisfy all expectations to the maximum extent possible. This is a noble pursuit and is unlikely to be fully realized all the time, but with the right Organizational Governance and leadership direction an organization can get close. What it results in is a visibly positive "state-of-being" and sends a good message to all Organizational Stakeholders.

As new and improved processes are experimented with and developed to instill more successful Project execution (i.e. to foster "Best Practices", or at least "Better Practices"), we become more productive, and our organizations become more profitable. So, how could such practices be resisted? Some potential issues are listed below.

- Paradigms could get in the way – "We have always done it a certain way, and that way has worked in the past, so why change?".

- Perceptions regarding our control being compromised might surface – and as managers we do not want to ever appear as if our roles are becoming less important.

- The "fear of change", in general.

- The additional work and/or costs associated with the use of different Tools & Techniques that we do not understand or want to accept.

Whether we acknowledge it or not, the usual approach is to resist, or at least to not fully (throughout the organization) embrace "change". Momentum is difficult to overcome, but it could be well worthwhile to attempt overcoming it.

One area where we, in the business world, seem to constantly improve is the PDP (Product Development Process) or PLC (Product Life Cycle) we implement – to basically "do more with less". The objective is to essentially out-perform our competition to the best of our ability. This includes diligently endeavoring to learn from our mistakes and implement "systemic changes" to ensure that we do not repeat those same mistakes in the future – as elaborated upon in Chapter 9 (Lessons Learned).

Without getting into too much detail here, be aware that two relatively recent trends in PDP innovation are: (1) the "Incremental" (or Iterative) Development Process; and (2) the "Agile" (or Adaptive) Development Process. The most common PDP employed in the past is referred to as "Waterfall", where Project Plans appear to resemble a waterfall when displayed on a Schedule Gantt Chart. One of the key distinguishing differences between these alternative PDPs is how Project Risk and uncertainty is treated. Another distinction is the way Project Teams are managed by the organization via Team Member accountability and empowerment. In the "Agile" Development Process, the tendency is to try to get more productivity out of people by empowering them – with the three-fold expectations that:

1. this will result in significant productivity improvements, and reductions in Product Development timeframes;

2. managers will be actively committed to breaking down "barriers to success", or impediments; and

3. it will result in a lasting improvement in the work environment.

To implement these processes well, the organization must endeavor to alter long-standing expectations and navigate through the issues associated with the general "resistance to change".

I was once at a training event where the facilitator mentioned something that has always stuck with me. He stated that there was a recent survey conducted to determine what people feared most. The number one fear was "speaking in front of a large audience". The number two fear was "change". And the number three most dreaded fear was "death". His take-away was that "people would rather die than change!" Interesting insight, and very telling.

One final note. The organization would be remiss if it were to place all the Product Development Process burden on the Project Teams, for these newer processes cannot be effective (to the extent possible) without the support provided by Organizational Governance. They imply a degree of empowerment is given to the Project Teams. Empowerment alone assumes a transfer of power to lower levels within the organization. This means that someone is consequentially losing power – something that may be difficult to swallow, especially if you are pushing this power down the organizational chain-of-command and are still held accountable (a concept very similar in nature to delegation). Thus, organizational maturity, collaboration and the establishment of fair managerial and Project Team expectations is key to true Strategic Project Management.

Is Your Organization Managing Projects Strategically?

Take the test, or at least see how your organization stacks up. An inventory of the key Strategic Project Management concepts espoused by this book can be kept, Chapter by Chapter. There is no established reference of good or bad, but you can see where your organization currently is, and use this tool to monitor progress. Each question starts with the phrase: To what extent does your organization......

6. foster **Healthy Organizational Conflict** to enable appropriate Project checks & balances?

1	2	3	4	5
O	O	O	O	O
Never	Rarely	Sometimes	Most of the Time	Always

7. recognize **Conflicting Stakeholder Requirements** and accept coordinated **Escalation?**

1	2	3	4	5
O	O	O	O	O
Never	Rarely	Sometimes	Most of the Time	Always

8. establish clear Project **Roles & Responsibilities** and **Decision-Making** authorities?

1	2	3	4	5
O	O	O	O	O
Never	Rarely	Sometimes	Most of the Time	Always

9. understand **Project Risks** and the need to **Proactively** and **Holistically** manage them?

1	2	3	4	5
O	O	O	O	O
Never	Rarely	Sometimes	Most of the Time	Always

10. promote productive Project Management **Governance Guidelines** and **Cultural Norms?**

1	2	3	4	5
O	O	O	O	O
Never	Rarely	Sometimes	Most of the Time	Always

CHAPTER 3

IT'S *PLANNING*

People who have "been around the block" a few times (relative to managing or working on Projects) know that even if the Project Plan is perfectly laid out, it may still have a very good chance of failing, especially if the Project is complex/risky. So, what does that say for poorly planned Projects? Bottom-line, you should give your Project Teams the best chance to succeed – plan well and everyone can win. By the way, planning is not easy – it is hard work, and the more complex the Project, the more difficult the job of planning. Add to this the intricacies of a Matrix Organization Structure and... well you get the picture. There is also the potential false impression that if you use the best available set of Project Management tools it will be a breeze to succeed. Remember that planning is only facilitated by the tools used, and that is important, but it is not sufficient in and of itself – you have got to put the right data into those tools and understand how to use them effectively. In this chapter we explore the more common pit-falls to Project planning, as well as some sound methodologies to enable greater chances of success.

THE BALANCING ACT

Chapter 6 will discuss the art of Maintaining a "Balanced" Project Plan, but in this chapter, we will discuss what it means to Establish a "Balanced"

ACHIEVING EPIC BUSINESS RESULTS

Project Plan first. Whether we have ever heard this phrase, we should be able to readily understand the intent of balancing a Project Plan. Before giving the masses (i.e. entire group of Project Team Members) the go-ahead to proceed on a Project, we should first develop a Project Plan for them to execute, in as much detail as necessary. And this Project Plan should be achievable. Balancing the key Project Constraints gets you to that point. As mentioned throughout this book, there are six key Project Constraints, and they are relatively straightforward to understand. These constraints are:

- *Project Costs* – the amount of Money (or Budget) necessary to cover Project Expenses

- *Project Schedule* – the amount of time necessary to meet Project Deliveries

- *Project Scope* – the specific sequence of tasks and/or activities to be performed throughout the Project Life Cycle

- *Project Resources* – the people (capabilities, capacity, and availability), facilities, equipment, and materials required to complete the Scope of Work

- *Product Quality* – the Product Requirements (i.e. features, technical performance, Product costs, etc.) to demonstrate vis-a-vis Product Compliance expectations

- *Project Risks* – the "threats" to Project success, as well as "opportunities" that could bolster Project success

Back "in the day", we referenced the "Triple Constraint", and endeavored to establish a Project Plan that satisfied all three – Project Cost, Schedule, and Scope. Additionally, a fourth important Project Constraint was recognized, Quality (i.e. Product Requirements). With these four constraints we could solve the "planning equation" – or we thought we could. But now, and more aptly, it is recognized by PMI® (Project Management Institute) Global Standards, that we must also consider Project Resources and Risks. To be totally honest, I first heard of the expansion to six Project Constraints when I read the PMI® PMBOK® (Project Management Body of Knowledge) Guide for the first time. After thinking this over, I concluded that it was absolutely genius, and commend the individual(s) who came up with this adjustment. My reasoning is this:

- This collection of **Six Constraints** enables you to conclude that "If one of the Project Constraints changes, it will affect at least one of the other Project Constraints" (PMI, 2013b). After pondering this for a while I agreed that the premise behind this "Rule of Thumb" seems to be indeed true. For example, if an issue arises and impacts a "critical path" task, whereby it causes a major Project Schedule delay, what can you do to get back on track?

  o Change Product **Quality** Requirements (e.g. remove a feature, and thus reduce Project **Scope** and pull the Project **Schedule** back in)?

  o How about adding more **Resources** (and consequently adding more Project **Cos**t/budget)?

  o Or do what is (in my opinion) more commonly done, change (condense) future task durations and essentially add more **Risk** to the Project?

  I can think of scenarios where a change to one Project Constraint can be off-set by affecting only one other Project Constraint but cannot think of a scenario where this fundamental "Rule of Thumb" would not apply, thus I support it whole-heartedly.

- These **Six Constraints** are therefore the logical foundation for a "Balanced" Project Plan. An initial "Balanced" Plan (or "Baseline") necessitates that you satisfy the following:

  1. Meet the Project Sponsor's **Schedule**/Delivery Expectations/Commitments

2. Meet the Project Sponsor's Budgetary/**Cost** Expectations/Commitments

3. Meet the Project Sponsor's Product **Quality**/Requirements Expectations/Commitments

4. Establish a **Scope** of Work that aligns with the above Expectations/Commitments

5. Secure **Resource** Expectations/Commitments (capabilities, capacities, and availabilities) to execute Project Scope within the Schedule and Budgetary Constraints

6. Stay within the Stakeholders' **Risk** Tolerances (i.e. Individual Risk Severity Tolerance level, and Overall Project Risk Threshold level)

Note that the words "Expectations" and "Commitments" are used in reference to the first five Project Constraints, and that "Tolerances" is used for the Risk Constraint. This is important, for Project Risk can be considered more "Variable" relative to the other five Project Constraints – nonetheless, it is important to also bound the risks (a topic of more in-depth discussion within Chapter 4: Managing Risks).

THE **BASIS** OF **ESTIMATE**

The Project Plan can only be as good as the estimates used to construct it. I was exposed to an interesting concept early in my career when I worked as a Deputy Program Manager at an Aerospace and Defense company – the "**Basis of Estimate**". In that world, the Government Program Offices (i.e. Sponsoring Agencies) have the right to conduct detailed assessments of proposal estimates and, in some cases, can commission the support of their auditing agency to perform an "independent" audit of the underlying organizational rates which were used to calculate the financials. We either negotiated the Product/Project Requirements or received a Request for Information/Proposal/Quote based on a sponsor-provided Statement of Work (along with the contract

Terms and Conditions) and Requirements. We were expected to provide reams of data to support our estimates of the detailed Project Scope, Resource Requirements, Schedule, and Costs. This was always an ordeal, and eventually, over the years, I got pretty good at it – from a Program Manager's stand-point. And now I appreciate the knowledge I received from not only preparing proposals/quotes but negotiating the related contracts as well.

A good BOE (Basis of Estimate) is inherently defendable. There are ways to develop defendable BOEs, but it is usually all about having credible SMEs (Subject Matter Experts) and good data on past Project performance, which is up-to-date and readily retrievable. The primary estimating methodologies are provided below.

Bottom-up Approach

Arguably the most common method of estimating is via the "Bottom-up" approach. This is basically a process that uses the combination of Expert Judgement from knowledgeable individuals or SMEs and preliminary quotes from suppliers. The SMEs involved may, or may not, use "Analogous" Data to facilitate the process – those who do are judicious, and their estimates are typically more credible and acceptable.

The pros of Bottom-up estimating:

- The process is relatively quick

- The process is not overly cumbersome

- This is the most appropriate methodology for very complex Projects with scope that has not necessarily been performed in the past (i.e. on prior Projects within that organization), or where past data was not necessarily/adequately collected or organized

- Judgements from SMEs are typically considered valid and credible

The cons of Bottom-up estimating:

- When obtaining inputs from more than one SME, the resulting estimates are likely to be inconsistent, since they are typically determined based on different "estimation biases" (i.e. propensity to be either "conservative", "aggressive" or "neutral" from a Project Risk perspective)

- "Unknown risks" are obviously not estimated per se (for they are not known – so how can they be estimated?), yet might be accounted for with budgetary "reserves" and/or schedule "buffers"

- The SMEs are not usually responsible for performing the tasks, thus they may over- or under-estimate if not aware of the skill level of the individuals who are slated to perform the work

- The estimates established without "Analogous" support data are usually difficult for PMs to defend – PMs can basically only defend SME data based on the estimators' Expert Judgement credibility

- Supplier quotes can be misleading (i.e. too "conservative" or "aggressive") since they are usually provided as "budgetary estimates" and may not be binding, or are NTEs (Not to Exceeds)

Top-down Approach

"Top-down" estimating is entirely valid for certain types of Projects, especially those where Products or Services are repeatedly produced or deployed. You basically "factor" (multiply or divide by an appropriately calculated number based on quantitative differences between past actual effort and the effort being estimated/planned) recurring costs (e.g. per Unit Production Costs) from past overall Project Cost data, to arrive at a new estimate for a different quantity. Top-down estimating (sometimes referred to as "parametric" estimating) can serve as a good general "sanity check" for an estimate derived from an alternative methodology.

The pros of Top-down estimating:

- Very simple, easy, and appropriate for recurring types of Projects

- May suffice for establishing "bogies" (i.e. budgetary estimates)

- Good potential "sanity-check" of estimates for more complex Projects with general similarities to past Projects

The cons of Top-down estimating:

- Requires accurate historical reference data that is readily available

- Generally, is not accurate for new or risky Projects (i.e. those with significantly different Scope of Work relative to any past Projects performed by the same organization)

- Estimates without enough back-up data are difficult to defend

Analogous Estimating

Fundamentally, BOEs for Project Cost and Schedule planning should include as much relevant "Analogous" past data as possible. Even if the input data is not a perfect match, the output is usually better than that estimated from a pure "Bottom-up" or "Top-down" approach. This methodology takes advantage of (to the maximum extent possible) data collected on past Projects. The past actual performance data is typically "factored" to arrive at the estimate.

For example, if it took 10 days to design a PCBA (Printed Circuit Board Assembly) which is 4 inches by 4 inches, with 4 ASICs (Application-Specific Integrated Circuits), 200 "passive" components (e.g. Resistors and Capacitors), no "through-hole" parts, and a 4-layer PCB (Printed Circuit Board), an SME might use this information and estimate that it takes 25 days to design a PCBA which is 4 inches by 6 inches, with 5 ASICs, 270 "passive" components, no "through-hole" parts, and a 6-layer PCB. For this above example, each technical difference could be assessed individually with "factors" to come up with the overall 2.5 times higher estimate (25 days versus 10 days).

These individual "factors" should be derived from a collection of relevant past data whenever possible. Theoretically, estimates get more accurate as you collect more data. Also, this data could potentially feed a Machine-Learning algorithm to assimilate the information and generate optimal "factor" values. The more relevant the data, the more accurate and credible the estimate.

There will likely be gaps in a total Project estimate that maximizes use of "Analogous" data – due to gaps associated with activities that lack relevant past data. A "Bottom-up" estimating methodology is usually employed to fill those gaps. This all sounds very sensible, but the underlying issue is "Does relevant past data exist?". There are ways of maximizing the amount of relevant past data – this is where the WBS (Work Breakdown Structure), organization's Data Warehouse and Project-Tracking processes come into play – to be discussed in the next section of this chapter.

The pros of Analogous estimating:

- Can be extremely accurate, given relevant past Project data exists and is retrievable

- Estimates are credible and relatively easy to defend

- Inherently includes the impact of materialized "unknown risks" – for past data includes the impact of those risks

The cons of Analogous estimating:

- Accuracy depends on the applicability and availability of past performance data

- Usually requires employing other estimating technique(s) for filling gaps in available "Analogous" data (a problem which is exasperated for very complex Projects with a lot of scope that has never been performed in the past by the estimating organization)

- Subtle or hidden gaps in data could cause issues. I experienced this on an important Strategic Project whereby some of the "Analogous" data was inadvertently omitted – and after a year into the Project, when the issue was discovered, the contract could not be completed and had to be cancelled.

Bridging Estimates

I found out early in my career, when managing Proposals (especially those for Projects that I would eventually have to manage), the best way to ensure that my Project Cost and Schedule estimates were valid was to establish both a pure "Bottom-up" estimate and an "Analogous" estimate – then "Bridge" the two. This is not necessarily applicable for Projects which use Incremental or "Agile" Product Development Processes (the topic of Chapter 7: Product Development Process) but can be extremely beneficial for contracted Projects with "Waterfall" (i.e. deterministic or predictive) Product Development Process requirements (i.e. where all Project and Product Requirements are solidified before the Project is kicked off, or very early in the Project Life Cycle), and whereby Project Team performance is highly scrutinized.

The "Bridging" methodology includes thoroughly comparing estimates down to the lowest level of activity – then determining (to the best of the estimating team's ability) why the differences exist. Differences between the estimates are likely, especially if the Project is large and complex. Reconciling the differences might mean increasing or decreasing estimates from either methodology (based on which approach appeared to make more sense) to arrive at a relatively consistent result for both – i.e. "Bridging" the estimates. Ideally, the "Analogous" estimate is higher – theoretically it should be, for the relevant past data used to arrive at those estimates included the impact of materialized "unknown risks", which are, by definition, impossible to estimate (other than to guess) when using a "Bottom-up" approach. Thus, if done well, the total difference should relate to the amount of Management Reserve (i.e. spare Project Budget) and Schedule Buffer to factor into the final estimates. Even if you do not go to this level of specificity, conducting a general comparative review of the two estimates can be helpful.

I learned a very important side-benefit from "Bridging" estimates – it prepared me well for contract negotiations. It enabled my team and me to justify our estimates using two different complementary methodologies; "Bottom-up" with Expert Judgment from SMEs; and "Analogous" estimates based on past actual data. This "Check-and-Balance" is hard to argue with – either to gain buy-in Internally for proposal submission approval, or in negotiating the final contract "terms and conditions" with the Project Customer/Sponsor.

The pros of Bridging:

- Typically, the most accurate estimating methodology, especially for large complex Projects

- Shares the benefits of both "Bottom-up" and "Analogous" methodologies

- Estimates are credible and defendable

The cons of Bridging:

- Most involved and time-consuming estimation process

- Necessitates a good database of information for the "Analogous" estimating portion

- May necessitate an objective facilitator (outside the estimating team) to manage potential bias/"not-invented-here" issues

THE WBS – A PATH TO USABLE DATA

The only time I was able to take advantage of past actual data to its fullest extent was when I worked in the Aerospace and Defense industry. We had to collect the data to bid on Government Contracts, and we were good about organizing the information so that it was readily retrievable and usable. It was all about the WBS (Work Breakdown Structure) and the Cost Control Matrix. In retrospect, the Information System was not perfect, but it did maximize use of the Information Technology available at that time. The "trick" was to codify the data via well-thought-out Cost Account numbering schemes (for use by employees to record their time and what they worked on). Today's technology enables us to greatly extend the capability and use more descriptive naming conventions, but we still need to be cognizant of data storage relational database needs (e.g. using features like "drop-down" menus to ensure consistency in naming/categorizing information to support effective and efficient "data-mining"). If you design the Cost Control Matrix well you can reap an additional benefit – better performance by the Functional Groups as a result of the more direct accountability for estimating, planning and executing the work. The following sub-paragraphs delve into these topics. But first, let's look at WBS and Cost Control Matrix examples to be clear about what the tools are.

Basically, the Figure 9 WBS chart looks like and Organization Chart but focusses on the hierarchy of Project work activities instead. [Note – I have also seen WBSs used to establish IPTs (Integrated Product Teams) on large Projects, and to facilitate development of a compatible Project Organization Chart]. Ideally, each activity represents a segregable piece of work (i.e. work that has high-level interdependencies relative to inputs (predecessor activities) and outputs (successor activities) – enabling "roll-ups" of data into larger groupings, and ultimately, for the entire Project Scope of Work. Being segregable enables estimating, planning, and executing Project work in smaller collective "chunks". It also supports the concept of functional accountability, discussed next.

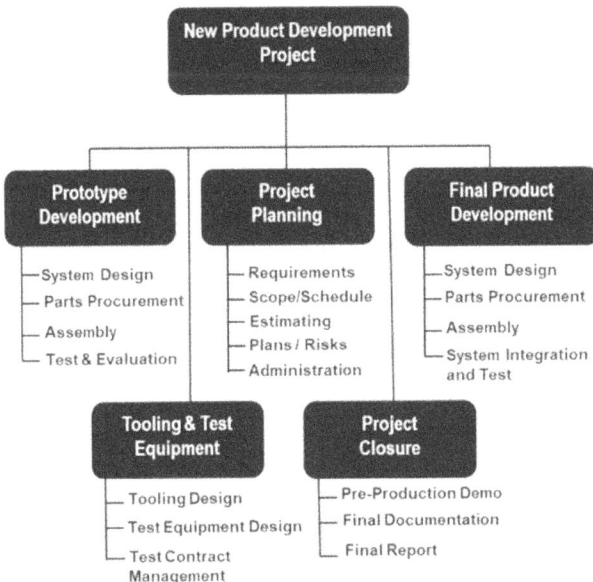

Figure 9. WBS (Work Breakdown Structure) Example

ACHIEVING EPIC BUSINESS RESULTS

Accountability through Objective Visibility

What happens when everything we do in our job is visible, especially if visible to those who evaluate our performance and consider us for raises and promotions? We tend to work hard to ensure that our performance data sends the "right" messages so that we reap the rewards becoming of good performers. A well designed WBS can enable this visibility, and this visibility becomes more important in organizations with Matrix Structures (i.e. where separate groups with specific expertise are combined as a "Function" that provides Project Resources for all the various Projects). Figure 10 provides a visual of how this kind of structure might be set up – by showing "solid" lines of accountability to the Functional Groups that we report to directly, and "dashed" lines to Projects that we support (i.e. indirect reporting relationships).

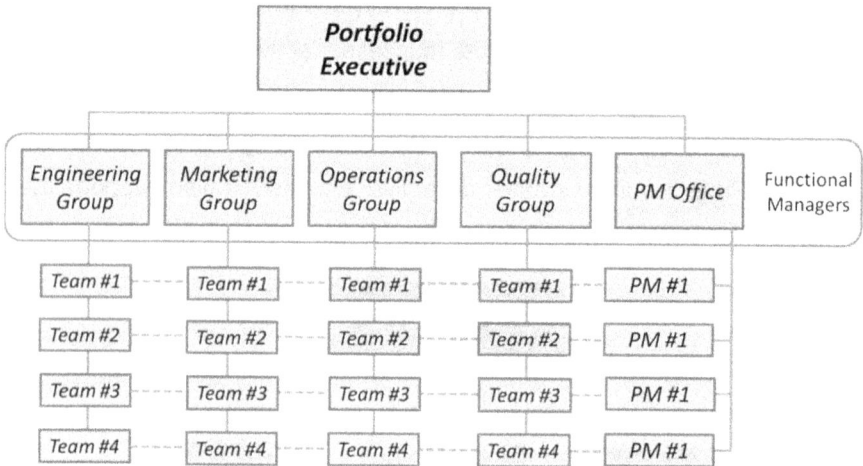

Figure 10. Example Generic Matrix Organization Structure

In today's complex world, with multi-national operations and diverse/dispersed Project Teams, larger companies tend to organize in Matrix Structures. There are several different kinds of Matrix Structures (e.g. Weak, Balanced and Strong) that are we introduced to in Chapter 2 (Managing Expectations). They are typically established in accordance with Organizational Leadership preferences. Regardless of the structure, what is most important is that we understand the concepts noted in the subsequent paragraphs.

If Projects are measured at the top level only (relative to overall Project Cost, Schedule and/or Technical performance), you put all the pressure on the Project Managers. And the Project Managers are not afforded much leverage to exert on the managers of support organizations, relative to the quality of their estimates, plans and execution for their Project responsibilities. This can cause a myriad of issues – and the only individuals with visible accountability are the Project Managers, who (by the way) typical have only a few "direct reports", if any. The Functional Managers are let "off the hook". To get around this issue and improve the probability of success on organizational Projects, it only makes sense that the Functional Managers are appropriately motivated to always put their best foot forward – this typically requires measuring and tracking their group's performance on Projects they support.

Collecting data per a well-designed WBS can remedy the above issue. This can be accomplished by setting up Cost Accounts (for charging time) with unique numerical or notational identifiers established for the various organizations performing the work – basically expanding the WBS as shown in Figure 11 (to include an Organization Chart tab and identifying [with and "X"] the effort those organizations conduct). With this methodology, functional performance on the Project is tracked separately to enable visibility at that level, and to instill accountability (for estimates, plans and execution) amongst the Functional Managers. This is not a "political move", but a fair and practical way of ensuring (at the organizational levels) that all Projects are receiving the appropriate level of support, and that potential problem areas are identified and judiciously fixed. This approach can lead to greater success across the enterprise.

Notional Project Cost Account Matrix (Organization Structure on Top Tab and WBS on Side Tab)	Management					Engineering					Operations				Procurement					Quality				
	Project Management	Finance Assistance	Contracts Administration	Data and Change Management Support	Technical Management	System Engineering	Mechanical Engineering	Electrical Engineering	Software Engineering	Test Engineering	NPI (New Product Introduction) Management	Manufacturing Engineering	Manufacturing	Logistics Support	Materials Management	Procurement Support	Subcontracts Administration	Subcontracts	Materials	Quality Assurance Management	Quality Engineering (Product Q & Rel., Test Dev.)	Shipping and Receiving	Supplier Quality Engineering	Quality Assurance (Product)
Project Planning	X	X	X	X	X						X				X					X				
Prototype Development	X	X	X	X	X						X				X					X				
Porotype Design						X	X	X	X	X		X				X	X	X	X		X		X	
Procure Parts (Initial Assembly)																X	X	X	X		X		X	
Procure Parts (Final Assembly)																					X		X	
Initial Assembly of Prototypes												X	X										X	X
Final Assembly of Prototypes												X	X										X	X
Engineering Test & Evaluation						X	X	X	X	X	X										X			X
Initial Design Review																								
Final Product Development	X	X	X	X	X						X				X					X				
Final Product Design						X	X	X	X	X	X					X	X	X	X		X		X	
Procure Long Lead Material																X	X	X	X		X		X	
Procure Remaining Material																					X		X	
Initial Assembly of POR Systems												X	X							X	X			X
Final Assembly of POR Systems												X	X										X	X
Conduct System Qualification						X	X	X	X	X	X													X
Verify Final Design Iterations						X	X	X	X	X	X										X			X
Final Design Review																								
Pre-Production	X	X	X	X	X						X				X					X				
Launch Readiness Review																								
Procure Remaining Production Material																X	X	X	X				X	
Project Closure	X	X	X	X	X						X				X					X				

Figure 11. Example Project Control Accounts Chart

Data is Useful if Well Organized and Cataloged

We are now in the era of "data analytics" and "machine-learning" – carried further, "artificial intelligence". Taking advantage of this type of analytical data manipulation and analysis is heavily dependent on the way data is organized. The question is: "Is the data supportive of relational database attributes – e.g. identification, cataloging, aggregation and retrieval "data-mining" functions?" This is important.

For example, if you have enough cataloged data, you can let the "machine" help determine "complexity factors" for "Analogous" estimates – and this could be invaluable for determining estimates and developing good plans. This means that, not only would you need activity descriptions (e.g. Printed Circuit Board Assembly [PCBA] layout descriptors, etc.), costs, and times/durations – you would need more specifics regarding key parameters which influence the Project Cost and Schedule, e.g. PCBA surface area, whether single- or double-sided, number of components within the various categories (e.g. "passives", ASICs, connectors, etc.), whether it is for "surface-mounted" parts or "through-hole" or both, number of PCB (Printed Circuit Board) layers, component "pick-and-place" feature sizes, etc.

Whether or not you are familiar with the above terms, you should get the picture. With that type of data for every PCBA design, an SME is afforded with the capability to derive some very good estimates of future design times and costs, especially if augmented by data relative to the type of HR (Human Resource) capability and equipment used to perform the work, as well. Using ERP (Enterprise Resource Planning) systems which necessitate electronic WADs (Work Authorization Documentations) with this type of descriptive information is one way to accomplish the data collection. There are other methods as well. The key is to design the process well and ensure that the data collection process is as useful as possible for supporting data analytics and improved estimating.

How About Data Collection of Work Effort (i.e. Time)?

We should recognize that many companies (especially small firms or those in certain industries, like Consumer Products and Services) do not require (or necessarily want) regimented time reporting practices which tie into their ERP financial systems to calculate and report spending. Some do, however, require "Effort" reporting by employees. Others may record such data via periodic generation of aggregate estimates by supervisors or Functional Managers, on behalf of their entire groups. From an estimating standpoint, any one of these alternatives is better than not performing data collection at all – even if it is just setting up a log/spreadsheet to record important Project performance information (e.g. start and end dates, changes experienced, outcomes achieved, etc.) at the completion of a Project. Or, if Phase Reviews are conducted, at least storing the presentation files in hard-copy and/or soft-copy folders, facilitates subsequent retrieval, when and if necessary.

ACHIEVING EPIC BUSINESS RESULTS

I have seen the effective use of a "home-grown" Effort Tracking system at a very large corporation, whereby employees were required to record (daily) the hours they worked on various Projects and On-going Operations, as well as their time-off from work (e.g. vacation, sick leave, bereavement, etc.). This data proved to be extremely useful in supporting management of BU (Business Unit) Portfolios (a topic included in Chapter 2: Managing Expectations). An Effort Tracking methodology like this can be readily extended for use in future Project Resource estimating.

THE PLC CRADLE-TO-GRAVE ACTIVITIES

Since all Projects, by definition, are "temporary endeavors" (PMI, 2013b) they have a distinct life cycle – naturally referred to as the "Project Life Cycle". This Project Life Cycle (or PLC, and not to be confused with the Product Life Cycle nomenclature sometimes used as well) is segmented into four distinct phases: Project Initiation, Project Planning, Project Execution, and Project Closure. Figure 12 depicts the general process.

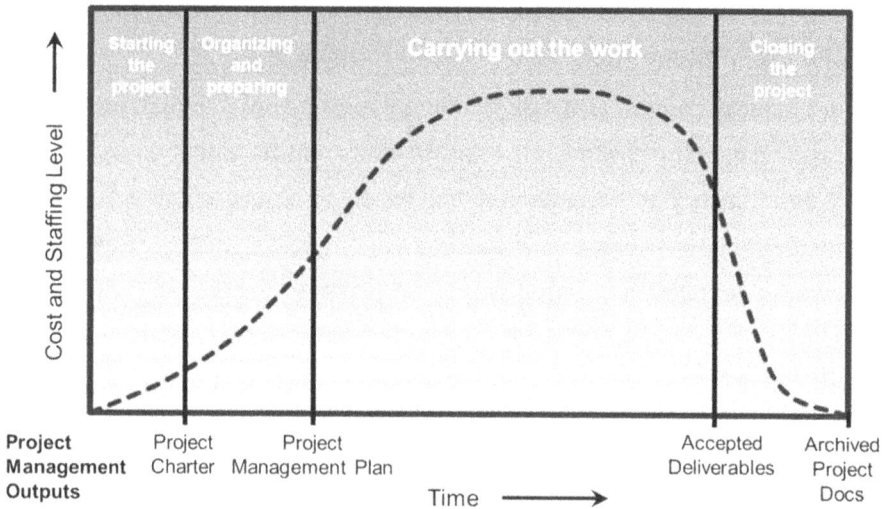

Figure 12. Generic PLC (Project Life Cycle). PMBOK® Guide - Fifth Edition (PMI, 2013b, p 39)

The key Project Life Cycle milestones are described in the subsequent sub-sections.

Project Initiation – the actual beginning of the Project. If the Project is established for development of a Strategic Product, it is likely to be driven by an approved Product Roadmap and supported by a Project Business Case. The high-level Product Requirements listed on a Product Roadmap (and included in the Business Case) drive the development of this phase's completion milestone, an approved Project Charter, which is discussed in detail within Chapter 1: Managing Requirements.

Start of Project Planning – the start of detailed Project planning is typically driven by receipt of an approved Project Charter by the assigned Project Manager (and Planning Team Members). Although the Project Charter is discussed in more detail in Chapter 1, suffice it to say that this document (or e-mail notification or verbal direction, etc.) contains all the essential information deemed necessary for beginning development of the detailed Project Plan. This phase typically culminates with a PMP (Project Management Plan) that lays out the detailed Project SOW (Scope of Work), Schedule, Budgets, Resource and Risk Plans approved by Sponsors and/or Organizational Managers as part of the Balanced/Baselined Project Plan. This plan is usually assumed to be thorough enough to support achievement of POR (Plan of Record) Product Requirements (per Product Quality expectations) within the organization's established Project Risk tolerances.

Project Kick-off – the meeting for (or announcement of) the start of Project execution by the Team-at-Large (i.e. various individuals assigned to the work on the Project). Ideally this is facilitated by an approved Project Management Plan (discussed in detail within the next section of this chapter). Bottom-line, the baselined Project Plan (a "Balanced" plan) is communicated to the key Project's Stakeholders (e.g. Function Managers and assigned Team Members, etc.), along with specific direction as to how the Project will be managed (e.g. Communication Protocols, Decision-Making Authorities, Periodic Meetings, Progress Update Reporting, Management Tools & Techniques employed, etc.).

ACHIEVING EPIC BUSINESS RESULTS

Project Completion/Wrap-up – an event typically marked by final delivery of end-Products, Services and/or Results (i.e. Project Deliverables). All subsequent effort (if expected) is typically referred to as post-Launch or post-Deployment, or Sustaining activities, whereby the receiving organizations assume the follow-on post-Project responsibilities and the Project Team Members quickly ramp down and are re-assigned to other organizational activities.

Project Closure – marks the end of the Project, where no further effort is deemed necessary. In some organizations, Project Postmortems are conducted and concluded by this time – a recognized "good practice". Key Team Members look back at past issues encountered and document Lessons Learned to determine (as appropriate) Systemic Cas (Corrective Actions) to ensure that those issues do not re-occur on future Projects – the subject of Chapter 10: Lessons Learned.

As you can see from this brief explanation of the Project Life Cycle, there are many elements to Project planning which are strategically important to Project Management activities enterprise-wide.

THE **PROJECT MANAGEMENT PLAN** VS. THE **PROJECT PLAN**

This topic was briefly introduced in the last section. Here we will delve a little deeper, for you may believe that the Project Management Plan and 'Kick-Off' are only about the establishment and communication of the initial baseline Project Plan – however, if done well, it is more involved than that. Documenting and communicating the Project Plan is certainly important, but the Project Management Plan should involve more than just comprehending/understanding the tasks to complete and their timing. It is also about how the Project will be managed, monitored, and controlled, including who will be engaged in these activities, what Tools & Techniques will be employed, and what the various roles, responsibilities and decision-making authorities are. In my experience I have found that most organizations that work hard to establish good Project Plans also tend to do a good job in communicating that plan to stakeholders. For some, the

"Plan" is all that matters, but leaving out the "Management" piece opens the door to potential stakeholder confusion and can ultimately jeopardize Project Team performance.

Figure 13 is a flow-chart example of the typical process steps taken to establish a Project Plan from its Charter, and the final Project Management Plan which kicks the Project off. That final Project Management Plan includes the Project Plan and elaborates upon how the Project will be managed. Without this latter piece (how the Project will be managed) the Project Management Plan is incomplete.

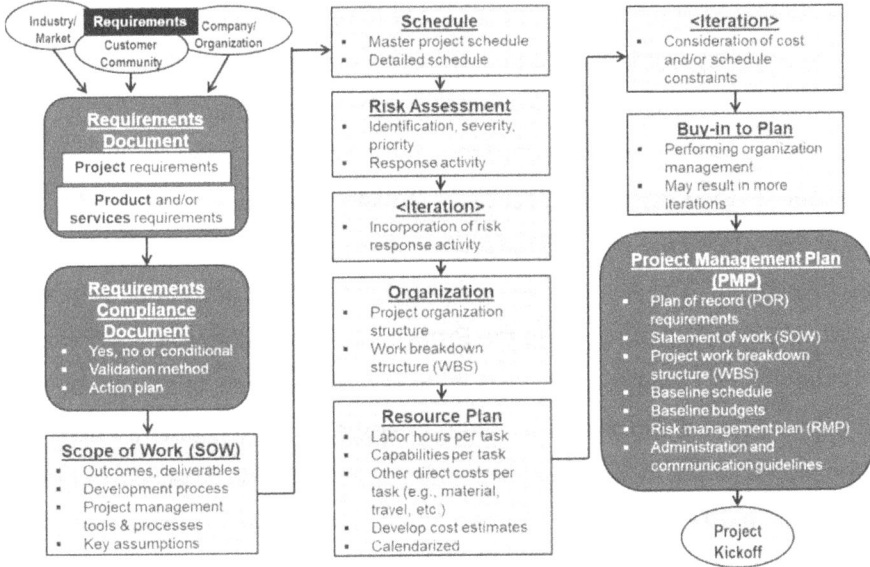

Figure 13. Example Project Planning Process Flow. *Project Risk Management (PMI, 2016, p. 28)*

The Project Plan

The Project Plan is essentially the culmination of the steps in the above process that produce a detailed Product description, Project Scope of Work, Baseline Schedule, Baseline Cost, Resource Plan, and Risk Assessment. This should be a "Balanced" Plan as discussed earlier in this chapter and should coincide with all key Project Charter directives. Note that for the various Product Development Processes employed (refer to Chapter 7: Product Development Process), a Balanced Project Plan is not necessarily fully deterministic, where all Project Constraints are definitively established up-front.

The Project Management Plan

As a Program Manager in the Aerospace and Defense industry I was always required to produce a Program/Project Management Plan document for the Project Sponsor's (and key Stakeholders') approval as a condition for starting Project execution by the Team-at-large. If the effort was internally approved using IR&D (Independent Research and Development) funds, we had to comply with certain documentation and procedural requirements for the company to receive financial credit for that work. And Government Contracts (or sub-Contracts) typically called out the submission of an official Project/Program Management Plan deliverable, per Military Standard requirements, which specified the content. In the Consumer Electronics industry, we typically provided a slide deck, briefed it at the Project Kick-off meeting, and saved it in an archive folder. The content was either established in compliance with an internal procedure or left up to the Project Managers' discretion. In smaller companies, or for smaller Projects in large organizations, this could be a much less formal process (e.g. e-mail or verbal communication). Regardless of the industry, organization, or Project type, I have concluded that, from a Strategic Project Management perspective it is best (or a "good practice") to establish a consistent process with standardized minimum basic information for initiating Project work.

The content of a thorough **Project Management Plan** might include (but is not limited to) the following:

- POR (Plan of Record) Project and Product Requirements and Change Management process
- Project Priorities and Key Assumptions
- Scope (including Product Development Process description) Baseline and Management
- Schedule Baseline and Management
- Budget Baseline and Management

- Resource Requirements and Management

- Risk Baseline and Management

- Operations (e.g. Manufacturing, Service Deployment, etc.) Readiness Plan

- Sourcing Strategy

- Quality Management Expectations

- Decision-Making and Communications Guidelines

- Sponsor and Team Meetings, and Key Reviews

- Documentation Requirements

- Project Management Tools & Techniques Employed

Notice all the "Plans" in the above list. These are due to the dynamic nature of Projects, and they may simply call out responsibilities and the processes for managing those aspects of the Project over the course of the Project Life Cycle. I would tell Program and Project Managers who worked for me that if they did not like planning and re-planning and re-planning and re-planning... (you get the point) then they are in the wrong job. We will touch on several of the above topics throughout this book. The PMBOK® Guide and my other book on **Project Risk Management** are good references for those interested in finding out more of the details. The key message here is that there is much more to Project Management than just putting a plan together, communicating it to the Project Stakeholders, and executing. Over the course of the Project Life Cycle teams will run into issues and will need to effectively deal with them. Much of this book is about how to do so in the most efficient way – with the most appropriate application of Strategic Project Management practices.

Is Your Organization Managing Projects Strategically?

Take the test, or at least see how your organization stacks up. An inventory of the key Strategic Project Management concepts espoused by this book can be kept, Chapter by Chapter. There is no established reference of good or bad, but you can see where your organization currently is, and use this tool to monitor progress. Each question starts with the phrase: To what extent does your organization......

11. ensure that **All Projects** start with a truly **"Balanced" Plan?**

1	2	3	4	5
O	O	O	O	O
Never	Rarely	Sometimes	Most of the Time	Always

12. estimate and establish **Credible** and **Justifiable Project Cost and Schedule Commitments?**

1	2	3	4	5
O	O	O	O	O
Never	Rarely	Sometimes	Most of the Time	Always

13. collect and store historical **Project Data** in organized, meaningful and retrievable ways?

1	2	3	4	5
O	O	O	O	O
Never	Rarely	Sometimes	Most of the Time	Always

14. initiate detailed **Project Planning** with a formal/documented **Project Charter?**

1	2	3	4	5
O	O	O	O	O
Never	Rarely	Sometimes	Most of the Time	Always

15. Kick-Off Projects with a formally communicated **Project Management Plan?**

1	2	3	4	5
O	O	O	O	O
Never	Rarely	Sometimes	Most of the Time	Always

CHAPTER 4

It's *MANAGING RISKS*

I remember when I was first required to officially manage Project Risks as part of a government contract with the DoD (Department of Defense). I was given templates to fill out as part of the MIL-STD (Military Standard) referenced by the contract. I recall flailing around trying to figure out what to do, and eventually finding my way. That was in the 1980's. Since then, the Project Management Institute (PMI®) has become increasingly more influential, and many of the Tools & Techniques originally established by the DoD have found their way into more industries, have become better understood and are more globally accepted. Project Risk Management Tools & Techniques are now much better defined. I wrote my first book on the subject, in part, to help practitioners: (1) better understand "Practical Implementation Approaches" to managing Project Risks; and (2) to select and implement the "practices" that can enable their Projects to be more successfully executed. In that book I elaborate on the "classical" (or basic) Project Risk Management processes but extended further – into the realm of "holistic" Risk Management – something I firmly believe is an essential ingredient to successful Strategic Project Management.

The following are a handful of observations I have made regarding the implementation of Project Risk Management practices.

ACHIEVING EPIC BUSINESS RESULTS

- Overall Project Cost and Schedule Risks (referred to as "Quantitative" Risks) are more typically determined in an "qualitative" manner – using Expert Judgement versus a more quantitative methodology like Modelling & Simulation.

- Project Risk Registers, Assumptions Registers and Risk Matrices are not overly complex tools for managing individual task (or activity) risks, thus from what I can tell, many organizations and Project Managers do indeed use them. One caution is that the detailed use of these tools should be governed, and not left to the discretion of the Project Managers and Teams to define Rating Criteria and Tolerance Zones.

- Organizational Managers tend to do a pretty good job of conducting Project Postmortems to learn from "technical" or Product Development Process issues but are not as honest and forthright about conducting Project Postmortems to learn from miscues originating from "managerial" or Organizational Management process deficiencies.

- Lack of Project Risk Management understanding at higher levels of management tends to result in putting the onus on Project Managers to determine the right management methodologies (i.e. Tools & Techniques) to employ – and Project Managers tend to have difficulty with this themselves, compelling them to revert to doing what they have always done, whether applicable or not. These "practices" should be handled via Organizational Governance and established as a guideline for all Project Teams to adhere to. The key is to do so without making them too bureaucratic and then potentially ignored – but this is not nearly as difficult as some people may think.

- Insurance companies have profited from consolidating (or pooling) risks into Portfolios to lower overall financial exposure. Organizations can do something similar, for this is one of the benefits of establishing Portfolios and/or Programs – the pooling of risks. Is this proactively done in your organization or is it more of an ad hoc process? – in my experience it tended to be the latter, or not done at all.

If your organization does manage Project Risks well, then I commend your leadership – but I have seen many organizations struggle with this "practice", and suspect that this situation is more common than not. In Chapter 1 (Managing Requirements) I allude to the fact that very few PMPs who I encounter at PMI® Chapter meetings have ever used Modelling & Simulation to manage Overall Project Risks. The realization that a clear "Best Practice" is not being employed by most organizations tells me that many are missing out on the full benefits of Strategic Project Management. More on this in Chapter 8 (Employing Best Practices).

If you would like to learn about more Project Risk Management specifics, I would encourage that you get my other book on the subject. Here, in this chapter, we will delve into the topic at a higher level, focusing on several of the bullet-point observations provided above.

RELATIONSHIP BETWEEN RISK MANAGEMENT AND THE IMS

A well-developed Project IMS (Integrated Master Schedule) can greatly facilitate Project Risk Management. Many practitioners realize this, and as such, the DoD commissioned a Group several years ago to establish "guidelines" which are now referred to as the DCMA (Defense Contractor Management Agency) 14-Point Metric (DCMA, 2012) to ensure that good IMS development practices were being followed to facilitate EVM (Earned Value Management). EVM is a very good Project Risk Management tool which, if employed well, provides beneficial Early Warning Indicators which can prompt proactive remedial action before the situation worsens (more on this in Chapter 5: Cost of Change).

Engaging in this discussion requires that we first define what constitutes a well-constructed IMS. Warning: the more popular Integrated Master Scheduling tools provide a plethora of options and features, and their developers tend to keep adding more features to enable almost any kind of schedule to be created, sensible or not. This can cause confusion and potential issues. Bottom-line, you can build a Project Schedule in so many ill-advised ways. Doing so negates some of the extended benefits

ACHIEVING EPIC BUSINESS RESULTS

of a well-constructed IMS. To demonstrate, please bear with me as I get into the "weeds" a bit with some examples of what I am alluding to:

- You can construct a schedule with ALL "fixed" dates (i.e. task Start and Finish dates for each task are "fixed" or Manually Scheduled) – this is not an "Integrated" schedule – it is basically a simple Gantt chart. It will not self-adjust as changes to the network of tasks are made.

- You can tie a task start date to the completion of a predecessor task assuming a "negative lag" that is greater than the previous task's total time duration (i.e. start a new task before the predecessor task is even started) – this is not how we normally work. You cannot go backwards in time.

- You can assign task time durations and interdependencies (i.e. Predecessor and Successor relationships) to Summary Tasks that are normally used to simply roll up a set of lower level task activities and are usually only "administrative". This is not appropriate for most conventional schedules, although some "Agile" process schedules may use this approach for fixing "Sprint" time-frames.

- You can manually fix the start dates of tasks that are driven by other "automatically" scheduled tasks, and in this case, you are defeating the benefit of automatically re-scheduling when the Project Schedule is adjusted.

- You can experience problems or "planning misunderstandings" if you do not use "Soft Constraints" like "Start as soon as Possible" – for there are several other options to potentially choose from, like "Start as late as Possible" or "Start no Later than", etc. – these might have utility in certain types of schedules, but not for those expected to be used or imported into Schedule Risk Analysis (SRA) tools or Earned Value Management (EVM) systems.

- You can plan and schedule work on weekends, whether your organization works on those days or not.

- You can plan and schedule work on Holidays or Company Shut-Down days if they are not input into the IMS calendar.

- You can input a task that does not lead to any other work (so why do it?), or that leads to work many months in the future (so why do it so early?)

The above schedule construction issues are some of the more common that I have run across. The good schedule construction practices that I advocate are those which avoid the above and do as prescribed below:

- Focus on ensuring that not only the CP (Critical Path) is well understood, but that all "near-CPs" and potential "near-CPs" are comprehended and included as well.

- Progressively elaborate upon the schedule detail over time (i.e. develop good task detail or fidelity on near-term activities and less on the longer-term activities, and as time progresses, continually elaborate in more detail on the pending near-term activities by converting them to a series of more manageable tasks).

- Do not worry about Level of Effort (LOE) activities for they do not drive the schedule (e.g. Project Management, Financial Analysis, Scheduling Support, or other similar support activities).

- Incorporate all key out-source dependencies (e.g. Product Materials, Consulting Services, Test Facilities/Services, etc.) – giving then visibility and interim deliverables to monitor progress. These can turn out to be the riskiest activities, for they are not necessarily under your organization's direct control.

- Provide enough fidelity (i.e. decompose large activities into a series of smaller more manageable tasks) to gain greater insight into Project progress in areas that warrant careful monitoring and control – especially those that act as Early Warning Indicators of key potential pending issues.

- Provide enough fidelity to segregate work performed by different Functional Organizations to ensure the appropriate level of visibility and accountability is established for tracking and data retention purposes. This can also be of benefit for future Project estimating.

- Do not dwell on so much granularity that it makes the Project Schedule maintenance activity overly cumbersome and bureaucratic.

So, let us now assume that you have a well-developed IMS. Usually, seasoned Project Managers, Team Leads, and Functional Managers can readily identify the tasks or activities which represent the most Project Schedule risk. Since IMS tools typically support "Resource Loading" as well, by applying Human Resource assumptions to each task, resource, and cost trade-offs (and risks) can be assessed. Having a complete Project Schedule in front of you provides a good visual of how to sequence tasks best (i.e. in series, parallel, or over-lapping) – which is useful for trying to figure out how to save time on certain activities, if necessary. An example of the classical "Waterfall" (or Predictive/Deterministic) Project Schedule is shown in Figure 14 below.

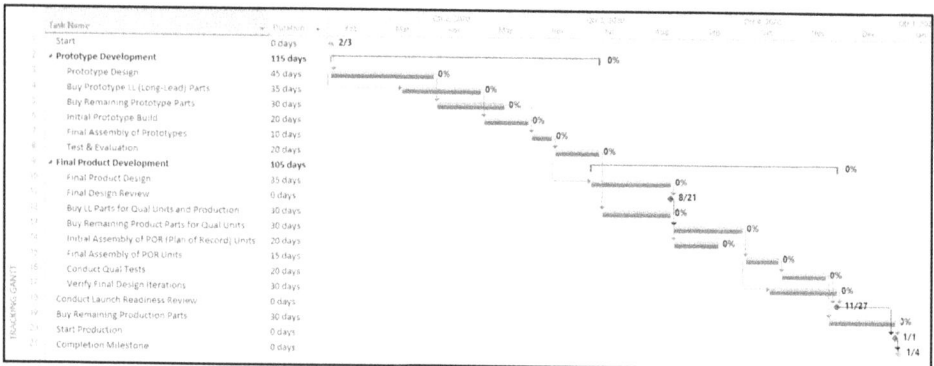

Figure 14. Example of IMS for a Waterfall Product Development Process

The connection between the Project IMS and Risk Management should be clear but is not generally well understood. In short, if your IMS is well-structured you can more effectively employ other "Bests Practices", i.e.:

- **Modelling & Simulation**, which provides the Project Team with the information necessary to evaluate Individual Project Risks more effectively, and to pro-actively conduct "what-ifs" to: (1) create better plans; (2) evaluate proposed Project changes; and (3) communicate % confidence in achieving Project objectives. This methodology has been around for decades, and basically involves the determination of Overall "Quantitative" Project Risks from the Individual Project Risks and Opportunities and using Modelling & Simulation to arrive at probabilistic solution sets – discussed in more detail within the next section.

  - o **SRA (Schedule Risk Analysis)**, which focusses on the Modelling & Simulation of schedule task duration (i.e. time) estimates and provides the Project Team with both Overall Project Schedule confidence (i.e. % confidence of achieving critical Project delivery commitments on time) and information necessary to effectively evaluate and analyze the Schedule Risks and Opportunities associated with individual Project tasks.

- **Project Status Updating**, which seems obvious, but is not necessarily done (or done appropriately) after the Project is "Baselined" and "Kicked-off". IMS updating is a fundamental Monitoring and Controlling process which, if done well, can provide greater insights into pending issues and facilitate pro-active Project Management. One of the most effective pro-active measures is EVM, or the practical ES (Earned Schedule) off-shoot mentioned later.

- **EVM (Earned Value Management)**, which was conceived for continually/periodically processing Project Resource and/or Cost performance data to produce Early Warning Metrics throughout the life of the Project – thus, this tool is dependent on Project status updating. The general idea is to evaluate how well the Project Team is performing against the original Project Plan (i.e. the "Baseline"

IMS) in completing the "work planned" over that time – referred to as the EV (Earned Value) compared against the "Planned Value". Knowing this enables you to compute Project Team efficiency metrics and extrapolate from "Actual" Project performance achieved to compute "Independent" (i.e. projected) end-states, which basically serve as Early Warning Indicators. Refer to Chapter 5 (Cost of Change) for more detail.

- ○ **ES (Earned Schedule)**, which is considered a practical expansion of EVM for schedule-related metrics. This methodology is espoused within the PMI® Inc. Global Standards on Project Management, as one of the "Trends and Emerging Practices in Project Cost Management" (*PMI, 2019*, p. 233). The ES methodology measures Project Time on a task-by-task basis and determines the cumulative Earned Schedule (from completed and active tasks) by calculating the amount of time taken (or expected to be taken) to complete the tasks (the "Actual" time) and comparing that result to the "Baseline" time estimates established for those tasks (the "Planned" time). This approach, in conjunction with IMS and SRA, provides the practical application of "Bests Practices" in planning and controlling schedules on "time-sensitive" Projects.

INDIVIDUAL (QUALITATIVE) RISK MANAGEMENT TOOLS

Project Managers and Teams have benefited from the use of practical tools developed to formally list, categorize, assess, act-upon and manage Project Risks (Threats) and Opportunities throughout the Project Life Cycle. Originally conceived of for use by the DoD, the Risk Register and Risk Matrix have found their way into many other industries, for they are not very complex or costly to employ. Thus, the use of these Tools & Techniques is considered a "good practice" due to their relative cost-effectiveness. Another complementary tool is the Assumption Register. Each is elaborated upon in more detail within this chapter.

Risk Register – Foundation of Classical Risk Management

The Risk Register is a simple table of information that is set up to log and track risks (threats) and opportunities. Ideally, this tool is maintained throughout the Project Life Cycle. Figure 15 shows an example template. In summary, Individual Project Risks are described, categorized, assessed, and responded to with "Action Plans" to lessen their "Severity".

	Risk (Threat) or Opportunity						
Item	Description	Project Objectives Potentially Impacted (cost, schedule, scope, quality)	Response Plan	Probability	Impact / Consequence	Severity
A						0
B						0
C						0
D						0
E						0
F						0
G						0
H						0
I						0
J						0
					Total	0

Figure 15. Example Risk Register Template

The Risk "Severity" level is derived from two key parameters of risk:

- the Likelihood or **Probability** of occurrence; and
- the Impact or **Consequence** to the Project should that risk materialize and become issue

The Risk Severity is typically represented as the product of these two parameters (i.e. Severity = Probability X Impact). You can thus establish a range of numerical levels of "Probability" and "Impact" to help quantify the Severity level of each risk (threat) and opportunity – and then display them on a grid; the Risk Matrix (discussed further in the next section).

A Meta-Language Statement can be formed to articulate the vital risk description parameters (i.e. Risk, Cause and Effect [or Impact]), and another Meta-Language Statement can be formed from this information to succinctly articulate the Individual Project Task Risk description. These two Meta-Language Statements are provided next.

> **As a result of <CAUSE>, <RISK> may occur, which will lead to <EFFECT>.**
>
> Risk Description**: <RISK> due to <CAUSE>**

Here is an example taken from my other book on *Project Risk Management*:

> "As a result of **more than expected test failures**, **more design-build-test cycles** may occur, which will lead to **schedule delays and added project costs**."
>
> Risk Description: **More design-build-test cycles** due to **more than expected test failures**.

Another use of this Risk Register is to provide insight into proposed "Action Plans" that can be established (i.e. Risk Responses) which either:

- decrease the Probability and/or Impact of a RISK (threat); or
- increase the Probability and/or Impact of an OPPORTUNITY.

Once the potential (or proposed) "Action Plans" are accepted, the Risk Severities are re-evaluated to show the effects of the implemented actions on the Project. If so inclined, the Project Team can identify the times/events when the effectiveness of these responses is expected to be realized, and track/monitor the Project Risk "Burn-Down" over the course of the Project's Life Cycle. More on this can be found in my *Project Risk Management* book. More on the numeric "Probability" and "Impact" ratings later in this chapter.

Project Assumptions Tend to Take Away Risks

An important (and sometimes-overlooked) Project Management Tool is the Assumption Register (or list of assumptions). Assumptions typically take away (i.e. eliminate) Project Risks (threats) – so this concept cannot be left out of the risk discussion, for it is an important element of Project Governance, and thus, Strategic Project Management. I am a believer in displaying Project Assumptions front-and-center in important Project documents and during key reviews (e.g. Project Business Cases, Project Charters, System Requirements Reviews, System Concept Reviews, System Design Reviews, Project Management Plans, Project Kick-Off Meetings, Phase Entry/Exit Reviews, Product Launch Reviews, etc.). These should be overt and not a surprise to anybody. I have seen push-back to this visibility, especially from the Project Stakeholders who approved the Project Assumptions and do not necessarily want that level of visibility. But it is important to make them very visible, for it cannot be made an excuse later – that a key Project Stakeholder "did not know or realize this was an Assumption, for if they did, they would not have agreed to it". Some Assumption examples are provided below.

- Government Furnished Equipment meets Technical Specs and is provided by a certain date

- Lower priority Product Requirement(s) can be jeopardized if necessary, to preserve Project Schedule

- "Equitable Adjustments" to Project Cost and Schedule will be granted if the Sponsor directs Requirements or Scope changes

- Weather Patterns are assumed to be those considered typical for the area and Time of Year, and extreme variances will allow the Project Team to re-Baseline the Project Plan, if necessary

- Critical/scarce resources will be made available within a certain window of time

- No surprise Regulatory Requirements changes are expected to be accommodated without re-Baselining the Project Plan, if necessary

The Risk Matrix – a Versatile and Easy-to-Use Tool

I have learned to both love and hate the Risk Matrix. I love it for its simplicity and visual appeal. I hate it when it gets too cluttered with risks. An example Risk Matrix is shown in Figure 16. This is the design I like best – a RED, ORANGE, YELLOW five-by-five matrix with "Probability" on the x-axis and "Consequence" on the y-axis and the five levels on each axis being denoted as 1 through 5. Someone else might prefer RED, YELLOW, GREEN three-by-three, "Probability" on the y-axis and "Consequence" on the x-axis, and with ratings on each axis ranging from 0 to 1, in fractions. [Note: from my stand-point I just do not believe risks should ever be categorized as GREEN until they are retired – thus the reason I prefer RED, ORANGE, YELLOW]. The structure of the Risk Matrix is not material ro this discussion. The numbers inside the colored cells in this below example are not normally shown. They are just for illustration – to show the Risk Severity of each Probability-Consequence combination (i.e. their mathematical "Products"). What is missing here are the Definitions of the various Risk Probability and Consequence ratings. These will be discussed a little later.

Risk Matrix					
5	5	10	15	20	25
4	4	8	12	16	20
3	3	6	9	12	15
2	2	4	6	8	10
1	1	2	3	4	5
	1	2	3	4	5

Consequence (or Impact)

Probability (or Likelihood)

Figure 16. Example 5X5 Risk (Threat) Matrix – with Severity Numbers Shown.
Project Risk Management (PMI, 2016, p. 84)

Examples of a filled-in Risk Matrix and corresponding Risk Register (simplified for a higher-level review) are provided in Figures 17 and 18 below.

	Project Risk Register Summary		Consequence	Likelihood	Severity Score
Item	Risk Description	Response Plan			
A	The need for an extra design/build/test cycle due to changing lead engineers.	(a) Build fast-turn prototypes to verify critical parameters early. (b) Include several peer reviews of design.	3	2	6
B	Only known material source may not give the necessary priority to our order due to raw material scarcity.	(a) Order material immediately. (b) Pay expedite premium to ensure on-time delivery.	3	2	6
C	Our fabrication needs might be out-prioritized by other projects due to our machine shop being over-booked by too many high priority projects.	Plan both internal (best shedule) and outside machine shop.	2	1	2
ALL					14

Figure 17. Notional Project Risk Register Example. *Project Risk Management (PMI, 2016, p. 92)*

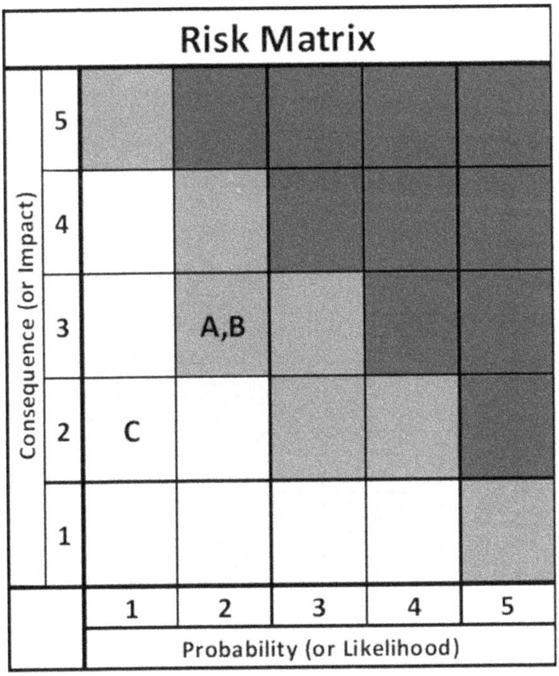

Figure 18. Notional Project Risk Matrix Example. *Project Risk Management (PMI, 2016, p. 92)*

Another Risk Matrix version is shown in Figure 19. This matrix is one established to accommodate the evaluation of both Risks (Threats) and Opportunities. Each half is a five-by-five matrix, and the rating levels are fractional values between 0.0 and 1.0.

Probability	Threats					Opportunities					Probability
Very High 0.90	0.05	0.09	0.18	0.36	0.72	0.72	0.36	0.18	0.09	0.05	Very High 0.90
High 0.70	0.04	0.07	0.14	0.28	0.56	0.56	0.28	0.14	0.07	0.04	High 0.70
Medium 0.50	0.03	0.05	0.10	0.20	0.40	0.40	0.20	0.10	0.05	0.03	Medium 0.50
Low 0.30	0.02	0.03	0.06	0.12	0.24	0.24	0.12	0.06	0.03	0.02	Low 0.30
Very Low 0.10	0.01	0.01	0.02	0.04	0.08	0.08	0.04	0.02	0.01	0.01	Very Low 0.10
	Very Low 0.05	Low 0.10	Moderate 0.20	High 0.40	Very High 0.80	Very High 0.80	High 0.40	Moderate 0.20	Low 0.10	Very Low 0.05	
	Negative Impact					Positive Impact					

Figure 19. Risk Matrix Example – Risks (Threats) and Opportunities. *PMBOK® Guide – Sixth Edition (PMI, 2017, p. 408)*

An example of the definitions of risk (threat) ratings is provided in Figure 20. Note that although the probability ratings are consistent for all categories of risk, the impacts are defined by category (i.e. Time, Cost and Quality). Each is individually described consistent with organizational expectations. Also, please note that it is not uncommon to identify Project Risks which impact more than one category, and normally the Project Team uses the highest Severity Rating within all affected categories to represent that risk in the most appropriate matrix. Use of multiple matrices (i.e. one for each of the categories) is sometimes done as well.

SCALE	PROBABILITY	+/- IMPACT ON PROJECT OBJECTIVES		
		TIME	COST	QUALITY
Very High	>70%	>6 months	>$5M	Very significant impact on overall functionality
High	51-70%	3-6 months	$1M-$5M	Significant impact on overall functionality
Medium	31-50%	1-3 months	$501K-$1M	Some impact in key functional areas
Low	11-30%	1-4 weeks	$100K-$500K	Minor impact on overall functionality
Very Low	1-10%	1 week	<$100K	Minor impact on secondary functions
Nil	<1%	No change	No change	No change in functionality

Figure 20. Sample Probability and Impact Ratings for 5X5 Risk Matrix. *PMBOK® Guide – Sixth Edition (PMI, 2017, p. 407)*

Now, not all tasks have risk and opportunities associated with their completion – thus, Project Teams should focus on those that do. Some of the more "risk-prone" tasks to consider are listed below:

- Design activities
- System Integration (e.g. merging of multiple Technologies, Components and/or sub-Systems)
- Test activities – especially Early Validation and Qualification Tests
- Approvals or Authorizations to proceed
- Design-Build-Test cycles
- Out-door Work – due to Weather
- Out-sourced activities and critical External Resources (e.g. Parts, Subject Matter Expertise, Fabrication or Test Facilities, etc.)

Some managers and organizations seem to be okay with seeing RED Individual Project Task Risks, and other RED metrics on Projects – and allow Project Teams to continually report RED Project Health. In the actual "Traffic Light" scenario (i.e. when we drive on the streets), RED means STOP, and if you do not you risk personal harm. So, you usually STOP and wait for the light to turn GREEN before proceeding. In Project Management you should STOP as well, to at least determine how to adjust the Project Plan to get to YELLOW, if not GREEN. If RED is okay, then the metric should not be RED, and the rating criteria should be appropriately adjusted, otherwise the message is confusing, and behaviors will adjust to it in a negative way. I have found that Project Teams that are allowed to report RED ratings repeatedly tend to conclude that they will not get the necessary help to fix the issue(s) and will not necessarily improve – for the attitude can denigrate to one where the rhetoric on the Project Team is "What does it matter if we do worse, we are still RED!". It should not be a surprise, therefore, that I am an advocate of requiring RED ratings to be dealt with immediately by the Project Team and Stakeholders outside the team (i.e. Functional Managers of Project Team Members and the executives concerned with jeopardizing achievement of Strategic Initiatives).

ACHIEVING EPIC BUSINESS RESULTS

If the organization is okay with RED risk ratings, I would advocate that the Leadership Team re-evaluate the RED "Tolerance Thresholds". The most appropriate way to do this from an Individual task Risks standpoint is to change the RED zone within the Risk Matrix. Figure 21 shows three different alternative rating criteria that could be considered depending on the organization's "Risk Appetite" – the darker shade is RED.

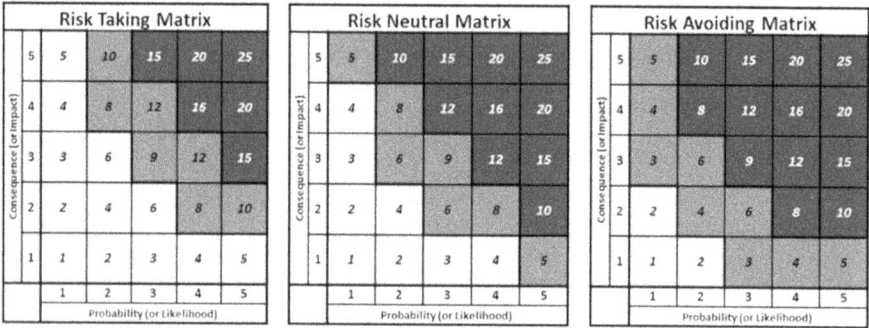

Figure 21. Risk Matrices Corresponding to Different Relative Risk Appetites

MODELLING AND SIMULATION TOOLS FOR OVERALL RISKS

The Modelling & Simulation process necessitates Individual Project Task Risk assessments – i.e. identification of duration (time) and/or resource (person-hours/days/etc.) risks and opportunities for completing the tasks relative to the Nominal (i.e. the most-likely) Project Cost and/or Schedule estimates. In doing so you can define task-level costs and duration estimates more appropriately, in terms of "Probability Distribution Function(s)" and use simulation methodologies to determine the "% Confidence" in achieving various results. This approach, if done well, provides a more accurate and useful picture of the combined effects of the Individual Project Task Risks, and can lead to better plans and more accurate commitment expectations.

As previously noted, SRA Modelling & Simulation tools work off IMS information, and are arguably the most powerful and under-utilized Project Risk Management Tools & Techniques available. They are powerful because they are basically the only legitimate and acceptable way that I know of to determine truly "quantitative" Overall Project Cost and/or

Schedule Risks – and their results are intuitively understandable. A problem associated with using this technique is that the methodology is dependent upon having a "valid and compatible" IMS. Modelling & Simulation processes can be easily sabotaged by incompatible scheduling nuances. These incompatibilities have a way of causing "user frustration" that can lead to decisions to abandon the methodology altogether. Thus, this tool, although a clear "Best-Practice" for most complex Projects (whereby the Project Team's performance is highly scrutinized), is not employed as much as I believe it could or should be.

I was exposed to Modelling & Simulation tools in the 1990's, when IMS tools were fairly new as well. This was in the day when computers were very large and slow (relative to today), and the tools themselves were not very fancy – i.e. they provided basic capabilities and were not real complicated. The benefit, however, was they consequently did not have all the "bells-and-whistles" which tend to cause confusion and mis-application that many of today's tools cause. I knew of "merge bias" before it had a name. And I learned about other important concepts described in this section, mostly through trial-and-error. Bottom-line, I used this methodology and benefitted greatly from it – and every Project I managed when employing this tool was successful. I never used Modelling & Simulation for Cost Risk Analysis, but did for Schedule Risk Analysis, since the tool that I used was of the SRA variety.

So, what exactly is Overall Project Risk Assessment via Modelling & Simulation as it relates to Project Risk Management? In its rawest form, it is the process of determining the accumulative effects of combining Project Task PDFs (Probability Density Functions) to determine the percentage confidence (% Confidence) in meeting Project Cost and/or Schedule commitments. Admittedly, I advocate use of this technique primarily for the latter – Project Schedule Risk Assessments. Although my **Project Risk Management** Book covers this topic in more detail, I will elaborate here to the degree I find necessarily, and if you desire more information, you know where to find it. First, we will discuss the process itself, then some of the key benefits.

ACHIEVING EPIC BUSINESS RESULTS

<u>Modelling & Simulation Mechanics</u>

As mentioned earlier, modern Project Management Modelling & Simulation techniques use IMS information as a starting point. You do not necessarily have to use the IMS to determine Overall Project <u>Cost</u> Risk with this methodology, but you do have to use the IMS for determining Overall Project <u>Schedule</u> Risk. Therefore, we will focus on the determination of Overall Project Schedule Risk. Note: you can use a financial spreadsheet tool to set up and run a Project Cost Risk Assessment, for you only need to aggregate Project Cost information per the Project's WBS, and do not necessarily need the IMS network – but you do need the IMS network (i.e. task interdependencies) for Project SRA (Schedule Risk Analysis).

If we have done a good job of constructing the Project IMS, and we have a good understanding of which tasks and activities carry the most risks (threats) and opportunities, we can use this information to create and execute the SRA Modelling & Simulation approach.

The first step is to determine task PDFs (Probability Density Functions) for each risky IMS task (some guidelines regarding which tasks are typically the more "risk-prone" were provided earlier in this chapter). We do this by assuming that the IMS task single-point duration estimate is the "Nominal" task duration, and from that starting point, determine the other parameters needed to form a PDF for each risky task. If you are not familiar with the statistics, do not fret too much – I will try to make this readily understandable.

I have concluded over the years that, given the degree of uncertainty that task durations typically have, Triangular Distributions are all we really need, even though some people might prefer to use the more complex distributions (e.g. Beta, Binomial, Poisson, etc.). From a "data accuracy" stand-point I believe that using those more complex distributions just gets us bogged down in trying to extract information necessary to figure out the right coefficients to use – and I have never considered this worth the effort.

The task duration that we normally input into the IMS is a single-point value at 100% probability – the "nominal" estimate. But we know that this is not right for the inherently risky tasks in our schedule – for those tasks have the potential for taking more (or less) time to complete – thus they can possess a range of potential durations. Figure 22 shows a simple Triangular Task Distribution. The "nominal" duration is 20 (we will assume this is work-days). In this scenario, there is both opportunity and risk (threat) to the completion of this task as planned. The SME (Subject Matter Expert) has indicated that if everything goes right (i.e. no missteps) the task can be completed in 10 work-days (the "best-case" opportunity relative to the "nominal" duration), and the "worst-case" scenario (due to the highest risk) indicates it will be completed in 40 work-days. These three points form a triangular Probability Density Function. Refer to the below chart.

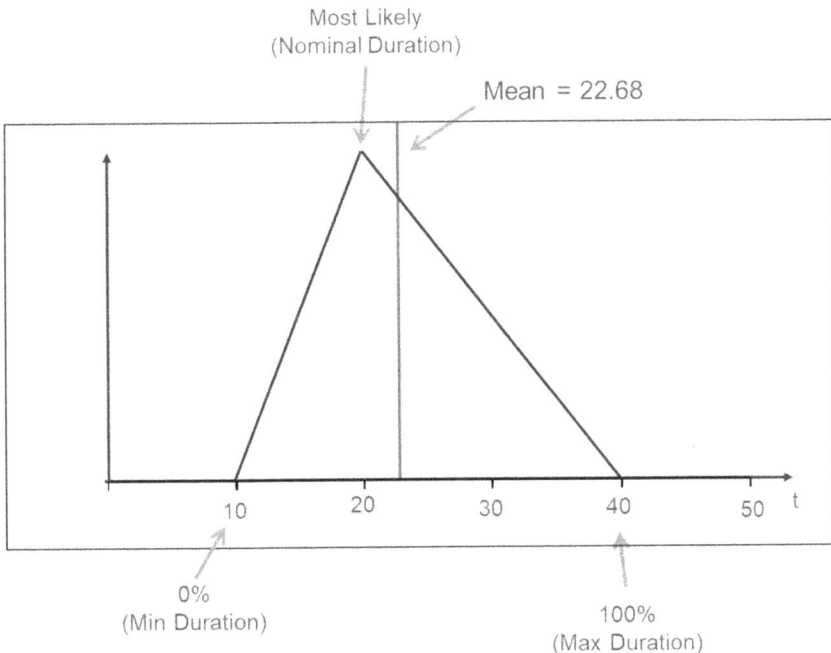

Figure 22. Triangular Task Distribution Example. Project Risk Management (PMI, 2016, p. 99)

Now, say that the area of this triangle is normalized to 1.0 (or 100%). It turns out (using a little algebra) that half of the area for this triangle (or the mathematical "Mean" of the distribution) is where the duration is 22.68 work-days. In other words, if I were to accumulate the area of the triangle gradually from left to right, I would start at 0% at the minimum duration (10 work-days). The 33.33% point would be at my "nominal" 20 work-day duration. The 50% point would be at 22.68 work-days. And the 100% point would be reached at 40 work-days (the maximum duration). The resulting curve that is produced is shown in Figure 23 and represents the Cumulative Probability Function – sometimes referred to as the 'S' Curve. This 'S' Curve basically says that I can determine the probability of completing the task by any duration (i.e. the number of work-days after the beginning the task) between 10 and 40 (e.g. my 50% confidence duration is 22.68 work-days). This is the basic building-block for the model we are setting up to simulate. It is called establishing task 3-point estimates.

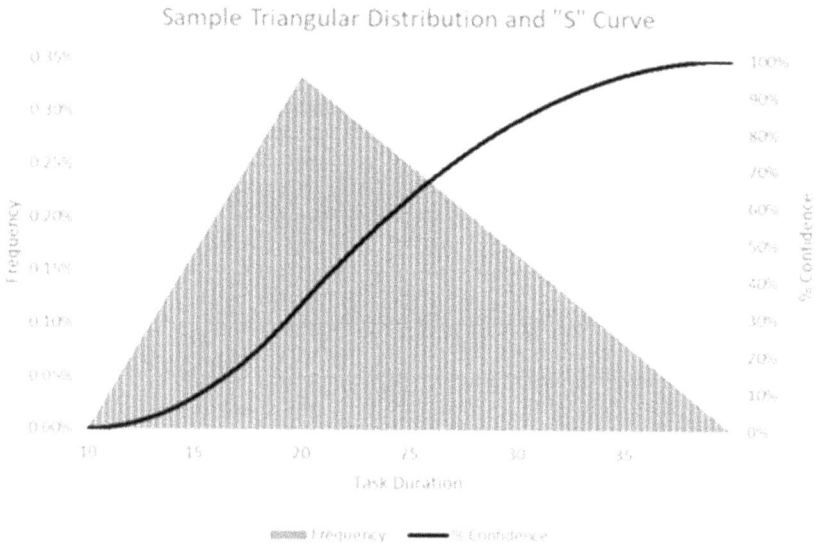

Figure 23. Example overlay of Cumulative Probability Function or 'S' Curve

Some people (especially Engineers and including me) seem to have difficulty with the 0% and 100% probability estimates for "best-case" and "worst-case", respectively. [Note: I feel that since I was (and still am to a degree) an Engineer, I can get away with picking on them a bit]. So, to accommodate this issue with determining "best-case" and "worst-case" task durations, I have migrated to using the triangular distribution derived from a 10% confident "best-case" duration and a 90% confident "worst-case" confidence duration, then generating the triangular distribution from those estimates. Figure 24 shows how this would be done for a 10% (10-day "best-case" duration), 50% (20-day "nominal" duration) and 90% (30-day "worst-case" duration) Probability Density Function. People seem to be better able to come up with 10% estimates versus 0% estimates, for 0% is theoretically unachievable and 10% is achievable. The same general argument works for "worst-case" (or "high-confidence") estimates – for some people, coming up with a 100% confidence estimate means factoring in the occurrence of very low probability disasters. Doing so is not productive, so asking for 90% confidence durations seems to get past that mental block or "estimation stigma".

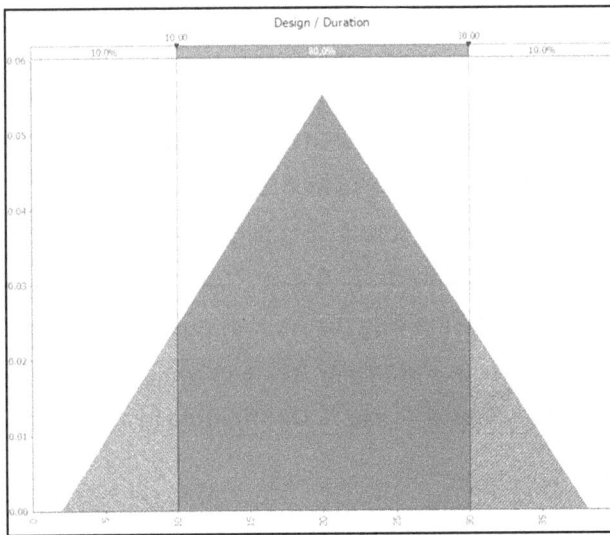

Figure 24. Triangular Distribution Generated from 10% and 90% Estimates.
Project Risk Management (PMI, 2016, p. 101)

The nice thing about task PDFs is that once generated they can be used to run many schedule simulations using the IMS to derive the range of end-dates (and their "frequency of occurrence") relative to a "milestone date" within the IMS – this basically turns out to be just another PDF with its superimposed 'S' Curve. This type of result is normally obtained using a Monte Carlo simulation. If there is no risk, each task duration value would be "fixed" (at 100% Confidence), and the simulation will always pick the same numbers (i.e. the "nominal" task duration values), resulting in the standard IMS CP (Critical Path) schedule output date 100% of the time. When you apply 3-Point triangular distributions to the risky tasks you now have many possible schedule scenarios and outcomes. When using a Monte Carlo simulation, the distribution of schedule outcomes over some range of dates will be based on how many schedule simulations (i.e. "iterations") you perform and how the simulation picked each task duration number (exercising Random Number Generation algorithms) between the minimum and maximum task durations within the task duration PDF.

The Monte Carlo simulation basically picks random durations for each task, based on the task's PDF (e.g. the same "nominal" duration will always be picked for tasks without 3-point estimates, but the duration of tasks with 3-point triangular PDFs will randomly change for each schedule Iteration based on the 'frequency of occurrence" dictated by their PDF). If you run one thousand schedule simulations the resulting end-milestone PDF will have 1,000 points distributed over a range of dates, forming a Histogram Probability Distribution which looks something like that which is shown in Figure 25 (for the Project Commitment Milestone). Notice the over-laid Cumulative Probability 'S' Curve. You can go to any point along this curve and determine the Cumulative Probability for meeting each date on the x-axis. That y-axis Probability Value (scale shown on the right-hand side secondary y-axis) is the **% Confidence** in meeting that date or any date earlier.

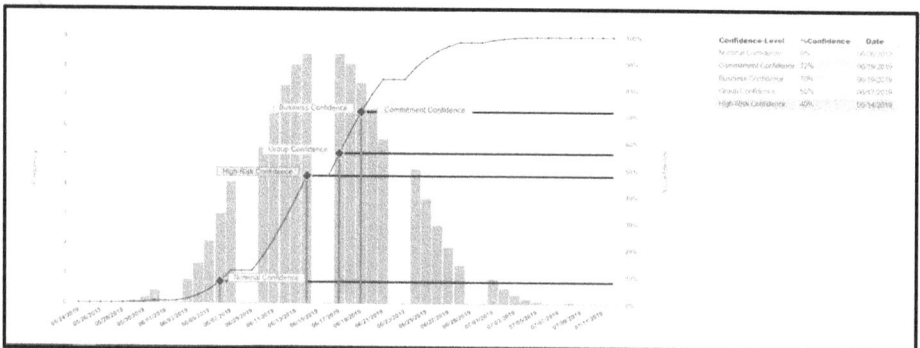

Figure 25. Example Milestone Distribution with 'S' Curve Superimposed

Key Benefits Derived from Modelling and Simulation

Hopefully, you are now seeing the value of this Modelling & Simulation process. If constructed properly, the Project Team IMS is modeled to consider task duration risks and to produce (i.e. simulate) "risk-adjusted" schedule results. This will enable the Project Team to better understand the Overall Project Schedule Risk by drawing a vertical line from the "Commitment Date" on the x-axis and observing the corresponding % Confidence where it intersects the 'S' Curve. Overall Project Risk is basically (100% minus the 'S' Curve % Confidence). If the % Confidence is too low (from an Organizational Governance preference standpoint) the Project Team can investigate alternative schedule adjustments (which might also include compromises to other Project Constraints – e.g. adding additional Project Budget to expedite parts deliveries, or adding more Resources to complete some tasks earlier, etc.) which could enable the preferred % Confidence result to be achieved.

Without going into too much more detail, other benefits derived from this process are:

- This methodology exposes Task Duration Estimation Biases

    o Over-Aggressiveness in making estimates – when Nominal Durations are very close to "Best-Case" Durations

    o Extreme Risk Avoidance (some refer to this as "Sand-Bagging") – when Nominal Durations are very close to "Worst-Case" (i.e. High-Confidence) Durations

- New Individual Project Task Risks that were not previously recorded in the Risk Register may be discovered – for the 3-point Task Duration estimates do indeed "point to" Individual Project Risks and Opportunities

- Risk Severities might have been incorrectly assessed before developing the 3-point estimates, and better risk assessments can be documented (i.e. a 1 month schedule task risk is not important if not on or near the CP, for the CP or near-CP tasks are the usual Issues)

- Too many near-CP tasks are driving the % Confidence down (i.e. a "Merge Bias" issue exists), and some scheduling changes (e.g. scheduling of tasks in parallel versus in series, or adding more Resources to reduce task durations, etc.) might be necessary.

- The Highest Risk tasks can be readily assessed via a "Tornado Diagram" (basically a Pareto Chart identifying those tasks with greatest impact to Overall Project Risk [and % Confidence]) – these are the tasks to focus on for improving the schedule.

- This methodology comprehends the diminishing effects of the Completion Milestone "Confidence Variance" over time (e.g. the range of completion dates between 10% and 90% Confidence) which tends to justify breaking the Project into "phases" to enable a better accounting for general Commitment Confidence uncertainty – exemplified by the different widths of the Project Milestone Distribution at different points along the Project Life Cycle – shown graphically in Figure 26.

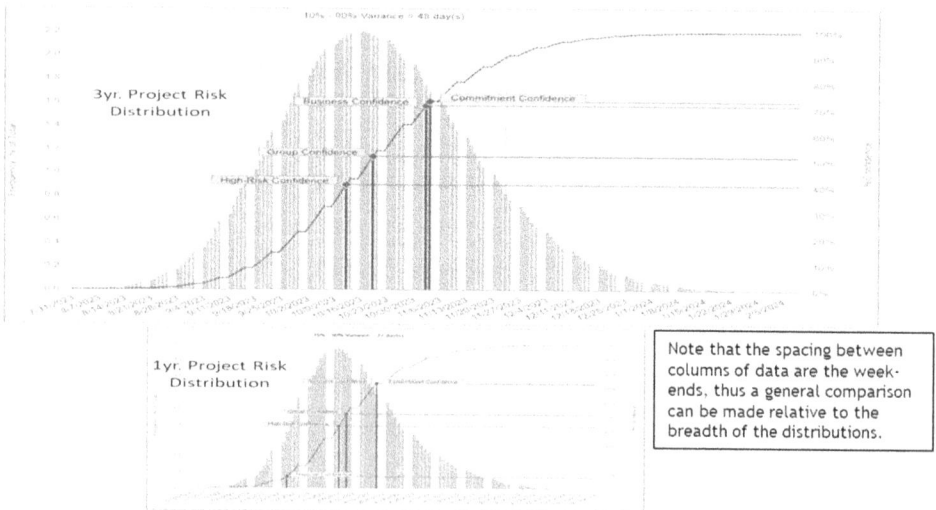

Note that the spacing between columns of data are the weekends, thus a general comparison can be made relative to the breadth of the distributions.

Figure 26. Breadth of Risk Distributions Supporting Project Phases

Again, if interested in more detail regarding this subject, please reference the **Project Risk Management** book.

Executives Understand % Confidence Better than Risk Matrix

I have held several different positions in my career, and I know that as an executive, even though I understand the Project Risk Matrix, I never seemed to have the patience to review it in detail, especially if it had a lot of identified risk items. I concluded that I just wanted to hear about the one or two highest level risks, and even at that, I usually did not fully comprehend the underlying Overall Project Risk concern unless I saw a corresponding Project Risk Assessment via an SRA % Confidence. It seemed like every time I asked a Project Manager who did not conduct SRAs how he or she would rate their Overall Project Risk they would say that it was about "50:50" (i.e. 50% Confidence) – and when the SRA analysis was completed it was usually less than 5%. I have found that most executives seem to readily understand % Confidence, and many tend to struggle, as I did, in figuring out the Risk Matrix message if not accompanied by an SRA result – for as long as there were no RED risks everything was OK, right? Well, in fact, that typically does not mean that all is OK, and we are remiss if we hold Project Managers and Teams to high standards but turn a "blind eye" to the risks being taken.

So, at what "% Confidence level" should I, as an executive, establish as a guideline for those managing and working on Strategically Important Projects? It behooves us, from a competitiveness stand-point, to endeavor to establish "aggressive Targets" (more on this in Chapter 10: Team Leadership), and we do not want to be too lax, for we could miss out on good Business Opportunities and fail to meet Strategic Goals and Objectives if we are too lax. I like a 70% Confidence (as depicted in Figure 26) for it is usually close to the highest linear part of the 'S' Curve. I do not accept anything near 100% (for the 'S' Curve starts flattening out and you are in the region of "diminishing returns"). I am also too much of a realist to want to see anything less than 30% or 40% Confidence. In fact, I am okay with 50% Confidence at times, for I know that given the inherent skews in "nominal" Critical Path schedules, the odds of meeting CP-based schedule commitments are relatively low (i.e. most risky schedules are less than 5% Confidence), and 50% Confidence is a much more achievable confidence level. Yet we still tend to believe that Project Teams should meet commitments based on "single-point-estimate" CP-based schedule results – then get upset or disappointed when they are not successful. More on these inherent skews in my *Project Risk Management* book, if interested.

OTHER OPTIONS FOR OBTAINING OVERALL PROJECT RISK

We do not <u>need</u> to use Modeling and Simulation techniques to determine Overall Project Risks. We could either use "Expert Judgement" or simply tally the individual risk (threat) "Severity" ratings from the Risk Register to derive "best-case" and "worst-case" bounds. I have seen both methods used, and "Expert Judgement" is arguably the methodology used the most out of these two options. I am not an advocate of either method, as I explain in the following sub-sections. In fact, as will be noted, tallying up risk "Severity" ratings is flat-out wrong, and totally inappropriate, yet I have seen it done on more than one occasion – so let's explore why.

Determining Overall Project Risk via Expert Judgement

Using Expert Judgement to assess Overall Project Cost and/or Schedule Risk is arguably the most common approach. Normally, as with Modelling & Simulation techniques, the Individual Project Task Risks have been previously assessed during the Project Planning process and those assessments are used as a starting point. Typically, a few experts (i.e. Technology Experts, Product Development Process Experts, etc.) and key Project Management Team Members assemble and decide on the Overall Project Risk based on past experiences and current level of Project complexity relative to other past Projects, if possible. The more comparable the past data, the more credible the estimates. Sometimes the Project Manager and key Project Stakeholders will decompose the Project Plan into more manageable chunks (maybe, per the WBS) and will interview different SMEs (Subject Matter Experts) separately to determine Overall Project Risk in more of an incremental manner.

As an example, Figure 27 shows a notional Overall Project Cost Risk Assessment for a Project separated into its three major activities. The typical reason for doing this is to get separate, more accurate estimates from the different groups slated to work on those specific activities. This is, in general, a "good practice". So let's see how this works out.

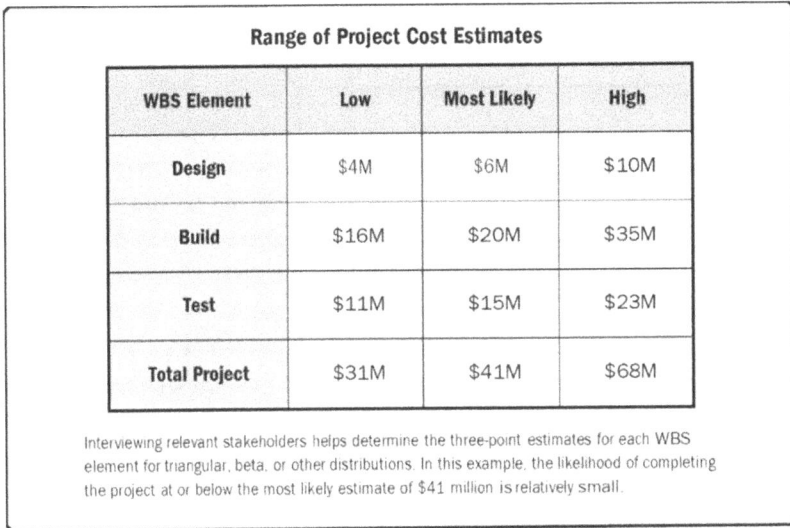

Range of Project Cost Estimates

WBS Element	Low	Most Likely	High
Design	$4M	$6M	$10M
Build	$16M	$20M	$35M
Test	$11M	$15M	$23M
Total Project	$31M	$41M	$68M

Interviewing relevant stakeholders helps determine the three-point estimates for each WBS element for triangular, beta, or other distributions. In this example, the likelihood of completing the project at or below the most likely estimate of $41 million is relatively small.

Figure 27. Example of Overall Project Cost Risk Using Expert Judgement.
PMBOK® Guide – Fifth Edition (PMI, 2013b, p. 336)

For the above example, the Expert Judgment methodology was employed to determine Low, Most Likely and High estimates for the three key activities, and then the results were added together to derive Overall Project Cost Risk – which does seem to make sense, right? The result could indicate that the organization should establish a $41M budget and set aside a $27M reserve ($68M minus $41M) for this proposed Project.

The question is, "Is the Most Likely Cost Target of $41M the right number or not (i.e. does it truly represent the 50:50 expectation)?", and if so, should the organization decide the fate of this Project based on the potential for a $68M total bill when all is said and done? Let us apply the Modelling & Simulation approach to this and see if this Expert Judgment data analysis truly makes sense. It is a relatively simple model to construct (we have the data to construct three Triangular Probability Distributions and can randomly select 3 dollar values (for Design, Build and Test) to add up per each Monte Carlo Iteration). The resultant "S" Curve is shown in Figure 28, along with some key Financial and % Confidence numbers.

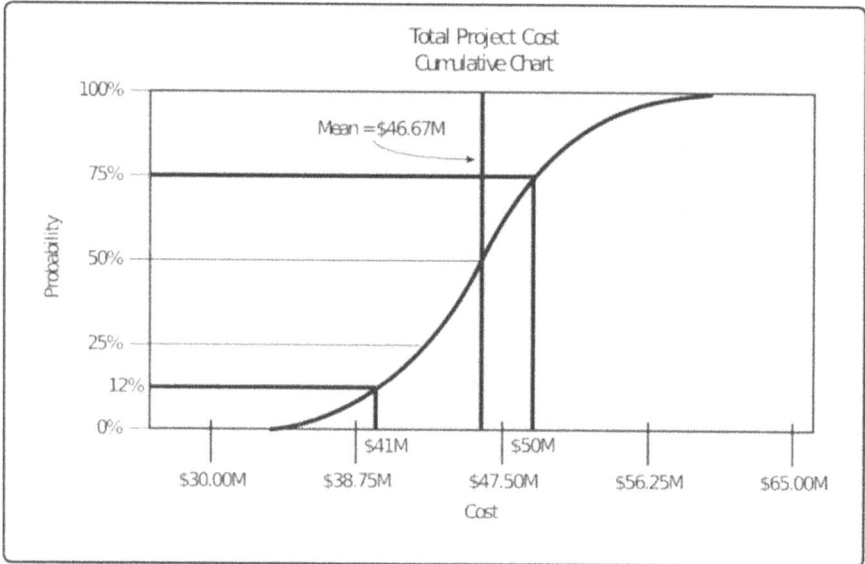

Figure 28. Overall Project Cost Risk Results Using Modelling & Simulation.
PMBOK® Guide – Fifth Edition (PMI, 2013b, p. 340)

The bottom line conclusions from this simple Modelling & Simulation exercise are:

- The $41M Most-Likely estimate is not the 50% Confidence estimate, it has only got a 12% Confidence

- The 50:50 estimate is $46.67M – almost 14% higher than the $41M Nominal estimate

- The $68M High-Cost case is well beyond the range of the chart (meaning its extremely pessimistic and should not be considered the "Worst-Case")

- Probabilistically, based on 70% Confidence criteria, we should expect this Project to be completed for $50M or less – not $68M

- If I were part of the Project Sponsor decision-making team, I would be more inclined to approve the proposed Project based on this simulation analysis – I would provide the Project Team with their requested $41M Budget and set aside a $9M Reserve – a more palatable Project approval strategy than that which simply uses the Expert Judgement data.

The differences between these two methodologies are a bit striking, and the Modelling & Simulation results expose some rational findings:

- The Estimates are "skewed to the right" – since the difference between Most-Likely estimates and mathematical "Worst-Case" estimates is usually always higher than the difference between the Most-Likely estimates and the mathematical "Best-Case" estimates

- Since the range of potential combinations tails off at the extremes of the PDF, the odds of meeting the mathematical "Best-Case" estimate is extremely low (very close to 0%), and the mathematical "Worst-Case" estimate at the other extreme is almost 100% (which is extremely unlikely and ultra-conservative)

The Modelling & Simulation outcome is more realistic. Think about this. If I ask someone to give me a "nominal" duration for completion of a task, and then ask for "best-case" and "worst-case", I'm likely to get a "worst-case" estimate that is twice the "nominal" duration, and a "best-case" that is half the "nominal" duration – this is not uncommon, unrealistic or unexpected. What it means, however, is that the % Confidence of meeting the "nominal" estimate is 33%, not 50% (check this out relative to the first Triangular Distribution we discussed earlier in this chapter). If you assume that most risky tasks are assessed this way, combining several tasks connected in a network will result in an Overall % Confidence much lower than 33% due to the cascading effects of this phenomena throughout the IMS network.

I hope you can follow all this, for it explains a lot regarding why Expert Judgement-based estimations (without the benefit of a more objective methodology, like Modelling & Simulation) can be deceptive. My experience is that when using Expert Judgement exclusively to make Project Cost or Schedule assessments, the "nominal" (or assumed 50:50) estimate is typically lower than 50% Confidence and the Probability Distribution is extremely broad, thus the "nominal" is typically understated and the "worst-case" tends to be exaggerated – which can potentially cause unnecessary angst, and result in a misinformed decision.

Overall Project Risk via Individual Risk Severity Ratings

Right from the start I want to re-iterate that adding up the potential risk impacts or "Severity" ratings of Individual Project Risks to determine Overall Project Risk is not appropriate. I'm purposely including this section to make that point and explain why, for I have seen it done to the detriment of a strategically important Project which was (in retrospect) inappropriately cancelled – so I know that people have done this. The following are a couple scenarios relating to why adding Individual Risk Severity rating is not appropriate.

a) Say that my Project Plan includes several parallel activities that extend over much of the Project Life Cycle. This is common on complex Projects. I have one key risk in each parallel activity that impacts the final schedule deliverable. One is relative to a task on the CP (Critical Path) which has a 30% chance of materializing, and if so, will result in a one-month push-out of the Project Schedule. On the other path (which is 5 work-days off the CP, thus, a near-CP task) there is a task having a risk with a 25% chance of materializing into a 2-month push-out of the Project Schedule. So, what is my worst-case Schedule Risk? If I add the two, I get 3 months. But if both were to occur, the worst-case impact I would expect is a 7-week push-out (based on assuming 4-week months). This is because they over-lap and the most significant impact will drive the schedule, and that turns out to be driven by the second near-CP task risk. And, although the total task risk is 2 months (i.e. 8 weeks), since this task is one week off the CP, the worst-case impact to the Project would be 7 weeks.

That 7 weeks is also based on a 25% probability, which is not even factored into this relatively simple example.

b) Another Project (which is six months long) basically follows a classical "Waterfall" process with all risky tasks sequentially aligned along the CP. The five risky tasks have the following risks (1: 5% for a 4-week slip, 2: 25% for a 2-week slip, 3: 60% for a 1-week slip, 4: 30% for a 3-week slip; and 5: 80% for a 1-week slip). If I add up all the worst-case impacts, we could have a worst-case impact/slippage of 11 weeks. If Marketing states that a 10-week slip would destroy our chances of receiving business, the money we invest in this Project would likely be wasted if that happened. Otherwise, if we stay within the 10-week deadline we can make a huge profit and grow the business. What should we do? I have seen a scenario like this in my past, and the decision was to scrap the Project. Had anyone performed a Modelling & Simulation Analysis, the decision would have been very different, for the odds that all five worst-case issues would occur during this process is extremely low, and the #1 risk (5% for a 4-week slip) has a probability that is quite low, yet its impact is the worst of all the risks, and this single factor drives the worst-case Project impact. Implementing some additional risk mitigation actions on of few of these tasks might be the best decision versus cancelling the Project altogether.

Note that there is one other related nuance relating to Individual Project Task Risks and their total Risk Severity scores – they can only be used to compare task risks on that specific Project only, and it is generally inappropriate be use them to compare the total Individual Project Task Risks associated with other Projects. Within a Project, task Risk Severities should be compared to determine where to apply resources to get the most Project benefit per $. The total Risk Severity score (or rating) is also appropriate for assessing risk "Burn-down" success on a Project throughout the Project Life Cycle. There are too many other factors to consider if trying to use this metric to evaluate and compare different Projects. It is therefore appropriate to compare task Risk Severities on a Project, but it is not appropriate to compare total Risk Severity scores between Projects.

BENEFITS OF PORTFOLIO PROJECT MANAGEMENT

Portfolio Management is the name given to groups of Programs, Projects and On-going Activities which have natural inter-dependencies. Whether it is called "Portfolio" or "Business Unit" or "Division" or "Group" or any other name, does not matter. It is the fact that there is typically an organizational construct that aligns all the work activities (Projects and On-going Activities) with the Organizational Strategic Goals, Objectives, and Initiatives. That activity is referred to as Portfolio Management, and when referencing Project Management activities, it is referred to here as Portfolio Project Management.

As far as Project Risks are concerned, you can consider Portfolio Project Management, in part, as a means for pooling risks, much like Insurance Companies do. In essence, when aggregating Projects into Programs and Portfolios, total Risk Reserves (including Schedule Buffers) are effectively reduced. The organization can manage the risks at a higher level, where accumulated Risk Severities can be effectively reduced based on the lower odds of all Projects overrunning by the maximum amount. Below is a simple example of how the math works for aggregating similar Projects into a Program group.

For simplicity, this analysis assumes that each Project has the same level of complexity and budget. Each has a "nominal" $10M Budget requirement and the risk assumptions conclude that there is a 10% (or "best-case") probability that each Project can be completed for as little as $8M and a 90% (or high % Confidence) probability that each Project will be completed for $15M or less. When considered individually, to account for at least a 90% Confidence, one would thus set aside $15M for each Project. As a group, given statistics, the Budget "set-aside" amount that is needed to maintain a 90% Confidence decreases incrementally with each additional Project (i.e. 2 Projects require $27.43M versus $30M, 3 Projects require $39.8M versus $45M, etc.) Further, if Risk Tolerance supports a lower Confidence Threshold (like 70%), less of a Budget "set-aside" is needed. See the Figure 29 graphic below.

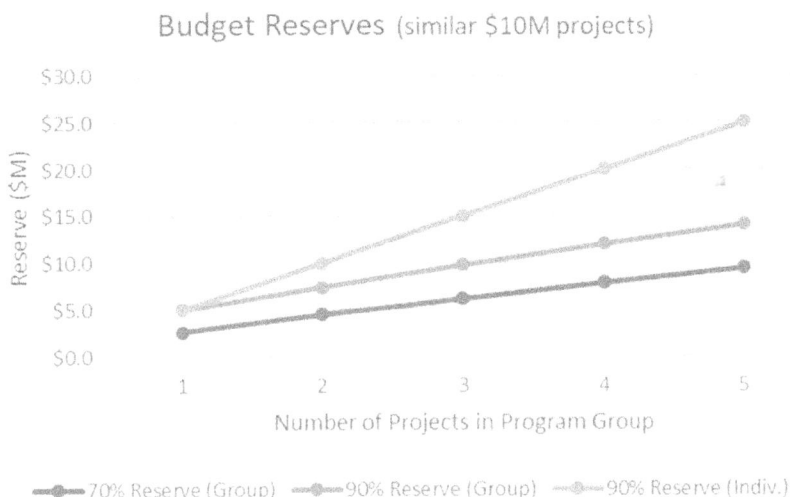

Figure 29. Example of Benefits Derived from Grouping/Pooling Project Risks

In addition to the above, there is another realizable aspect of pro-active Project Risk Management when Project inter-dependencies are factored into the equation. Typically, inter-dependencies exist between Projects in Program groupings (e.g. 90% of a motor design for one car model might be transferable to another, or a less expensive computer can be basically established by de-featuring the higher-end offerings, etc.), for that is why they are grouped. Once an issue surfaces on a preceding Project, because of the materialization of a shared risk, its impact ripples through to all subsequent Projects. Management of these situations can thus be laser-focused, and since arriving at an expedient remedy is beneficial to of all Projects, this can foster more cooperation and more efficient and effective teamwork to get to an acceptable solution quicker.

RATIONALE FOR GOVERNING PROJECT RISK MANAGEMENT

Project Risk Management is not easy. And it is arguably one of the most difficult Project Management tasks to perform well. This job is made more difficult and inconsistent when not governed well within the organization. Again, I am not one to advocate for unnecessary bureaucratic processes, but this is where lack of process controls can make a tremendous difference to both organizational performance and employee job satisfaction. The Governance Guidelines I believe to be the most important are:

- Dictating the Tools & Techniques to employ, e.g.:
    - Risk Register
    - Risk Matrix
    - Modelling & Simulation for high priorities (Project Schedule and/or Cost)
    - IMS to support Modelling & Simulation and/or EVM
- Establish/document and communicate use of consistent Risk Impact and Probability "rating scales"
- Establish/document and communicate Risk Tolerance levels
    - RED zone of Risk Matrix as the "Keep-Out" zone
    - RED & YELLOW % Confidence levels along the SRA 'S' Curve
- Expectations regarding Project Status report content and Project Review content
- Expectations regarding On-Going Project Risk Management activities
    - Establishment of Risk Management "Review Boards"
    - Periodic and "event-based" Project Progress Updating

HOLISTIC PROJECT RISK MANAGEMENT

A discussion of Project Risk Management by me would not be complete without the mention of Holistic Project Risk Management. This is also brought up in Chapter 1 (Managing Requirements), but now that we have gone through the Risk Management fundamentals, it is worth reiterating the value of Holistic Project Risk Management here. I have espoused, for some time now, that Project Management Is "All about Risk Management." If there were no risks to manage, there would be no need for this book. But realistically, in this highly competitive, global, and dispersed, dynamic market-place we now engage in, he or she who manages Project Risks the best wins. Time-to-Market, Time-to-Quality, Time-to-Cost Leaders prevail – and this is largely due to their Holistic Project Risk Management approach, which then feeds into their high performance Strategic Project Management approach to Portfolio Project Management.

Due to the importance of Holistic Project Risk Management, almost every chapter in this book addresses some aspect of the topic. It is a vital element of Strategic Project Management, and those who understand this will improve their organization's performance, competitiveness, and customer satisfaction metrics. Executives will be pleased with the resulting business success and employee morale will be bolstered.

Is Your Organization Managing Projects Strategically?

Take the test, or at least see how your organization stacks up. An inventory of the key Strategic Project Management concepts espoused by this book can be kept, Chapter by Chapter. There is no established reference of good or bad, but you can see where your organization currently is, and use this tool to monitor progress. Each question starts with the phrase: To what extent does your organization......

16. drive **Project Risk Management** with complimentary **IMS Tools & Techniques?**

1	2	3	4	5
O	O	O	O	O
Never	Rarely	Sometimes	Most of the Time	Always

17. use **Risk Registers**, **Assumptions Registers** and **Risk Matrices** to manage **Project Risks?**

1	2	3	4	5
O	O	O	O	O
Never	Rarely	Sometimes	Most of the Time	Always

18. use **Modelling & Simulation** (e.g. Schedule Risk Analysis) techniques to manage **Overall Project Cost & Schedule Risks?**

1	2	3	4	5
O	O	O	O	O
Never	Rarely	Sometimes	Most of the Time	Always

19. use **Program** and/or **Portfolio Management** to effectively **Manage (Pool) Project Risks?**

1	2	3	4	5
O	O	O	O	O
Never	Rarely	Sometimes	Most of the Time	Always

20. establish **Risk Management Governance Guidelines** to ensure reporting consistency?

1	2	3	4	5
O	O	O	O	O
Never	Rarely	Sometimes	Most of the Time	Always

CHAPTER 5

It's *THE COST* of *CHANGE*

The classical shape of the "Cost of Change" curve over the course of the Project Life Cycle is eye-opening. It is simple to understand, and when coupled with an overlay of the "Risk and Uncertainty" curve as shown in Figure 30, the message becomes very clear. It is just logical. The earlier we implement a Project Change the less it costs. As time goes by and uncertainties (i.e. risks) are either eliminated or reduced, the risk goes down – and as the need for making changes to address issues diminishes (due to completion of Project Scope/Work and realizing progress), our chances for successful Project execution increases. If risks materialize it behooves us to resolve the resulting issues as soon as possible. The term "Cost" can refer to actual "Financial" Cost, but in the bigger picture, it also includes the amount of "Effort" (i.e. Scope of Work), and "Time" (i.e. Schedule) as well. This simple concept should influence what we do from a Strategic Project Management perspective to manage Project Requirements and Change. In general, we should:

- Endeavor to understand Project Risks well and reduce them as soon as possible (i.e. shift the "Risk and Uncertainty" curve to the left)

- Identify necessary changes (due to issues impacting Product Requirements and Project Scope) as soon as possible

- Gain as much insight as possible regarding "pending" issues – via Early Warning Indicators/Metrics

- Access issues quickly and effectively

- Decide on, and implement remedial Corrective Actions as soon as possible/practical

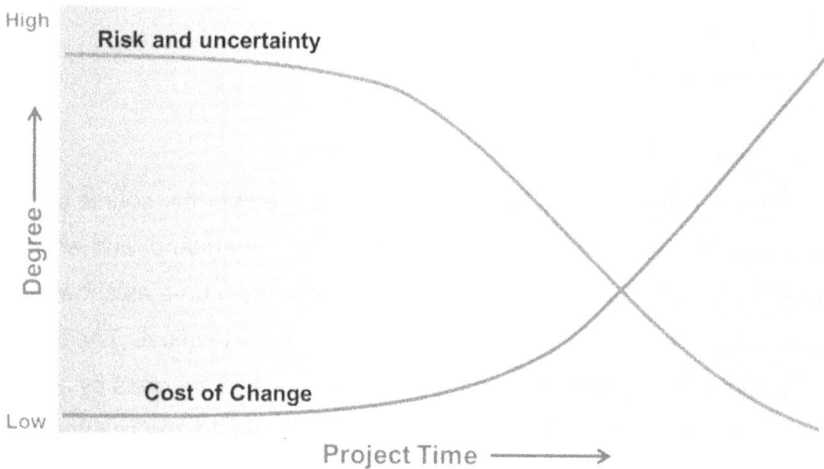

Figure 30. Cost of Change versus Risk and Uncertainty Curves over the PLC.
PMBOK® Guide – Fifth Edition (PMI, 2013b, p. 40)

Having been in several different executive positions, I have had the luxury of being exposed to "Change" arguments from "both sides of the fence" when issues and resultant conflicts arise. Below is a realistic notional scenario to demonstrate the dilemma.

When the "competitive landscape" changes and our Marketing folks realize that the Product Features and number of SKUs being offered are insufficient to gain the business that we projected in our Project Business Case, something needs to be done. We (the Development

Team) are now six months from Product launch (on an 18-month Project), and we are asked to implement Product Requirements changes and keep our original Product launch date – the infamous "both" request. The entire organization wants this, and the Project Team is perplexed. A review of the situation reveals that the costs for making this change are great (i.e. the commitment Schedule, given no additional Resources and/or Funds is improbable to meet). We could by-pass some Product Quality Requirements, add more Project Resources and spend more funds to improve our chances. Nobody wants to make those compromises, but the executives eventually elect to do so, draining key resources from other Project Teams and putting those other Project Commitments at risk.

The reality is that the Marketing Organization had to determine Product Requirements more than a year earlier and did the best they could with the data available but found out later that they needed to change these requirements to provide a competitive Product Offering. The Project Team could have greatly reduced the impact if it was identified 6 months earlier, but at this time there are no "good" options. Even with the changes, the risk of meeting the required launch date with the requisite Product Quality is much higher now.

Did everyone do everything they could have to minimize the damages in that above situation? Maybe, but what should have been, or could have been done better? The only real option was mitigating the impact by finding out about the competitive situation sooner and making all the change decisions quicker to prevent some of the rippling affects to other Projects. The subsequent subsections delve into these options.

KPIs KEEP YOU AHEAD OF THE COST OF CHANGE CURVE

The ultimate way to address (and potentially prevent) Project Changes is to detect the issues that could lead to them before they materialize, via Early Warning Indicators – using metrics or KPIs (Key Performance Indicators) which can foretell pending issues. Seeing an indication of a pending issue before it materializes can enable you to take immediate actions to either "nip it in the bud" (i.e. prevent the issue from occurring altogether), suppress the issue's escalation, or minimize the probability of occurrence and/or potential impact. The Health Care industry focusses on this to save and extend people's lives. One of the most note-worthy sets of Project management KPIs are the indices calculated from EVM (Earned Value Management) tracking – CPI (Cost Performance Index) and SPI (Schedule Performance Index). Performance measurement "trends" over time provide additional Early Warning Indications.

Early Warning via EVM Cost and Schedule Indicators

Many individuals who have had to meet EVMS (EVM System) requirements on a Government Contract tend to cringe when they see that acronym, and some have learned to want no part of using EVM on their Projects if optional to do so. I can certainly understand this stance, for I implemented EVMS for many years and fully understand the rigor associated with the process' application – it can be onerous. Regardless, I still learned to value this set of metrics. My problem was with the way the data was derived (seemed very bureaucratic and overly involved) and used (i.e. was thought to be more than an "indicator", and sometimes used as a precise projection or estimate of the future state of the Project). Also, in my opinion the EVM process and indices can be much easier to manage and derive. And the process can be more practical to use if stakeholders understand that these metrics are only indications of a potential future state and the numbers are not to be taken as literal expectations, but as "calls to action" to improve Project success.

Some of you who have never been exposed to EVM might conclude from the above paragraph that this is probably something that you should avoid. But before making that judgment, let me illustrate the process, and show how the EVM methodology can be simplified to meet organizational needs. The results might cause you to re-consider.

The subsequent set of charts (collectively, Figure 31) illustrate what I mean. I constructed an 8-month notional Project Plan and then created three different Status Update Scenarios from that Plan. The three scenarios are compared at the halve-way point of the Project Life Cycle, and their general descriptors are:

Scenario A: The Project is behind Schedule and over-Budget

Scenario B: The Project is right on Schedule and Budget

Scenario C: The Project is ahead of Schedule and under-Budget

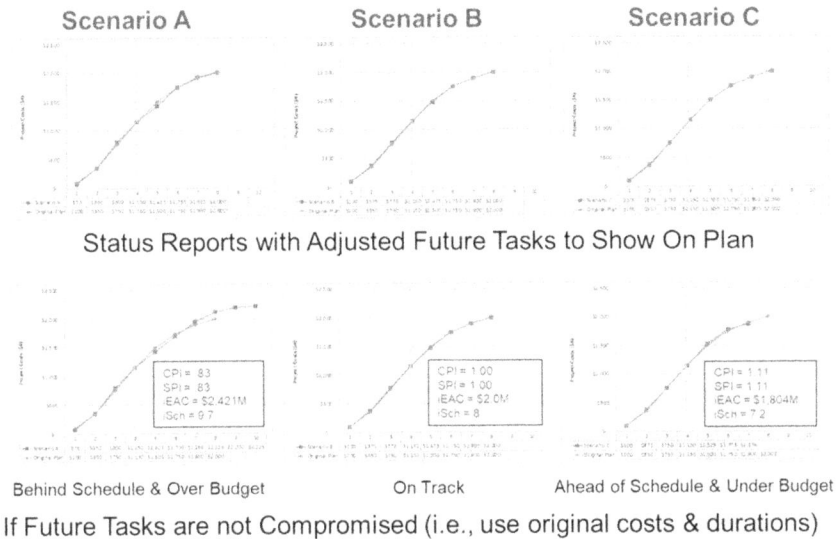

Status Reports with Adjusted Future Tasks to Show On Plan

If Future Tasks are not Compromised (i.e., use original costs & durations)

Figure 31. Example of Insight Gained from Use of Simple EVM Methodologies. Project Risk Management (PMI, 2016, p. 153)

The top row of charts is what the Project Team might present to Management at the Status Update Review, and the bottom row provides supplemental EVM data using two relatively simple methodologies: EVM – Estimates using Original Plan; and EVM – Estimates using CPI and SPI. Each of the six charts show the same basic information. The original Project cumulative planned spending for each month is provided – which is the same for all six charts. The "status date" is indicated with a dashed vertical line at month 4. The cumulative "actual costs" for each month are plotted up to the "status date". The remaining "planned cumulative Project Costs" are provided from the "status date" to the projected Project completion date.

ACHIEVING EPIC BUSINESS RESULTS

Note that the charts in the top row all look similar – and the message portrayed in each scenario is that the Project is proceeding as originally planned. But please realize that although the spending can be as planned, the amount of "work completed" is not necessarily as planned. The data under-pinning the three scenarios is indeed different, yet the status update charts are virtually identical. How can this be? The bottom row of charts is created using some additional data which provides insight.

So, let us look at the bottom row of charts which relate to those on the top row, respectively. The first EVM method (Estimates using Original Data) produces the additional "future data" displayed on the chart, corresponding to the tabulated data in the below tables. This data shows that:

- Scenario A is projected to Over-Spend by US$225K and to be late by two months;

- Scenario B is projected to be On-Schedule and meet Budget expectations; and

- Scenario C is projected to Under-Spend by US$125K and be completed one month early.

This method basically incorporates the "current estimated completion costs" for the "open" tasks and assumes the future task durations and costs per the original "Baseline" Project Plan. Thus, this method assumes no change to the future tasks, whether they were actually changed or not.

The second EVM method (Estimates Using CPI and SPI) shows that:

- Scenario A is projected to Over-Spend by US$421K and be late by two months;

- Scenario B is projected to be On-Schedule and meet Budget expectations; and

- Scenario C is projected to Under-Spend by US$196K and be completed one month early.

This second method basically follows an approach which applies the same over-run or under-run percentages that were experienced on prior effort to future estimates of durations and costs (and assuming no interim changes to these estimates relative to the original "Baseline" Project Plan estimates).

Several observations can be made regarding both sets of the above EVM data:

- In all three scenarios the **actual-plus-plan vs. time** Cost Profiles (top row of charts) indicate that the Project Team is "on-target" to meet its Project Cost and Schedule commitments in all scenarios.

- The EVM data shown in the bottom row indicates that:
  - Scenario A is **behind** Schedule and **over** Budget
  - Scenario B is **on** Schedule and Budget
  - Scenario C is **ahead of** Schedule and **under** Budget

- The two EVM metrics give the same indications

- The two EVM metrics give different estimates regarding the potential magnitude of the problem (the second being the more conservative approach)

So, the question is, "Why is the data in the top row so deceptive when the Project is off its plan?". The answer is quite simple – and it is not due to Project Managers trying to pull a "fast one" on everybody. Project Managers realize that their job is to continually work/alter the Project Plan when it veers off course, so that it eventually re-aligns with (and meets) expectations. This usually entails altering future task durations and cost estimates and might require some re-structuring of the Project activities (e.g. over-lapping task activities and/or performing more tasks in parallel). If the Project Manager does not make these changes, someone higher up will probably "help" him or her – something we tend to want to avoid at almost all costs. The problem is that the act of changing future planned tasks tends to add risk and:

- some Project Team Members are not well-schooled in managing Project Risks and may just absorb the risk without fully realizing the extent to which that might jeopardize the Project's success;

- most Organizational Managers do not care to review the Risk Register and Matrix information, and even if they do, there is a pretty good chance that they do not understand what the data really means;

- most Project Teams do not use Modelling & Simulation methodologies to determine the % Confidence of meeting Overall Project Cost and Schedule commitments that result from changes made to the Project Plan;

- there might not be a good set of Risk Tolerance Thresholds established (via Organizational Governance) to aid in limiting the amount of Project Risk that can be absorbed;

- there is usually a limit to the amount of Project Resources available to remedy issues

- we (Project Managers, Team Members and Functional Managers) tend to avoid recommending Product Requirements changes; and

- to avoid changes to Product Requirements we would rather figure out how to change the Product Development Process (i.e. Project Scope) – which is usually the same as adding more risk to the Project.

So, after all that, isn't it worth considering some simple EVM metrics? In both cases, you are just looking at the available data in a different (more objective) way to enable greater insight into Project Team performance, and Project Risk levels over time. And even though the EVM data does not tell you the true magnitude of the problem, you and your Project Stakeholders are still provided objective Early Warning Indicators, which can prompt further investigation and consideration of mitigating actions/changes as soon as possible. The idea is to establish these metrics via Project Governance Guidelines to gain more visibility and transparency into "pending" issues (i.e. risks). And taking actions prompted by Early Warning Indicators can lower the eventual "Cost of Change" on the Project.

Early Warning via Modelling and Simulation

The best metric I have ever used to manage complex Product Development Projects is the "% Confidence" in meeting major schedule commitments. This "figure-of-merit" is basically derived from Individual Project Task Risks and is considered a "quantitative" Overall Project Schedule Risk metric. As such, it is discussed in detail within Chapter 4: Managing Risks. But in this chapter, I will give you the rationale for why I consider Modelling & Simulation metrics the best Project Management Early Warning Indicators. In short, the "% Confidence" metric is produced using IMS (Integrated Master Schedule) and Modelling & Simulation tools. The result looks something like the Figure 32 histogram chart.

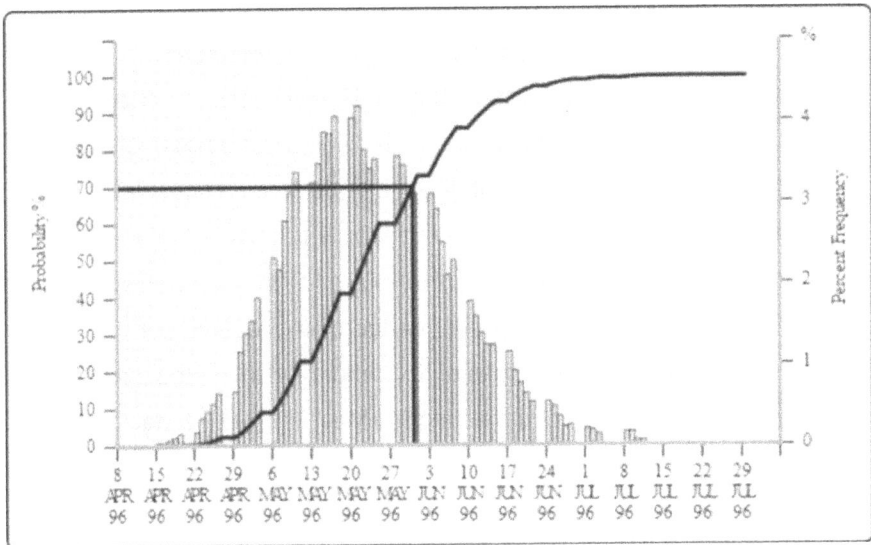

Figure 32. Overall Project Schedule Risk Modelling & Simulation Example.
Project Risk Management (PMI, 2016, p. 100)

This histogram was generated by running thousands of Project schedule simulations and stacking the result of each "iteration" in a "date bin" for a specific Project Milestone event. The chart shown represents the number of occurrences (on each work-day) that the final Product Delivery is theoretically completed, based on 10,000 simulation "iterations". When you accumulate this information from the left-most date to the right-most you generate a Cumulative Probability curve (referred to as the 'S' Curve) that starts at zero % and concludes at 100%. You can then go to any point along this curve and see what the Probability % (or "% Confidence") is for meeting a certain completion date. This example shows that the Project Plan established by the Project Team had a 70% chance of meeting the final contract delivery on May 31, 1996.

So, how was this "% Confidence" metric used as an Early Warning Indicator? To answer that question, we must go back in time to a date two years earlier, when the Project Manager (who happened to be me) was first exposed to the Modelling & Simulation methodology.

> We had already negotiated the contract with our customer (an Aerospace and Defense industry Prime Contractor) and were getting ready to kick-off the Project within the next month. The president of our division brought in a new Schedule Support Manager who wanted to introduce Modelling & Simulation. Integrated Master Scheduling had been introduced a few years earlier with a fair amount of success, and I had become a believer in the methodology, so I decided to use the new "Monte Carlo" Simulation capability to ensure that my Project Plan was "sound" (for this was a Firm-Fixed-Price contract, so as far as I was concerned, I could never be too over-precautious).
>
> To my surprise, the results of the simulation indicated that we had only an 12% confidence in meeting my May 31, 1996 "Final Delivery" commitment. My team and I first spent a fair amount of time trying to ensure that we interpreted the results properly and did not make any "data entry" mistakes. We discovered some phenomena associated with how the Modelling & Simulation probabilities exposed "real" scheduling problems (discussed in more detail within Chapter 4 and in my book on **Project Risk Management**) and concluded that we had a major schedule issue (i.e. the Early Warning Indication). So, we spent

about 2 weeks working the Project Schedule (i.e. putting as many activities as we could in parallel, attempted to remove "near-Critical" Paths, decided to begin the Project with more Design Engineering resources, and coordinated having critical designers working overtime and Saturdays starting day-one of the contract). This revised Project Plan was eventually approved, and Figure 31 was the resultant approved "Baseline" Project Plan. By the way, our CP (Critical Path) end-date was April 10th (which has a 0% confidence of being achieved according to this analysis, but since it was based on the "nominal" estimates, we used it as our Project Team's "target" schedule).

Fast forward – we ended up making our final contract delivery one and a half weeks early. The Project was a huge success story, and my young career was boosted "big time". Things would have been a lot different had it not been for that Modelling & Simulation Early Warning Indicators – so you can see why I am such an advocate for this Strategic Project Management approach.

Some Other Early Warning Indicators

There are several other Early Warning Indicators that can be established or considered. I do not profess to know all that can be conceived of, but below is a listing that I have compiled from my past experiences. These metrics primarily pertain to Product Quality, Product Development Processes, and Customer Satisfaction concerns:

- Statistical process control chart data
- Product first-pass-yields
- Product Cost of Goods Sold
- Incoming inspection failure rates
- Field return rates
- Field failure rates
- Number of software bugs opened, closed
- Ave. time to close software bugs
- Particle counts and size
- Temperature and humidity levels

- Production cycle times
- Production throughput by line, product, team
- On-going reliability testing
- Out-of-box auditing
- User trials (i.e. alpha/beta testing, conference room pilots, etc.)
- Pilot production runs
- On-time delivery performance
- Industry performance benchmark testing
- Inventory turns
- Customer service response times (broken out by touch points)
- Warranty costs per product costs
- Gross Margins per product sales units

Many of the above Early Warning Indicators can be supplemented by a corresponding "trend analysis" – the topic of the next section.

Using Trends as Performance Measurement Indicators

Sometimes the most useful data to track over time for "early warning" insight are "trends". I find that three points of data can serve as a very useful trend to draw preliminary conclusions from. Figure 33 shows a set of charts that were constructed from the Notional Project with EVM scenarios in Figure 31 to explain the CPI and SPI EVM Indices.

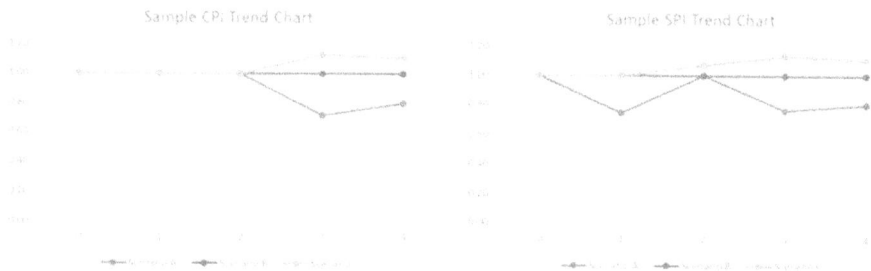

Figure 33. EVM CPI and SPI Trend Charts – Notional Example Scenarios.
Project Risk Management (PMI, 2016, p. 132)

So, what does the above data indicate? Recall that Indices > 1.0 are Positive (i.e. means you are either ahead of Schedule or under-Budget), and < 1.0 are Negative (i.e. behind Schedule or over-Budget). In the Figure 33 Performance Indicators, you can infer that:

- For month 3, the Cost and Schedule Variance trends for both Scenario A and C are pronounced (i.e. > 10% variance)

  - In Scenario A this data is positive – good, but do not get too exited

  - In Scenario C this data is negative – something to keep an eye on

- By month 4 there is a slight change to both scenario A and B data

  - In Scenario A the Trend is slightly negative, but not alarming – still positive

  - In Scenario C the Trend is slightly positive, but still a concern – may prompt further investigation

The next logical level of trend analysis is at the Overall Project level. Figure 34 (a Project Status Update Template I have used) was constructed to elaborate on the Scenario A notional Project status over time. This status update reflects the Cost and Schedule EVM trends as of the "status date" and paints a deteriorating picture of Project Health. From a positive stand-point, at least all the information is on the table, visible and being addressed. The Project Team might even be able to recover to a degree. If the team were more alert, they could have acted a month earlier. Many times we tend to discount sudden "blips" in the data (especially at the onset of the Project), and this sometimes turns into a bigger problem – but we choose to "wait and see" at times before taking action and potentially "causing a stir" in the organization.

	Overall Status					RECOVERY PLAN
	Month -3	Month -2	Month -1	Current	Future Trend	*Future Trend:* Steady ⇔, Improving ⇧, Worsening ⇩
Overall Project Health	Y	G	R	R	⇔	Overall project is in serious jeopardy of missing commitments. Meeting tomorrow morning with all stakeholders to assess.
Schedule	R	G	R	R	⇧	Slight improvement in SPI – Team to Evaluate (to report on next week).
Scope	Y	Y	Y	R	⇩	Additional scope required to recover. Increase in concern over last month's report.
Technical / Quality	G	G	G	Y	⇩	Considering product spec changes to meet schedule and budget.
Resources	G	G	Y	G	⇩	Resource concern resolved, but scope change might require that this is re-visited.
Finances	G	G	R	R	⇧	Slight improvement expected, but additional scope changes are expected to be required to recover.
Risk	Y	G	Y	R	⇧	Risk materialized regarding completion of design. Impacts to project performance is expected to Increase – under review.

Figure 34. Project Status Update – EVM Scenario A Notional Example. From *Project Risk Management (PMI, 2016, p. 134)*

Think about what this above chart might have looked like if the EVM data was not used to reflect Project Cost and Schedule status. Last month's report would have probably been GREEN, and this month's report might have been GREEN or YELLOW, but not necessarily RED. In that situation you would had a "false sense of security" and would not have seen the need or sense of urgency in evaluating change options and implementing them as expediently as possible – a much worse outcome.

Now you could probably say, well this is just a notional example and does not really happen in real life. I would have to beg to differ with you if that were your opinion. I have seen this happen more often than I would have liked, especially for Projects that were under my purview. Usually the reality would "set in" at about the half-way point in the Project and it would change almost instantly from being "right on track" to being "in disaster-mode" – a surprise which no Manager likes. This is no-doubt a big part of the reason (I am sure) for the proliferation of EVM in the Aerospace and Defense industry.

Establishment of good, tried, and proven KPIs and "trend tracking" methodologies can therefore enable Project Teams to get ahead of the "Cost of Change" curve. But this is not where the story ends, for getting an "early warning" is of marginal benefit if the Project Team and Organizational Management do not act quickly to address the pending issues – our topic in the next section.

ASSESSING CHANGES QUICKLY AND EFFECTIVELY

If you really understand the "Cost of Change" curve, you realize that it is always more beneficial to identify pending issues and implement necessary changes as soon as possible. The problem is, we do not want to jump to conclusions and act rash – then live to regret it. So, what should we do? First, we need to collect the facts and assess the options as quickly and as thoroughly as possible/practical.

Collecting the Facts

In the words of the highly esteemed W. Edwards Deming "In God we Trust, all others bring data". Data (i.e. facts) are what I consider the key to good decision-making. When we make decisions without facts we are guessing or relying on "gut instincts". Most of us realize that these types of decisions are risky and difficult to defend. In the "business world", we endeavor to collect as much data as possible/practical to help us in making decisions. This does not ensure that all our decisions will be right, but they should be rational and defendable the majority of the time.

So, what is meant by "as much data as possible/practical"? This is where we tend to get "hung up". Getting as much data as possible may take a lot more time than we can afford to expend – remember the "Cost of Change" curve. We do not want to become victims to "analysis paralysis", for data collection is typically the culprit behind that notion. There are no "silver bullet" solutions to this, but my acid test is: "Did I consider all the data available and all the data that was able to be acquired within a reasonable amount of time?". The word "reasonable" is a bit vague, but this is where judgement comes into play. Below are some self-reflective questions to consider, to help avoid being second-guessed:

- Have all the pertinent Project Stakeholders been consulted – to determine if they are aware of other readily available data which could (or should) be considered?

- Is there some additional relevant information that could be readily acquired to provide valuable insight?

- Are there any SMEs (Subject Matter Experts) available to consult with?

- How urgent is it to decide on this matter?

- How important and potentially impactful can this decision be to Project success or failure?

Assessing the Options

There are a couple of common mistakes made by Project Team Members: 1) believing that they have no choice other than just absorbing the risks caused by issues and/or "Change Requests"; and 2) jumping to a conclusion (or decision on a solution) without assessing all pertinent and viable options. There are typically many options available for solving such problems. I have found that by considering a few viable options, many times you settle on some sort of compromise between them that turns out to be better than any one of the options alone. The idea is to perform this assessment both effectively and efficiently – with the goal of making a good decision as quickly as possible/practical. Some ideas to consider are:

- assess changes to each of the Project Constraints – Product Requirements, Scope, Resources, Costs, Schedule and Risks;

- assess changes to a combination of Project Constraints – does not have to be one-dimensional;

- force-rank the Project Constraints by priority to help decide – it is important to ensure all the key Project Stakeholders are on-board with this ranking;

- sort the Product Requirements by Priority Groupings, e.g. Must-have, Highly-desired, Nice-to-have;

- do not by-pass the risk assessment process – know the impact of all considered options;

- consider using the Delphi Method of evaluating alternatives (i.e. to deal with personal biases) by having all key Project Stakeholders evaluate and select their choices without knowing the originator of the ideas; and

- as Project Manager, try to gain consensus to the best of your ability, and if not possible, make the one best for the Project and communicate dissenting views.

TIMELY DECISIONS AND EXECUTION OF REMEDIAL ACTIONS

If the Project Team has done a good job of assessing options, a decision on which option to follow-through on might be immediate (e.g. for those options which the Project Team is authorized to decide upon) or take some time (e.g. for those options which require higher-level authorization). Usually the authorization level is dictated by Organizational Governance, either formally established and communicated or informally implied. The catch is, even if a Project Manager has the authority to decide on certain types of changes, if escalated (due to lack of consensus) it can be "kicked up" to the next level of management (or higher) to decide – discussed in Chapter 2: Managing Expectations (within the discussion on "escalation"). From a "Cost of Change" perspective, it behooves the Project Manager to work diligently to arrive at an amicable compromise to avoid the added time associated with the escalation processes. Good Project Managers will stage (i.e. prepare the Project Team for) the remedial actions before obtaining final approval to minimize the negative effects of the "Cost of Change."

When a "change" decision is pushed up to higher-level management levels, the Project Manager should take a few key actions:

- ensure that this is done as soon as possible;

- prepare a concise "review package" with an "Executive Summary" for a quick decision and relevant support data – to include a clear Project Team recommendation and proposed action plan to execute (i.e. the supporting data and various options that were assessed, and detailed rationale for the Recommendation); and

- pre-brief the various decision-makers, if possible.

The Organizational Management Team should also take all necessary steps to facilitate expedient decision-making, including showing support of the proposed recommendation. Note that the data and/or recommendations should not surprise any of the key Project Stakeholders, otherwise the process is likely to be extended.

THE ROLE OF GOVERNANCE IN CHANGE MANAGEMENT

Some of the fact-collecting, assessing and decision-making relative to Project Change issues can be accomplished ahead of (or in conjunction with) certain changes (e.g. "directed" changes, "requested" changes, or incidental/self-imposed changes). Well-designed and relatively simple organizational processes can help cut down on the number of changes requested, considered, and implemented – as well as abating the pressure placed on Project Team Members to satisfy those requests. Below are some thoughts.

Pro-Active Change Request Processes

Incremental Product Requirements and Scope changes are sometimes hard to control, for Project Teams tend to want to satisfy all Project Stakeholders and automatically abide by their requests. So, make these requests visible, and require that justification data is provided before they can be considered. System Requirements Review processes (discussed in Chapter 1: Requirements Management) are beneficial, but not necessarily sufficient. There are likely to be Product Requirements changes requested mid-stream during a Project's Life Cycle. These arise primarily due to "market dynamics", and Project Teams are sometimes pressured to add them, absorb the risk (as discussed in Chapter 2: Managing Expectations) and potentially jeopardize Project commitments as a result. To avoid this, the organization can establish a Change Control process which highlights and documents all requests. A good process also considers decision-making escalation, as appropriate.

Scope Creep Prevention via Stand-up Meetings

If only I had a dollar for every time I saw "scope creep" voluntarily inflicted on a Project by its own Team Members! The only way I have ever seen this effectively dealt with is through the imposition of periodic "stand-up" meetings to frequently status activities – for tasks completed and near-term tasks to be performed. This tends to "nip the issue in the bud" by discovering details that might not be otherwise realized or detected. Being a relatively good engineer myself, I was a perfectionist, and I have learned that most good engineers are. The problem is, good engineers have a hard time gauging when they are "done" – for we can always improve upon our work output. I had this same problem when I oil-paint. My instructor told me that he had a self-imposed policy of never touching a painting after signing it – after I adopted that policy, I became much more prolific. The point is, many times it takes others (e.g. Leads or Manager) to convince the good engineers that they are done, or the likely result could be "scope creep".

Handshakes Between Project "Suppliers" and "Customers"

We discuss this same topic in Chapter 1: Managing Requirements. Have you ever worked on a task for someone, turned in the completed work, and then was told that what you did was not right, or it was missing something – then must either redo it completely or fix the parts that were not completed to your "customer's" expectations? Most of us have. This is an example of a scenario where there was not a good "handshake", or maybe there was from your perspective, but not from the other person's, and there was nothing in writing to corroborate either position. This happens on multi-disciplined (or cross-functional) Projects all too often. When it happens, it signifies the manifestation of an unexpected Project issue, and if that task is on or near the Critical Path it is likely that some sort of Project change is needed to rectify the situation. And sometimes the amount of change is significant/disruptive. My other way of stating this is, ensure that all Project Stakeholders understand what constitutes acceptable "completion" of a task.

This sounds like a "no-brainer", but it is always a good idea to document your "handshakes" regarding Intra-Project deliverables, especially when they are made to a group outside of your manager's jurisdiction. This should be done in both the Planning Phase of the Project, and whenever Project changes are made which might materially affect the expectations regarding task deliverables. Further, adherence to this process should be an overt expectation passed down by Organizational Management and Project Managers.

The Portfolio Alignment Processes

Strategically, all Project Objectives should be well-aligned with Organizational Strategic Goals, Objectives, and Initiatives. In large organizations, this is typically accomplished via "Portfolio" Management. This alignment process is discussed in detail within Chapter 1: Managing Requirements. I will re-address some of this here, for Portfolio alignment is entirely germane to the Project "Cost of Change" topic.

Many organizations adjust their Business Strategies and Operating Plan details monthly to stay ahead of the "Cost of Change" curve at a higher level. These Strategic Plan adjustments can (and do) often-times lead to "directed" Project changes. This adjustment process is typically iterative and inclusive of key Portfolio Management individuals. Scenarios are evaluated, and usually require mid-level management involvement to determine specific impacts of the change decisions as they relate to

Project Charters, On-Going Operations, and the potential rippling impacts on Human Resource staffing. It thus behooves the Management Team to prepare for changes and implement them as expediently as possible. Changes to Project Charters have typically been evaluated by the time those changes are officially approved. Thus, that foreknowledge can enable those changes to be implemented quickly. Sometimes, however, the information is considered too sensitive to disseminate early, and some changes are likely to be a surprise to most – thus they become much more difficult to implement in an expedient way.

Portfolio alignment is not typically a Project Management training topic, per se, but when discussing Strategic Project Management, you cannot omit it. As can be deduced by this chapter's content, managing the "Cost of Change" well, at the Project level, certainly calls for a fair amount of Organizational Governance and Management involvement. Portfolio alignment "flow-down" processes should therefore be well understood and implemented by those who are responsible for this aspect of the "connective tissue" between Organizational Strategy and Project definition.

Is Your Organization Managing Projects Strategically?

Take the test, or at least see how your organization stacks up. An inventory of the key Strategic Project Management concepts espoused by this book can be kept, Chapter by Chapter. There is no established reference of good or bad, but you can see where your organization currently is, and use this tool to monitor progress. Each question starts with the phrase: To what extent does your organization......

21. focus on the **"Cost of Change"** and **Risk/Uncertainty Curves** to improve **Project Success?**

1	2	3	4	5
O	O	O	O	O
Never	Rarely	Sometimes	Most of the Time	Always

22. establish and use objective **Project Performance KPIs as Early Warning Signs?**

1	2	3	4	5
O	O	O	O	O
Never	Rarely	Sometimes	Most of the Time	Always

23. continuously monitor/evaluate **Project Performance Trends as Early Warning Indicators?**

1	2	3	4	5
O	O	O	O	O
Never	Rarely	Sometimes	Most of the Time	Always

24. establish **Requirements and Change Processes** that enable **Expedient Change Decisions?**

1	2	3	4	5
O	O	O	O	O
Never	Rarely	Sometimes	Most of the Time	Always

25. quickly convey **Change Decisions** enacted to ensure **Alignment with Strategic Objectives and Initiatives?**

1	2	3	4	5
O	O	O	O	O
Never	Rarely	Sometimes	Most of the Time	Always

CHAPTER 6

IT'S *MAINTAINING A BALANCED PLAN*

In a perfect world, every time a "blip" occurs with respect to Project performance the Project Team assesses the impact relative to the key Project Constraints, determines corrective actions (if necessary) and immediately implements the recovery plan. This does not always happen, however. Usually, the Project Team expects that there will be variances to the Project Plan throughout the Project Life Cycle, but if a variance is within "tolerance" it should be okay to wait before taking serious action. Once there is an indication that the variance Tolerance Threshold may be in jeopardy or a major issue surfaces, the Project Team is expected to immediately take steps to minimize the damages and/or recover. So, under what conditions do you, as Project Manager, "re-Balance" the Project Plan, and what are your options for doing so? Within this chapter we explore the concept of re-Balancing the Project Plan.

TOLERANCE THRESHOLDS Should be GOVERNED

Let us first recap what constitutes an Initial "Balanced Plan". From Chapter 3 we see that an initial Balanced Plan necessitates that you satisfy the following conditions:

- Meet Sponsor's **Schedule**/Delivery expectations/commitments

- Meet Sponsor's Budgetary/**Cost** expectations/commitments

- Meet Sponsor's Product **Quality**/Requirements expectations/commitments

- Establish a **Scope** of Work that aligns with the above expectations/commitments

- Secure **Resource** expectations/commitments (capabilities, capacities, and availabilities) to execute the Scope of Work within said Schedule and Budgetary Constraints

- Stay within the Stakeholders' **Risk** Tolerances (i.e. Individual Project Task Risk Severity Tolerance level and Overall Project Risk Threshold level)

One of the key observations to note from the above list is that the first five conditions are required to be "fully compliant" and as such, are reflective of the Project Team's "commitments". If all five of these conditions are met throughout the Project Life Cycle the Project Plan will have been flawlessly executed. This rarely occurs, especially on Projects that are complex and risky. We typically attribute most of the miscues on complex Projects as issues that arise from "known risks" (i.e. pre-determined "threats" to meeting any of the other five Project Constraints). Unknown or unforeseen risks might materialize as well – these are "threats" that were either missed at the time the Project Plan was "Baselined" or those which are generally too vast and random to predict. Further, some Product Development Processes (i.e. Incremental and Agile) have built-in expectations regarding key Project Constraints that are expected to be "traded off" if necessary – e.g. the "Agile" Development

Process tends to assume that some lower priority Product Requirements might have to be dropped to meet Product launch date requirements – more about this in Chapter 7: Product Development Process.

Regardless of the type of Product Development Process employed on a Project, when we veer off course a little, we should not panic – everyone should realize that this happens, and expectations should not be unreasonable (i.e. so rigid as to believe that issues will not arise). We should start getting concerned when we veer off course too much for our own comfort (i.e. when one or more of the Project Constraints changes too much and in the wrong direction). And we should be greatly concerned when this variance is large enough to seriously jeopardize the Project Team's chances of meeting all its established commitments and/or expectations. The key is, how do we define these conditions so that every Project Stakeholder involved knows when and how to act when the Project Team veers off plan? The phrases "to much for our own comfort" and "large enough to seriously jeopardize the Project Team's chances" are too vague and ambiguous. The answer should be "via specific Organizational or Contractual Guidelines" – i.e. Project Governance. Leaving this up to the individual Project Teams to decide can result in Project-to-Project inconsistencies and opens the door to unnecessary misunderstandings and conflicts. Examples are provided below.

General Guidelines Provide Consistency

I have always preferred reviewing good "visual" representations of data versus spreadsheets loaded with arrays of abstract numbers, or presentation slides with nothing but words (and tiny font to fit everything on the page). Well-designed "visuals" can readily enable others to "pin-point" the most relevant information, assist in high level data analysis, enable comparison of alternative solutions, facilitate expedient decisions, and generally save time. What makes this even better is when all Project Teams are required to report the same type of data, in the same format, and via the same "language". By "language", I am referring to the use of Words, Colors, Symbols, Graphs and/or Ratings that mean the same for every Project. We tend to like using RED, YELLOW and GREEN to indicate ISSUES, CONCERNS and GOODNESS, respectively. I realize that this is somewhat obvious, but if we can define these color categories in enough detail, we can then use them to create specific and consistent Project Governess Reporting Guidelines – and reap the benefits mentioned earlier. Below are examples of "general" guidelines – narratives and "objective" measures.

GREEN = The Project is "on-target" and satisfying Project Constraints/ expectations.

> **Measure:** within 95% of goals/commitments on every non-Risk Constraint and at least 50% or higher confidence in meeting Project Cost and Schedule expectations – AND no Individual Project Task Risks in the RED zone

YELLOW = There are Project concerns or additional risks identified for the Project Team to address. The Project Manager and Team have a "plan of action" that they believe will resolve or satisfactorily mitigate the concern/risk.

> **Measure:** within 90% of goals/commitments on every non-Risk Constraint, at least 40% or higher confidence in meeting Project Cost and Schedule expectations – AND no Individual Project Task Risks in the RED zone

RED = The Project is experiencing one or more issue relative to satisfying Project Constraints/expectations. The Project Manager and Team have a "plan of action." Action by one or more of the organization's Functional Managers is required to help resolve or mitigate the resulting impact(s).

> **Measure:** meeting less than 90% of Goals/commitments on at least one non-Risk Constraint OR below 40% confidence in meeting Project Cost or Schedule expectations, OR one or more Individual Project Task Risk(s) in the RED zone

Specific guidelines for each Project Constraint/expectation are provided in the subsequent sections. Please take note that there should be some leeway or latitude in the measures that constitute a GREEN Rating. This prevents being overly bureaucratic and worrying about every single little "blip" in the Project Plan – i.e. prevents unnecessary (and potentially over-burdening) micro-management.

Project Cost Variance Guideline Examples

Some organizations do not track Project Costs per se. Some track recorded "effort" (i.e. resource time), or "effort" is estimated by Functional Managers. Others keep meticulous records of time worked via "timecards" (physical or electronic). Sometimes Direct Material Costs and/or Indirect Costs (e.g. Travel, Supplies, Symposium Expenses, etc.) are important to track even if Labor Costs are not. If the organization does not track Project Cost or "effort" at all, then no need to worry about this Project Constraint. But, for whatever Project Cost data (i.e. financies) are tracked, below is an example of how those Project Cost commitments/expectations might be evaluated or categorized throughout the Project Life Cycle.

GREEN = Finances are stable or have been improved upon thus far.

Measure: within 95% of Overall Cost/Budget commitments/ expectations (e.g. EAC [Estimate at Completion] is not greater than Budget/.95) – AND if using EVM (Earned Value Management) indices, have a CPI (Cost Performance Index) of no less than .95

YELLOW = Budgets for Labor, Material and/or Other Direct Project Expenses are tight or higher than planned, but the Project Manager and Team have a plan to stay on track.

Measure: within 90% of Overall Cost/Budget commitments/expectations – AND if using EVM indices, have a CPI of no less than .90

ACHIEVING EPIC BUSINESS RESULTS

RED = Budgets for Labor, Material or Other Direct Project Expenses are determined to be insufficient to meet all Project Objectives.

Measure: below 90% of Overall Cost/Budget commitments/expectations, OR if using EVM indices, have a CPI of less than .90

Project Schedule Variance Guideline Examples

As with Project Costs, there are several different approaches to establishing Project Schedules and tracking Project Schedule performance over the course of the Project's Life Cycle. Some organizations might not track schedule performance at all. Others might use Milestone Charts or Simple Gantt Charts. IMS (Integrated Master Schedule) usage has become popular due to the automated features which support both Project Schedule construction and Project Status Updating, and is thus especially handy when managing complex, risky, strategically important Projects. Assuming an IMS scheduling tool is being used, the example below shows those Project Schedule commitments/expectations which might be evaluated or categorized during Project execution.

GREEN = The Project is on or ahead of Schedule or slightly behind and reasonably able to be recovered.

Measure: within 95% of Overall Project Schedule commitments/expectations for key Deliverables (e.g. total Project duration is no greater than [Baseline Project duration]/.95) – AND if using EVM (Earned Value Management) indices, have a SPI (Schedule Performance Index) of no less than .95

YELLOW = A slip to a key Project Deliverable is impending but there is a plan in place to potentially recover.

Measure: within 90% of Overall Schedule commitments/expectations for key Deliverables – AND if using EVM indices, have a SPI of no less than .90

RED = A key Project Deliverable and/or Schedule commitment/expectation has been missed or is likely to be missed. The recovery plan needs Functional Management help to mitigate or get the Project back on track.

> **Measure:** below 90% of Overall Schedule commitments/expectations for key Deliverables – OR if using EVM indices, have a CPI of less than .90

Project Scope Variance Guideline Examples

Project Scope is typically dictated by the PDP (Product Development Process), in conjunction with the other key Project Constraints. The sequence of activities and amount of effort required to conduct them is basically the Scope of Work. The Scope of Work, when completed, should validate that all Project and Product Requirements have been satisfactorily met. When Product Requirements change, the Scope of Work typically changes. When issues materialize from risks or misunderstandings about Project Task Completion Definitions, more Project Scope is likely needed to remedy the situation. If the Project Schedule is extended, the amount of management oversight (i.e. the "marching army") extends. Therefore, there is usually a consequential impact from changes in other Project Constraints, and Project Scope changes typically have a consequential impact to one or more of the other Project Constraints. When Project Scope is planned to be added due to inadvertent omissions or changing Project Requirements, Stakeholders should be informed, in part, to exercise their rights to consider other alternative solutions relative to accommodating the changes. Thus, pending Project Scope changes (due to issues or Project Requirements changes) are usually productive metrics to track. An example of how Project Scope might be evaluated or categorized is provided below.

> **GREEN** = The Project Plan is still valid, and/or reserves are not foreseen as needed to complete the Project's planned Scope of Work.

Measure: no changes, adjustments or pending changes that would materially change the Project Scope of Work are currently foreseen or contemplated.

YELLOW = Additional minor tasks have been identified as necessary to satisfy an existing Project commitment and/or new Project Requirement. The Project Manager and Team have a plan to contain this within Project reserves and/or Risk Thresholds.

Measure: some changes, adjustments or pending changes to Project Scope have either been implemented or are being contemplated and are causing one or more other key Project Constraint to be in the YELLOW zone, but do not (or are not expected to) cause any of the other key Project Constraints to be in the RED zone.

RED = Additional major tasks have been identified as necessary to satisfy an existing Project commitment and/or new Project Requirement, and not likely to be contained within Project reserves and/or Risk Thresholds.

Measure: some changes, adjustments or pending changes to Project Scope have either been implemented or are being contemplated and have caused (or are expected to cause) one or more other key Project Constraint to be in the RED zone.

Project Resource Variance Guideline Examples

The nicest aspect of a Project-Oriented Organization Structure is that the toughest Project Resources to manage (people) are typically dedicated to the Project. Personnel resource management gets much more complex and difficult to control in a Matrix Organization. So, if managing necessary Human Resources directly, and having virtually 100% control over their activities/assignments, the Project Manager might not have to worry about this Project Constraint. This is typically the complete opposite in a Matrix Structure, for personnel resource management can prove be a huge factor for success in organizations that conduct a multitude of Projects via pools of Project Resources controlled by Functional Managers outside the Projects. In addition to Human Resources, other factors (e.g. Facilities, Equipment, Out-Sourced Specialties and Funding) should be considered. An example of how Project Resources might be evaluated or categorized is provided below.

GREEN = All required Project Resources are in place or there is an achievable plan in place to have them available in a timeframe that will not affect Project performance.

> **Measure:** no lack of required Project Resources, or if there is, the Project Plan can be easily adjusted to accommodate Project Resource availability without impact to other key Project Constraints.

YELLOW = There are some Project Resource shortfalls that are impacting Project performance but there is an agreed-to recovery plan with a good likelihood of success.

> **Measure:** specific Project Resources with capabilities (that were assumed when Project estimates were determined) to complete Project Scope are either currently unavailable or are in jeopardy of being available, and this shortfall causes (or will cause) one or more other key Project Constraints to be in the YELLOW zone, but do not (or are not expected to) cause any of the other key Project Constraints to be in the RED zone.

RED = There is a significant Project Resource shortfall which is impacting Project performance, and the recovery plan does not enable the Project to get back on track without resolution of the shortfall.

> **Measure:** specific Project Resources with capabilities (that were assumed when Project estimates were determined) to complete Project Scope are either currently unavailable or are in serious jeopardy of being available, and this shortfall causes (or is

expected to cause) one or more other key Project Constraint to be in the RED zone.

Product Quality/Technical Variance Guideline Examples

Technical Product Requirement changes can cause the most devastating problems to Project performance. These types of changes, especially when significant, can either add undue risk (if "absorbed") and/or result in a major impact to Project Scope, which in turn, can lead to Project Cost and/or Schedule consequences – and potentially lead to Project Resource issues as well. Therefore, I cannot over-state the importance of managing Project Requirements and changes – the subject of Chapters 1 and 5 (Managing Requirements, and Cost of Change), respectively. Project Quality/Technical Requirements evaluations are handled similarly to Project Scope, as shown in the below examples.

GREEN = There are no "technical" issues that are significant enough to impact deliveries or impact the Product performance requirements.

Measure: no changes, adjustments or pending changes are currently foreseen or contemplated that would materially change the Project Scope of Work or other key Constraints.

YELLOW = There are "technical" issues (or pending "technical" issues) impacting deliveries or Project performance but there is an achievable plan to recover within Project Constraints.

Measure: some changes, adjustments or pending changes to Product Requirements have either been implemented or are being contemplated and are causing one or more other key Project Constraint to be in the YELLOW zone but does not (or are not expected to) cause any of the other key Project Constraints to be in the RED zone.

RED = There are major "technical" issues (or pending issues) that are impacting Project performance and Deliveries. There is a low probability of resolving the issues without additional organizational help.

> **Measure:** some changes, adjustments or pending changes to Product Requirements have either been implemented or are being contemplated and have caused (or are expected to cause) one or more other key Project Constraint to be in the RED zone.

Project Risk Variance Guideline Examples

As discussed in more detail in Chapter 3 (Planning), Overall Project Risk tends to be the "variable", and "absorbing" risks tends to be the first consideration when issues arise, and Project changes are needed. However, there is (or should be) a limit to how much risk can be absorbed before it becomes a major issue itself and leads to eminent Project failure. I am an advocate of establishing two Risk Thresholds, one for the number (and "Severity") of Individual Project Risks (typically associated with specific tasks or activities) and a second which comprehends the Overall Project Cost and/or Schedule Risks. More on this in Chapter 4 (Managing Risks) and my first book **Project Risk Management**. An example of how these risks might be evaluated or categorized is provided below.

> **GREEN** = There are only a few "Medium" Residual Risks identified as a result of implementing all risk "mitigation" actions, and Overall Project Cost and Schedule Risks are within "tolerances" established for GREEN Risk ratings.

> > **Measure:** be within at least 60% (or higher) confidence in meeting Cost and Schedule expectations – AND no Individual Project Risks in the RED zone – AND no more than two Individual Project Risks in the Medium Risk zone of the Risk Matrix.

> **YELLOW** = There are no "High" Residual Risks identified as a result of implementing all "mitigation" actions, AND/OR the Overall Project Cost and Schedule Risks are within "tolerances" established for the YELLOW Risk ratings.

Measure: be within at least 60% confidence in meeting Cost and Schedule expectations – AND no Individual Project Risks in the RED zone of the Risk Matrix.

RED = There is an unmitigated "High" Risk and/or excessive "Medium" Risks with no "mitigation" or "contingency" plans, AND/OR the Overall Project Cost and Schedule Risks are lower than the "tolerances" established for the YELLOW Risk rating.

Measure: be below 50% confidence in meeting Cost or Schedule expectations, AND/OR one or more Individual Project Risk(s) in the RED zone of the Risk Matrix.

GOVERNING TOLERANCE THRESHOLDS

Tolerances should be established by Organizational Management (via Procedures or Directives) and consistently applied to Projects throughout the organization – a key aspect of Strategic Project Management. The above examples assume certain tolerances which apply to changes in Project Constraints and suggests the corresponding "action plans" to be initiated. These "action plans" may be as benign as keeping a close eye on certain activities or as disruptive as re-Balancing (or even to the extent of re-Baselining) the entire Project Plan. The "threshold-of-change" levels are typically derived from organizational tolerances and may differ for different types of Projects (e.g. Strategically Important Projects, versus Process Improvement Projects, versus long-term Research and Development Projects, etc.). High-risk/high-reward Projects tend to warrant looser tolerances and lower-risk/strategically-important Projects might necessitate tighter tolerances to ensure commitments are met.

The specific tolerances are either numeric values by nature or levels of change which could correspond to numerical values, if desired. The "Spider Chart" shown in Figure 35 below is an example of how these numerical tolerance levels could be portrayed, if all are converted to a 0 to 100 numerical scale. Figure 35 depicts the original Project Baseline Plan at the time the Project is kicked off – Overall Project Risk (% confidence in

Cost and Schedule) is 95% (65% confidence plus 30%) and all other Project Constraints are at 100%. Figure 36 depicts a notional in-progress Project Status Update scenario -- where Project Risk confidence has dropped to 92% (still in the Green zone), Project Cost has dropped to 85% (in the middle of the Yellow zone), Project Schedule has dropped to 78% (high end of the Red zone), Project Scope has dropped to 75% (in the Red zone) Product Quality/Requirements has dropped to 95% (middle of the Green zone), and Project Resources have dropped to 95% (middle of the Green zone).

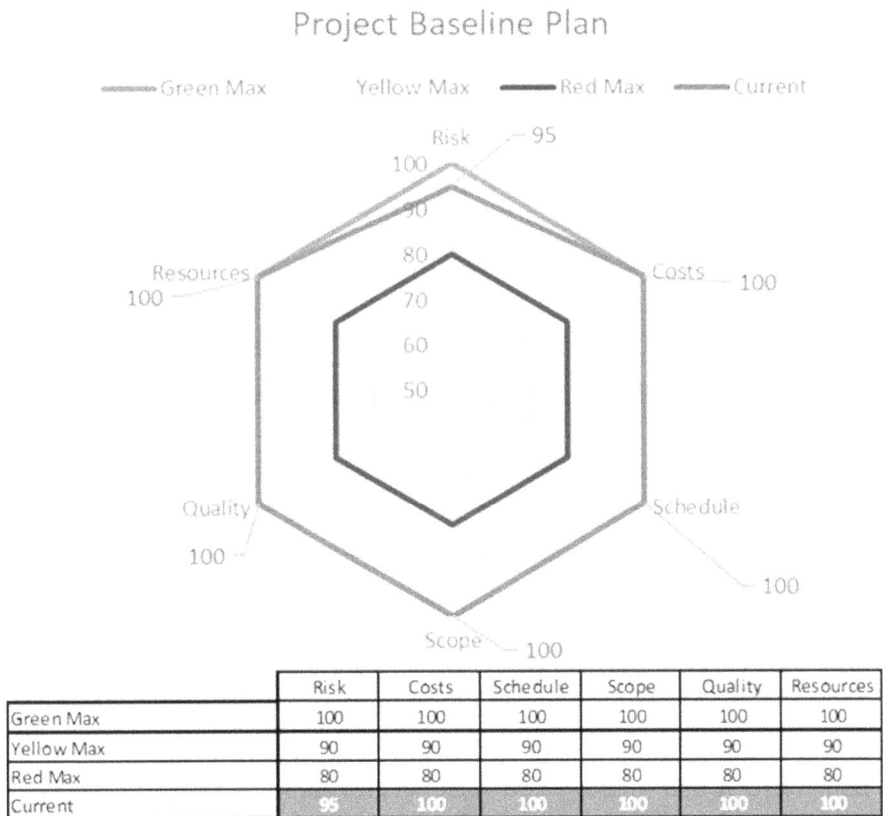

Project Baseline Plan

	Risk	Costs	Schedule	Scope	Quality	Resources
Green Max	100	100	100	100	100	100
Yellow Max	90	90	90	90	90	90
Red Max	80	80	80	80	80	80
Current	95	100	100	100	100	100

Figure 35. Spider Diagram Depicting Baseline Project Constraints

Project Progress Update Status

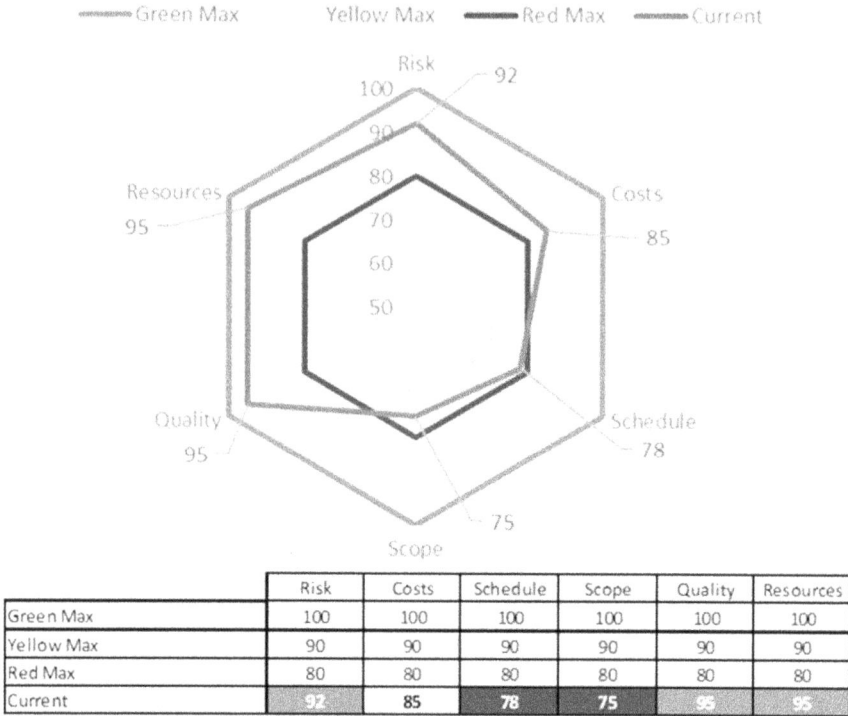

Figure 36. Spider Diagram Depicting In-Progress Project Constraints

	Risk	Costs	Schedule	Scope	Quality	Resources
Green Max	100	100	100	100	100	100
Yellow Max	90	90	90	90	90	90
Red Max	80	80	80	80	80	80
Current	92	85	78	75	95	95

Defining Overall Project % Confidence

Note that in the original "Baseline" Project Plan the only non-100% level is Overall Project Risk (or in this case: 65% Confidence + 30% = 95% and the 30% adder is just a simple factor to get the metric up to 100% when a 70% Confidence or higher is achieved). As mentioned earlier in Chapter 4 (Managing Risks), risk is typically the variable in our "Baseline" Project Plans, thus it tends to be based on Organizational Tolerance expectations. Bottom-line is that we commonly assume that our Project Schedules and Costs have at least a 50:50 chance of being met (which equates to 80% on this scale, or 50% + 30%), and to get beyond 70% Confidence (i.e. 100% on the Spider Diagram) would typically incur too much of an expense. So realistically, we tend to accept a certain level of risk to keep the Project Plan from "exploding", and any confidence level "north of" 50% is likely to be a good compromise. I pick 70% confidence for the 100%

because it is typically on the linear slope at the top part of the 'S' Curve and is the level I have used in the past with very good success. Figure 37 below shows how the Overall Schedule Risk metric can be tracked over time. It also provides to a "confidence-level" variance (the number of work-days between 10% and 90%), which was elaborated upon in Chapter 4 (Managing Risks).

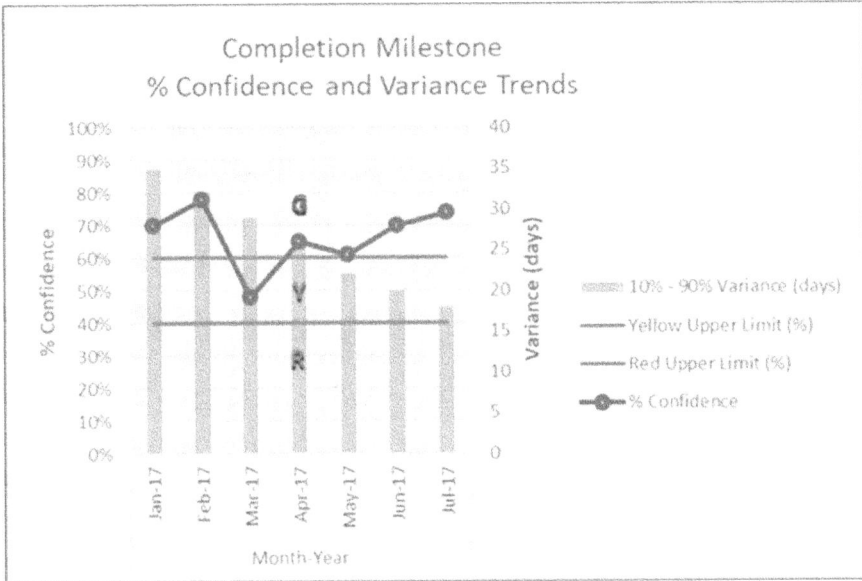

Figure 37. Trend Chart Showing Overall Project Schedule Risk History

Defining the RED Zone of the Risk Matrix

As noted in the previous section, there are actually two key Project Risk metrics that I tend to advise people to use, one for Overall Project Risk (as noted above) and the other for the Individual Project Risks per task. Both can be used for determining the RED, YELLOW, GREEN ratings (which is my preference), or just one of them can be used. The Individual Project Risk metric relates to the number of individual tasks or activities with risks within "High" and "Medium" zones of the Risk Matrix (a popular tool discussed in Chapter 4: Managing Risks). The Risk Matrix that I prefer to use is a 5x5 matrix – five "probability" zones and five "impact" zones (example shown in Chapter 4). An example of how an organization could define the zones, and especially the RED (i.e. "keep-out") zone in this Risk Matrix, is provided in Figure 38 below.

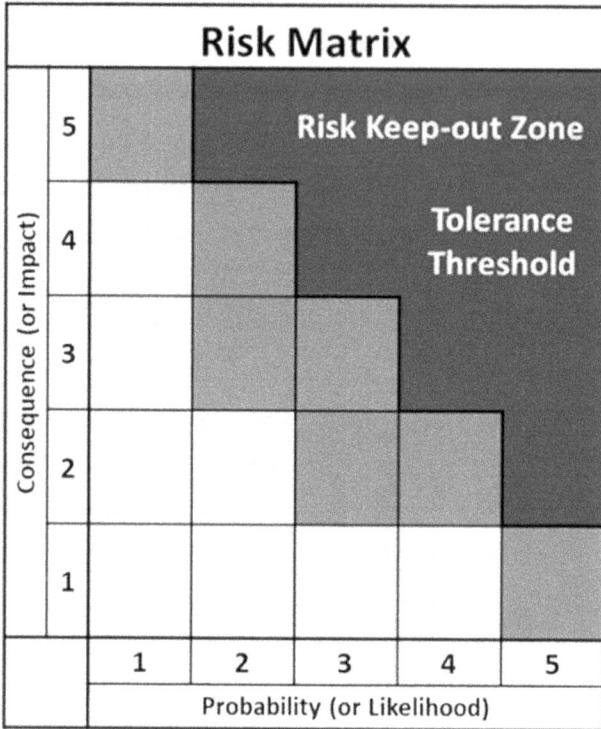

Figure 38. 5X5 Risk Matrix Showing Tolerance Threshold and Keep-out Zone

I am a firm believer that the "RED" zone of the Risk Matrix should be established as the "keep-out" zone for Individual Project Risks. Think about it – is it acceptable to be okay with a Project Plan that is expected to have a major issue, resulting in adding months to a schedule, especially on a Project that is tightly controlled and scrutinized? Obviously, not. This scenario is representative of the upper right-hand corner of the Risk Matrix. So, what **is** an acceptable Project Risk? The organization should determine the range of "Probability X Impact" combinations that should be avoided – to call into question the practicality of establishing a Project Plan which is, from the start, on a path of almost certain failure. But the Risk Matrix allows those risks. So, the Risk Matrix should have a "keep-out" zone and using the RED (i.e. High-Risk) zone as that guideline makes utter sense. What this means is, if a risk is accessed to be in any of the "probability" X "impact" cells of the RED zone (i.e. High-Risk zone), the Project Team and Functional Managers with vested interest should be given notice to remedy the situation within some set timeframe (e.g. one or two weeks). Thus, Individual Project Risks which show up in the RED zone should be dealt with immediately to steer the Project back on track, or at least onto the right trajectory. This will likely impact one or more of the other key Project Constraints.

The Risk Matrix design should therefore be constructed per the organization's "Risk Appetite". Figure 21 (back in Chapter 4) shows a comparison of how the Risk Matrix might be constructed to accommodate three different "Risk Appetites" – Risk Taking, Risk Neutral and Risk Avoiding. Note the corresponding changes in the three risk zones. Organizational Governance guidelines should be established to set the most appropriate expectations, based on senior management preferences, biases and opinions. Also, it is best (logically and ascetically) to create zones which have non-overlapping numerical ranges. For example, in the center matrix: Low Risk "severity" is 1 to 4; Medium is 5 to 9; and High is 10 to 25.

WHY AND WHEN TO RE-BASELINE A PROJECT

The primary goal of Strategic Project Management should be to enable all Organizational Strategic Goals and Objectives to have the highest possible "probability of success". Everybody wins in that scenario. The "Baseline" Project Plan should not be used as a tool for "keeping score" and pushing Team Members to the maximum extent possible. We want improved productivity, but we should also want our employees to feel valued and excited about working for our organization. Metrics are good to establish and track ["you cannot improve what you do not measure" – Posted by Todd Smith (2018)], but there should be a degree of discernment applied relative to how to effectively use the information, learn from our mistakes, and move forward with refreshed confidence. Re-Baselining a Project Plan can accomplish this goal.

ACHIEVING EPIC BUSINESS RESULTS

Why Consider Re-Baselining?

Years ago, as a key executive within a company, I noticed that the organization's executives and the Sales Force were always given a clean slate to start at each fiscal year, yet the Product Development Teams were not. Project Teams had to carry forward the baggage of the past years' performance shortfalls. Everyone else got an automatic reset in their metrics. I also noticed that there were no established Organizational Governance guidelines for reporting status or managing Project Risks. Risks were assumed to "be taken care of" or "made go away" somehow. Ultimately, most Projects were eventually in the "RED" zone and had no available way of getting out of the "RED" zone. The Team Members were all labelled as poor performers according to the CEO (a prior salesperson) and did not necessarily deserve to receive bonuses from his stand-point but were given bonuses, nonetheless. The problem that this caused was lack of motivation to improve, and a temptation to falsely report Project Team performance (the other division's solution to the problem). I championed establishment of Organizational Governance guidelines and re-setting (i.e. re-Baselining) all the Projects at the start of the new fiscal year, and the performance improvements (and attitudes) were striking.

This has left a lasting impression on me – re-Baselining should not be a "dirty word", but a practical necessity, when warranted. Think about this a little more. If the Project Progress Status is continually RED, how can we discern if other issues are surfacing and being responsibly dealt with? They just tend to get lost in the Project Status Updates, and this can lead to the attitude "since the status is already RED why worry about it?".

When Should a Project Team Re-Baseline?

A Project Team should re-Baseline whenever the Project Plan needs major changes to get back on track (i.e. when the current Project Status is "RED" and one or more of the Key Objectives can no longer be achieved). Making a few changes to just barely get back into the YELLOW zone, if possible, could be acceptable to avoid re-Baselining, but re-Baselining might still be worthwhile to re-energize the Project Team.

The onus for figuring out how to get out of the RED zone should not be placed solely on the shoulders of the Project Manager and key Project Leads. It should be an organizational endeavor, involving all key Project Stakeholders who have a vested interest in the change options. Sometimes, simply pushing out a date or changing a Product Requirement is all that is needed to get the Project back to a reasonable "state of health" (i.e. YELLOW). But if you do decide to re-Baseline, diligently try to re-set to a GREEN Project Plan – the best "strategic" option for all involved. To help facilitate this decision process consider a Project Health metric. Figure 39 is a simple table that basically counts the number of RED, YELLOW and GREEN ratings with respect to the six key Project Constraints. There are 28 levels – 17 REDs, 7 YELLOWs and 4 GREENs (refer to the far-right column). Pick a threshold. I tend to wait until the resulting Project Health is in the RED zone before considering re-Baselining. You can adjust the Red zone boundary to establish your own criteria, and you may want to add more categories, as well – e.g. Customer Satisfaction, Contract/Funding Status, etc.

Any Combination of Schedule/Scope/Technical/Resource/Finance/Risk							
R	R	R	R	R	R	=	R
R	R	R	R	R	Y	=	R
R	R	R	R	R	G	=	R
R	R	R	R	Y	Y	=	R
R	R	R	R	Y	G	=	R
R	R	R	R	G	G	=	R
R	R	R	Y	Y	Y	=	R
R	R	R	Y	Y	G	=	R
R	R	R	Y	G	G	=	R
R	R	R	G	G	G	=	R
R	R	Y	Y	Y	Y	=	R
R	R	Y	Y	Y	G	=	R
R	R	Y	Y	G	G	=	R
R	R	Y	G	G	G	=	R
R	R	G	G	G	G	=	R
R	Y	Y	Y	Y	Y	=	R
R	Y	Y	Y	Y	G	=	R
R	Y	Y	Y	G	G	=	Y
R	Y	Y	G	G	G	=	Y
R	Y	G	G	G	G	=	Y
R	G	G	G	G	G	=	Y
Y	Y	Y	Y	Y	Y	=	Y
Y	Y	Y	Y	Y	G	=	Y
Y	Y	Y	Y	G	G	=	Y
Y	Y	Y	G	G	G	=	G
Y	Y	G	G	G	G	=	G
Y	G	G	G	G	G	=	G
G	G	G	G	G	G	=	G

Figure 39. Example Overall Project Health Ratings Chart Definitions. Project Risk Management (PMI, 2016, p. 230)

It's Wise to Retain Baseline Change History

Re-Baselining is warranted at times, and for some very good reasons. Organizations that endeavor to continually improve should not, however, over-look the "Root Cause" issues behind those decisions. A "mini-Postmortem" might be appropriate – i.e. an exercise to investigate a specific "causal incident" versus the entire Project. Consider answering the following questions:

- What was (were) the underlying Cause(s)?

- What could be done to either prevent this from occurring, or at least lower the likelihood of it happening again?

- Does this warrant a Systemic Change, and if so:
  - What is the Action Plan?
  - Who is the Owner?
  - How will we know the Action Plan worked?

Retaining the Project Baseline history is important for a few reasons:

- Per the above Postmortem Process, Systemic Changes can prevent re-occurrence of issues on the same or other Projects, but the impact and rationale should be retained, especially if the Systemic Change does not turn out to be 100% effective.

- Some Contracts require the "paper trail" to be retained for future reference, if necessary.

- Teams should be motivated to avoid having to re-Baseline and keeping track is a potential deterrent.

- Functional groups should be motivated to avoid causing a re-Baselining action – again acting as a potential deterrent.

- An analysis of Project re-Baselining reasons can lead the organization to conclude that there is a gap in Organizational Training or Personnel Development.

Whatever position you take relative to Project re-Baselining, think of the behaviors that you want to reinforce. There are good reasons why public companies reset financial goals (e.g. Product Sales and Revenue, Gross Margins and Profit Targets) each year – it is hard and discouraging when trying to continuously get out of a deep hole, and executives want to motivate the workforce to improve "Financials" by giving new targets and bonus opportunities. Do we do the same for the Project Teams?

> I ran a Business Segment at a High Tech company where the Product Development Teams were never allowed to re-Baseline. If they were in the RED they had to just keep "taking it on the chin" for past performance issues – and for some less-than-visible Product Requirements changes imposed on them. You can just imagine the morale. So, I decided to reset all Projects at the beginning of the new Fiscal Year – this ended up being one of the best actions I ever took.

Is Your Organization Managing Projects Strategically?

Take the test, or at least see how your organization stacks up. An inventory of the key Strategic Project Management concepts espoused by this book can be kept, Chapter by Chapter. There is no established reference of good or bad, but you can see where your organization currently is, and use this tool to monitor progress. Each question starts with the phrase: To what extent does your organization......

26. avoid leaving Project management **Governance Guidelines** up to Teams to decide?

1	2	3	4	5
O	O	O	O	O
Never	Rarely	Sometimes	Most of the Time	Always

27. require all key Project Constraints to be **Maintained within a Specific Range?**

1	2	3	4	5
O	O	O	O	O
Never	Rarely	Sometimes	Most of the Time	Always

28. specify **RED, YELLOW and GREEN** Status Update Definitions and **Objective Measures?**

1	2	3	4	5
O	O	O	O	O
Never	Rarely	Sometimes	Most of the Time	Always

29. set **Risk Tolerance Guidelines** – Risk Matrix keep-out (i.e. RED) zone and **Project % Confidence?**

1	2	3	4	5
O	O	O	O	O
Never	Rarely	Sometimes	Most of the Time	Always

30. have a fair and practical **Project Re-Baselining** Policy and Procedure?

1	2	3	4	5
O	O	O	O	O
Never	Rarely	Sometimes	Most of the Time	Always

CHAPTER 7

It's *THE PRODUCT DEVELOPMENT PROCESS*

As is discussed in Chapter 3 (Planning), the Project's Scope of Work is largely dependent on the PDP (Product Development Process) implemented. The PDP is the process by which Products (including Services) are developed and brought to market, in concert with the other over-arching Project Constraints. In some industries and/or organizations the PDP is referred to as the Product-Oriented Process (PMI®, Inc.), the NPI (New Product Introduction) process, or the PLC (Product Life Cycle) process. The different fundamental types of PDPs are commonly referred to in terms of their key Characteristics (i.e. Waterfall [or Predictive/Deterministic], Incremental [or Iterative], Agile [or Adaptive], and Hybrid [or combination of types]). The PDP used might be sponsor-directed, derived based on an SME's (Subject Matter Expert's) assessment, or selected because it is considered a "Best Practice" that has worked in the past. "Best Practices" are recognized as those which are consistently found to be best suited for driving successful achievement of the specific Project's over-arching objectives within its recognized Project Constraints (i.e. treatment of Product Requirements, importance of achieving a Schedule and/or meeting a specific Budget, the types of Resources needed, and the degree of Risk accepted).

Given the breadth and variety of Project types, there are likely to be uniqueness's to every specific PDP employed. Standard PDPs are sometimes established within industries and/or organizations. These standard PDPs are typically designed to be tailorable (i.e. adjustable) to meet unique or detailed Project/Product Requirements. The general types of PDPs noted above are the most common employed at the time of this publication, but others may emerge over time. As with most Project Management Tools & Techniques, there are some common general needs that are addressed by them, and some specific differences which should drive their selection. Some PDP options are straight-forward and simple to implement, and others are more complex and may need greater organizational support and/or resources to successfully plan for and execute. So, it is conceivable to develop a table of PDP options to aid in the selection process, and thus, one is provided in the last section of this chapter.

My caution to those aspiring to ensure that their organization embraces the over-arching concept of Strategic Project Management is that "there is no one size fits all" approach when it comes to PDPs. Some people may disagree with this assertion, but if there was, we would not see so many different PDP implementation options being effectively used in different scenarios. I choose to address this topic head-on, for I do believe that a basic Strategic Project Management tenet is that "it's all about the Product Development Process", and I feel that it would be remiss of me to omit it.

THE COMMON DRIVERS BEHIND PDP SELECTION

The PDP selected by a Project Team is typically a primary driver to the determination of Project Scope. The Scope of Work planned for meeting over-arching Project and Product Requirements is driven by the collective work activities derived by the organization or Project Team to ultimately validate that Project Deliverables meet all the advertised Project and Product Requirements. This is typically facilitated by the development of a Project/Product Requirements document (per Chapter 1: Managing Requirements). Requirements documents are established and maintained to ensure that Project Stakeholders are aligned with Project and Product Goals and Objectives, and specifically, the corresponding Product Technical/Quality specifications. These documents therefore provide visibility into potential Product Requirements misalignments with the product validation methodologies that are employed.

Project Management Processes and Knowledge Areas

Product Development activities are a vital subset of the over-arching Project Management processes which specifically relate to determining Project Scope and enabling a "Balanced" Project Plan. As such, the fundamental Project Management Process Groups and Knowledge Areas espoused by the PMBOK® Guide and other PMI® Practice Standards apply irrespective of the type of PDP methodology employed.

Systematic Requirements Reviews

When developing a Project Plan there is a good chance that Project Stakeholders disagree on some of the Project/Product Requirements. Disagreements are sometimes due to the specific descriptions and/or specification limits. Some proposed requirements might be too vague to accept (e.g. a statement like "the software must be compatible with all current and future computer architectures" would cause a problem since the Project Team cannot control future computer architecture designs by other companies). Other proposed requirements might not provide enough Safety Margin (e.g. relative to dimensions, or range of environmental conditions, and needs for meeting regulatory requirements, etc.) to ensure factory equipment reliably and repeatedly produce high-yielding saleable Products – a situation that could potentially compromise or jeopardize Project Business Case objectives. Still other requirements may impose an inordinate amount of risk (e.g. relying on the development of a new system that includes several unproven technological innovations), making it literally impossible to "Balance" the Project Plan without changing one or more of the other key Project Constraints (e.g. Completion Schedule, Costs/Budget or Resource capabilities). Thus, conducting System Requirements Reviews (SRRs), as detailed in Chapter 1 (Managing Requirements), early in a Product Development Process is a good/appropriate practice to follow to settle disagreements, solidify Project Scope, and establish a "Balanced" Project Plan.

Project Risk Tolerances Influence PDP Methods

Here is a thought to contemplate: I believe that a Project Team can theoretically establish a viable Project Plan based on any set of Project Cost, Schedule, Scope, Resource, Product Quality constraints provided there is no limit to the Project's Risk. It is all about Managing Risks (Chapter 4), and the PDP method selected is therefore highly dependent on Project Risk Tolerances. Some scenarios are provided below.

Scenario A: Project with Almost Zero Risk. In the fifth year of production, a Contract Manufacturer is given an order to build half the usual volume of Product in the same amount of time normally given for double that volume. The company has enough material on-hand to build 4 times that amount of Product. The contract is set up to pay all costs at an agreed to Overhead Rate, and with an agreed to Profit Margin. This is a very low risk Project, and one that should be straight-forward to execute.

Scenario B: Project with Tremendous Risk. According to marketing intelligence a New Product must be developed within the next year to meet a critical Strategic Objective. Similar past Projects have taken two years to complete due to the number of iterations required to arrive at a Product Design that meets all the stringent Quality Requirements. The Project Team is also given half the budget of similar past Projects and concludes that it has about a 10% confidence in getting the Product Design right the first time. This Project Plan is the product of "wishful thinking" and given the demand to meet all Product Requirements it is not likely that the Project Team will be successful. Hopefully, the organization's management recognizes all the risks. If they do and make it clear (preferably in writing) to the Project Team that the Management Team just wants them to do the best that they can, you have a palatable situation. If they do not recognize the risk and expect the Project Team to somehow "make the risks go away", the next year-or-so is likely to be a tumultuous time for this entire organization – for a very probable "no-win" potentially de-moralizing situation has been established.

Scenario C: Project with Reasonably Containable Risk. The Project Team has produced a Project Plan to develop a new, fairly-complex device. There is no new technology per se, but this specific type of device has never been previously produced by the organization. All the Project/Product Requirements have been established and prioritized, but regardless of priority all are expected to be met. The Project Team has developed Products in the past with similar complexity and have factored the past data (Schedule, Cost, Scope and Resource requirements) into their estimates, along with establishing the appropriate amount of Risk Reserves (Budget Reserves and Schedule Buffers). The schedule is admittedly tight, but the Project Team believes they can meet it based on their solid Individual Project Task Risk assessments (i.e. no RED task risks) and overall Project Risk assessment of $\geq$ 70% confidence in meeting both Project Cost and Schedule commitments (factoring in the Risk Reserves). This Project Plan also assumes (with Project Sponsor buy-in) that a critical sub-component provided by a sponsor-directed key supplier will be provided on time and in accordance with its specifications (and no on-sight manager is required to over-see that supplier's activities on a continuous basis). This scenario represents a Project with a "Balanced" Project Plan, established with all Project/Product Requirements known and accounted for up front.

ACHIEVING EPIC BUSINESS RESULTS

The above Scenarios, specifically Scenario B and C are referenced further, in subsequent sections. You might think that Scenario B is exaggerated, but it is indeed realistic (for I have experienced this situation). Scenarios B and C can therefore serve to demonstrate how PDPs might be selected. The bottom-line is that Project Risk is typically the most significant influencing factor. Another key factor is the make-up of the organization's resource pool. It does make a difference if your Human Resources are (or are not) all capable and versatile enough to support most of the Project's technical activities (Question: Is the Project Team mostly "Functional" or "Cross-Functional"?). More on this as we discuss PDP methodologies.

THE DIFFERENT PDPs

The most significant differentiator between the previously noted PDP types is inherent Project Risk and tolerance to changes, due primarily to the rigidity and certainty (or lack thereof) of Project/Product Requirements. Other factors which influence the PDP selection decision include: Resource mix and availability, Time-to-Market considerations (i.e. schedule pressures), and Project Cost considerations (i.e. budget pressures). These influences are frequently a response to competitive pressures (i.e. how well our competitors execute their Product Development Plans), and thus, they usually dictate the general flow or sequence of activities to complete Project Scope (i.e. PDP). The four predominant PDPs are described within the subsequent sub-sections.

Waterfall (or Predictive) Product Development Process

Predictive PDPs are typically time-sequenced activities and/or tasks which are substantially serial, and thus, when displayed on a chart chronologically, from top to bottom, resemble a waterfall. These processes are referred to as "predictive" or "deterministic" since they represent Product Development Process sequences which are normally planned based on well-established Product Requirements, a specific Scope of Work, and with definitive Project Schedule and Budget commitments. This is typical of many large multi-disciplined Aerospace and Defense Projects, and for decades has been considered a "Best Practice" for most complex "Research and Development" Projects.

If the overall Product Plan is extremely complex and risky, it might make sense to segment it into sequential Projects of cascading/ diminishing Project Risk – in Project Phases, grouped to comprise an overall Program. For example, consider a new Product which could potentially utilize any one of several competing technologies (i.e. a Targeting System for a Military Aircraft which could use competing Imaging Infrared Sensor technologies). A prudent Project Sponsor might establish a competition whereby several competing technical designs from different companies are funded via competitive Feasibility Demonstration Projects. These Projects could lead to follow-on Advanced Development Projects (the next Phase of the Program) whereby the two most promising technologies are funded via a "head-to-head" competition. The plan would be to fund the winner of the "head-to-head" competition for a Production Readiness Project and potential subsequent Field/User Demonstration Projects, leading up to eventual Product Production and Support Projects. These individual Projects in this example are each established to proactively manage the cascading technological risks, with contingency options, and they end up comprising an over-arching Program that is established with distinct phases of development.

One key short-fall associated with this "Waterfall" approach is that it necessitates prior determination of all significant Project and Product Requirements, meaning uncertainties (i.e. risks) must be well understood and accounted for with Schedule Buffers, Budget Reserves and Product Performance Margins at the start of each Program Phase. Thus, this type of Product Development Process is prone to execution problems if estimates for Project Scope, Time and/or Costs are inaccurate, and if risks are not well understood or adequately managed. The off-setting benefit, however, is that the requirements are derived for a Product and/or Service satisfying a specific purpose within the sponsoring organization and is not necessarily driven by potentially volatile Market Dynamics, as in the Consumer Products industry.

The "Waterfall" process is one in which the resulting Product (or System) is systematically/sequentially built and tested, enabled by Product Requirements "flow-down" to the key sub-systems and components. Because of this "build-up" approach, major issues discovered late in the process (i.e. during Final System Integration, Validation or Qualification Testing) can lead to high-cost negative consequences (i.e. Budgetary, Schedule, and/or Product Requirements changes). This can justifiably lead to very conservative estimating practices, especially in organizations that highly scrutinize Project Team performance. Such Project Teams spend a significant amount of time determining the Scope of Work and tend to factor in very detailed up-front analyses to ensure that the "flow-down" of requirements is sound and as complete as possible. As alluded to earlier, in many such Projects, the performance of components is validated prior to sub-system integration, and sub-systems are validated prior to higher-level sub-system and/or final system-level integration. The Figure 40 Gantt chart depicts a sample "Waterfall" process.

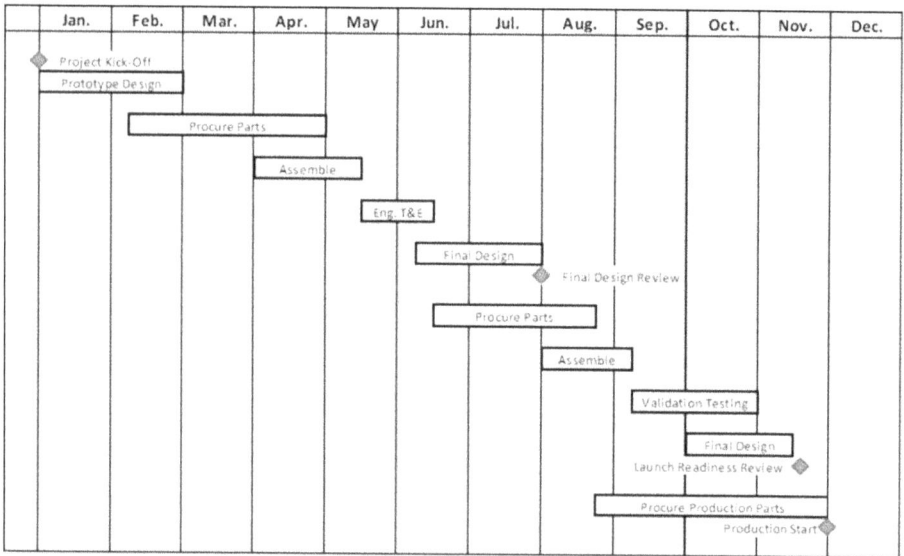

Figure 40. Waterfall Product Development Process Example. Project Risk Management (PMI, 2016, p. 148)

Development of one or more "prototype" system(s) is typically included in a "Waterfall" schedule as a risk reduction strategy, and to manage the "Cost of Change" (Chapter 5). The idea is to first develop initial prototype systems to demonstrate performance under nominal conditions (e.g. normal use, room temperature, normal humidity, no harsh shock and/or vibration, etc.). These prototype systems might also be tested under more extreme conditions to identify the most obvious technical issues to fix when endeavoring to finalize the design. Follow-on "Qualification Units" are usually expected to meet all Environmental and Qualification Requirements with minimal changes and regression testing. More interim or subsequent levels of Product maturity testing (beyond tests established for the initial prototype design, but not yet to the final Plan of Record (POR) configuration of the "Qualification Units", may be performed as well – this then starts to resemble the "Incremental" (or Iterative) Product Development Process discussed in the next section.

The previously described Scenario C Project (with reasonably containable risk) represents an example of a complex Project that might utilize a traditional "Waterfall" PDP described above. All key Project Constraints are determined (i.e. negotiated) up front and a reasonable amount of Project Risk is usually tolerated – and is typical of a Product Development Program performed under contract for a single sponsoring organization (i.e. customer or agency, etc.).

A common variation to the classical "Waterfall" Product Development Process is to "progressively elaborate" on Product Requirements definitions and detailed Project Scope versus solidifying all lower-level requirements and corresponding task scope up-front. As Project work is completed, the detailed Project Plan for up-coming near-term future tasks/activities is "fine-tuned", or "elaborated" upon in more detail.

A "Waterfall" PDP is typically more applicable for a Project that not only has firm Product Requirements but has firm Cost and/or Schedule and/or Scope Constraints as well. The idea is for the Project Manager and Team Leads to initiate the Project by collecting all proposed Organizational Requirements from the various affected departments (e.g.

Manufacturing, Quality, Marketing, Engineering, Procurement, etc.) and sponsors or customers, and assessing each to determine those which can be met and those which may have to be "limit-bound" or reconsidered. Prioritization of Product Requirements (e.g. separating those which are "must-have", "highly-desired" and "nice-to-have") and prioritization of the key Project Constraints (i.e. Delivery Schedules, Project Costs, and Product Requirements) can facilitate this process. An example of this Overall Project Planning process flow is provided in Chapter 1 (Managing Requirements).

Incremental (or Iterative) Product Development Process

Think of the above Scenario B situation as an "internal" Project that was established to meet competitive market needs. Assume further that the "competitive landscape" changes, whereby your key sub-system supplier is now able to expedite its delivery of POR (Plan of Record) samples by three months, and your organization's Executive Team members are informed that two of your biggest competitors (who use that same supplier) have committed to provide high-priority customers with "Qualification Units" three months earlier, as a result. What do you do? The Executive Team might ask you (the PM) to convey to them what you need to accelerate your Project Team's efforts and enable a competitive response. And you realize that you will always have to be ready to respond to similar requests in the future once this precedent is established. In fact, Middle Managers and all Team Leaders will likely be asked to figure out how to pro-actively inflict this same level of "pain" on your competitors the next time. This is the type of situation that has led to the "Incremental" PDP. Be it TTM (Time-to-Market), TTC (Time-to-Cost), TTQ (Time-to-Quality), TTV (Time-to-Value) or any other "TTx", whatever the critical business criteria are, you try to maximize those Project Constraints (i.e. time expedience to get to "Best-in-Class" "x" performance within the industry). This tends to compromise other Project Constraints. Thus, it naturally leads to greater risk-taking, and higher tolerance toward compromising the other Project and Product Requirements. I lived in this type of corporate environment for over a decade and was constantly requested to determine how to best enable "organizational competitive leadership" in accordance with the industry's highest priority business criteria.

An Incremental PDP is, thus, one which enables greater risk-taking and less stringent Product Requirements control than a "Waterfall" (i.e. Deterministic) PDP, while incrementally achieving faster Product maturity and the establishment of more definitive Product Requirements over time, as the Project Plan is executed. This process does not typically allow time to conduct extensive up-front analyses. Instead of conducting a thorough design analysis, you take a prior working design and incrementally change it to gain knowledge of other required changes, as soon as possible. As the end-Product Design gets closer to the POR configuration, more strenuous testing can be conducted to evaluate Product performance under increasingly more extreme conditions, enabling design-expedient issue identification and resolution. Typically, pre-determined minimum Product Quality performance criteria and Product Costs are targeted. And once a "candidate" POR design configuration is achieved, final qualification testing can be conducted to identify any additional minor alterations, if necessary. Once those changes are incorporated and regression testing is conducted, the Product is ready for conditional or final release for production/deployment. In a highly competitive "TTx" market, conditional releases which compromise Product Quality are typically necessary to meet competitive schedule/delivery pressures – as such, some of the other Product Requirements (e.g. Product Cost and/or Quality, etc.) are waived/deferred to a later Product version release.

If performed well, this process enables very rapid Product development. It is employed in the Consumer Products industries where there exists a higher level of tolerance for Product performance issues – i.e. where achievement of faster (or more competitive) Time-to-Market out-prioritizes Product Quality and Reliability (e.g. Product features, Production yield issues, low-risk code bugs, less Safety Margin regarding Product Reliability under certain environmental conditions, etc.). Thus, organizations using this "Iterative" PDP approach tend to have a higher tolerance for Product development and launch risks, and pro-actively plan on engaging in post-launch issue resolution efforts to continuously improve Product performance and competitive positioning over time (via subsequent Product Version releases).

A computer HDD (Hard Disk Drive) Incremental PDP example is provided below.

HDDs are rapidly being displaced by SSDs (Solid State Devices) in the market-place, but during the industries "hay-day" competition was incredibly intense and necessitated the establishment and implementation of an "Iterative" PDP for competitive viability, up and down the Supply Chain. Subsequent generations of HDDs needed significantly improved Storage Capacity to provide a lower $/bit Product offering as technology advanced. Product Access Times, Benchmark Performance, Quality and Reliability are key as well, but to keep this simple, let us fixate on Storage Capacity (or Areal-Density – the number of bits of storage per square inch of disk space). If you can double the Areal-Density you can drop the $/bit by almost half – not exactly halve for there are other costs associated with New Product Development (e.g. more expensive/elaborate manufacturing processes, parts using more expensive technology, new tooling and test equipment, lower yields, more scrap, etc.). To double Areal-Density you should be able to simply change the spinning Disks and Read/Write Heads (think of an old "record player" with vinyl records – the process is kind of like that, but without the continuous physical touching of the disk) and produce a new, higher-performing Product. Well, it was not quite that easy, for these finer geometric tolerances necessitated that you fine-tune almost everything in the HDD, including the Actuator Arms, Spindle Motors, Pivots, PCBA (Printed Circuit Board Assembly) and Firmware (Software coded and burned into a memory device). Some revolutionary technology transitions would require even more extensive changes. But think about it; we were launching New Products about every 6 to 8 months at one point in the history of the industry. How do you do that? Well, not by the conventional method of developing all the drawings, analyzing the design, then ordering the parts, then assembling and testing, and then developing a final Product design, which requires ordering revised parts, assembling and testing (with some further analysis, fine-tuning and regression testing, as required). We by-passed all those steps and simply swapped Heads and Disks in the prior Product Design and tried running the newly-configured HDD. As we got basic functions to work, we would change other parts (e.g. the Actuator, the PCBA, the Firmware, etc.). Every change resulted in a new series of test articles to evaluate, and identified further changes for the next design iteration. The process for sequencing changes became better understood over time, Project to Project. Much of this was supported by (and coordinated with) suppliers of key sub-systems or parts to enable fast turn-around. In general, the process was hectic, but effective. We had some firm requirements, but many of the Product Requirements were adjustable to a degree, on the fly, as needed to meet market/business priority requirements. We also had "phase-gates" for entering a new stage of development when we could demonstrate requisite Product performance maturity (and our definition of "requisite" allowed for some degree of deviation in meeting Product Requirements). Ultimately, we provided early "engineering samples" for customers to assist in their computer system Product Development, and "qualification samples" to demonstrate system "functional integrity" within key customers' pre-launch test systems.

I cannot help but make an editorial comment here. Some of you are probably amazed by the process just explained, but can you imagine coming into this after having lived for almost two decades in the Aerospace and Defense industry? What a paradigm shift! Well, the story does not stop here.

Today, when I go to an electronics supply store and decide on a Product to pick from the shelf, I ask myself "Is this my lucky day?", knowing that there are likely some Products on that shelf that will not work when they are brought home and used. Others might work for a while, but then have a problem due to a "latent defect" (e.g. maybe a bad solder joint that seems okay at first, but later fails). The reason I go into this is to make a point; Consumer Products are as affordable as they are because consumers tend to accept the fact that to pay lower prices we must deal with potential quality and reliability issues. Suppliers tend to want to keep these issues to a minimum to endear brand loyalty, and ultimately make more money. So, we all tend to accept a degree of failure (i.e. compromise) to meet our more important needs. When I finally figured this out, I was able to establish a PDP that maximized the organization's ability to meet competitive requirements associated with TTM, TTQ, and TTC, in that order.

Figure 41 shows an example "Iterative" (Incremental) Product Development Process approach, where the number of design-build-test iterations (annotated as "Unit Builds" within the design phases) may change as the Project progresses and the Product design matures. Although this approach typically necessitates less up-front analysis than the "Waterfall" approach, it is not uncommon for organizations utilizing this approach to expend significant resources on Technology Staging activities (both internal and in conjunction with key suppliers or business partners) to ensure the most expedient Time-to-Market performance in the industry.

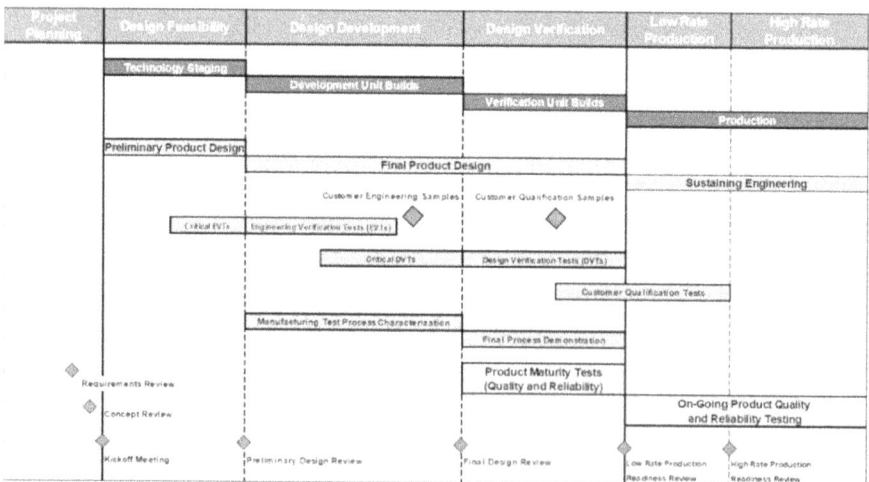

Figure 41.Example Iterative (Incremental) Development Process. Project Risk Management (PMI, 2016, p. 13)

Engaging multiple suppliers of key parts or sub-systems is a key Product Development Strategy to both improve probability of "Best-in-Class" Time-to-Market success and in achieving Product Cost targets -- even when home-grown in-house-developed options are pursued as well. For example, an HDD company might be vertically integrated (e.g. capable of designing and manufacturing Head Stack Assemblies and Disks for use in their own Hard Disk Drives) but will nonetheless typically engage with other merchant suppliers of these same sub-assemblies/components to reduce risk of meeting Product launch dates – and will split/share production supply quantities (i.e. purchase from 1 or more out-side suppliers) to ensure future engagements and competitive costs. Each combination of parts can constitute a unique Product SKU (Stock Keeping Unit), which usually necessitates its own set of qualification tests, and this typically causes over-lapping qualifications of the various SKUs during an "Iterative" Product Development Process. As a result, in this type of scenario it is important to construct a Project Plan based on a well-honed Sourcing Strategy for all key components and sub-systems – as well as a precise Configuration Control Matrix defining all resulting SKUs to be qualified to meet production needs.

As a final note, "Iterative" PDPs have characteristics that bridge the gap between the "Waterfall" and "Agile" processes. "Iterative" PDPs tend to build off predictive requirements management processes (e.g. up-front Requirements Reviews, Compliance Matrices, etc.), but recognize that compromises to some Product Quality requirements will likely be necessary to meet "TTx" priorities. The key is to keep these compromises to a minimum and prioritize features that are most important to the market and key customers. This mind-set is emphasized to a greater degree in the "Agile" process discussed next. One of the more noticeable differences between "Iterative" and "Agile" PDPs is that even within the "Iterative" approach all key Product Requirements can (and many times, must) be solidified early in the Project Life Cycle, whereas the "Agile" process can theoretically accommodate Product Requirements changes right up until the time that the Product is released.

Agile (Adaptive) Product Development Process

The PDP that is arguably the best for managing uncertain (or ever-changing) Project Requirements is the "Agile" (or Adaptive) process. This is a methodology that originally emerged for adaptation in highly complex Software Development Projects, referred to as the **Manifesto for Agile Software Development** (https://agilemanifesto.org/).

> "**Agile software development** is a set of principles for software development in which requirements and solutions evolve through collaboration between self-organizing, cross-functional teams. It promotes adaptive planning, evolutionary development, early delivery, and continuous improvement, and it encourages rapid and flexible response to change." (Wikipedia, 2018).

The fundamental difference between "Waterfall" Product Development versus "Agile" Product Development is that the highest value items are developed first in the "Agile" process. The benefit is that risks are "front-loaded" and incremental versions of the Product can be created and deployable per the needs of the business. Subsequently, development of the Product stops when sufficient value has been delivered to the business. As can be inferred from this above definition, the "Agile" Product Development Process is designed to accommodate Projects with Product Requirements that continually evolve and are not 100% solidified until very late in the process. This Product Development Process is branching out to other types of development activities as well (e.g. Home-Building, Education, etc.) – *SCRUM* (Crown Business, 2014).

In a nut-shell, here is a brief explanation of the process. General, high-level Product Requirements are used to initiate development, and as more details are added, the Product Solution is re-evaluated by stakeholders/users to determine how to modify and iterate the Product until an acceptable offering is produced, or a delivery schedule is met, or both. This process is intended to empower Team Members and enable continuous improvement in estimating "remaining work" based on iterative

Project Team accomplishments and learning. There is also an element of stakeholder participation which is solicited continuously throughout the Project. Stakeholders include people representing the business as well as management. In the Scrum Framework, the Scrum Master is in charge of addressing and resolving the Scrum Team's impediments. They are charged with talking with anyone in the organization to get help in resolving the Project Team's impediments – a Strategic Project Management approach.

Two Agile sub-process types have emerged over time: Kanban and Scrum. The most significant difference between these two methodologies is that Scrum Teams are set up a little different and work in a standardized cadence referred to as a Sprint, whereas the Kanban approach tends to work on activities that are not necessarily synchronized to a standard cadence. The objective of the Sprint is to complete the highest priority User Stories within the iteration, which includes design, development, and test of the User Story. Kanban, similarly, "front-loads" the highest priority items, but unlike Scrum, Kanban avoids overloading the team by limiting the number of items that the Project Team can work on at one time, sometime called WIP (Work in Progress) – in other words, limiting the Project Team's "queue depth". The remainder of this section will focus on the Scrum approach.

So, let us first go back to Scenario B discussed earlier, and use it as an example, again. This is the scenario referred to as the "Project with Tremendous Risk".

In Scenario B we have a classical clash between meeting a very aggressive Product launch request (dictated by competitive Market Dynamics), while at the same time providing a very complex Product (i.e. with numerous Product Requirements deemed necessary to attain maximum customer acceptance). The Management Team must do something, so it settles on an approach which enables Product launch in the market-driven "Launch Window", but all the stakeholders must understand (and accept) that some of the Product features might have to be sacrificed. The Project Team will focus on the highest priority

Product Requirements and will provide incremental releases of the Product over time to assess its user appeal/acceptability and gain a more informed understanding of Product design priorities (i.e. they will not spend a lot of up-front time analyzing existing information and formulating a predictive build-up schedule). Scaled Agile Framework (SAFe), which is used on large multi-team Projects has an event called Program Increment (PI) planning to plan out approximately 12 weeks of work, so that the team is working to a specific business timeline. In addition, the Management Team empowers the Project Team Members to manage their work, and at any time, communicate organizational issues that are impeding progress. The Management Team commits to set up "Task Forces" to address these impediments as they surface. This above solution is essentially the "Agile" process.

Although this "Agile" process is much less predictive (from a Product Requirements stand-point), it is accepted as a "Best Practice" for rapid development of Products which necessitate accommodating ever-changing and uncertain requirements. This process is powerful but does take a higher level of management tolerance and involvement to ensure that potential impediments are understood and expediently dealt with to improve Project Team performance. There is also a need for a high relative tolerance of Product Design (or Product Requirements) risk and changes, given the high overall Project Cost and Schedule uncertainty for achieving all requirements. On the other hand, "Agile" Project Teams tend to be more transparent to the business because the work completed after each Sprint is demonstrated to the stakeholders. If progress is slow, management knows right away and can assist early (i.e. before it is too late) to recover the schedule. Proponents of this PDP methodology [SCRUM (Crown Business, 2014)] stress that there should be a general recognition that the "Agile" process, if performed well, can inherently yield better Project Team results than other process alternatives – so the expectation is that even though Project Constraints are not necessarily predictive, much more Project Scope is being accomplished in a much shorter amount of time (vis-a-vis other PDP methodologies). The factors that make Scrum more productive include "front-loading" of risks, developing complex systems in "vertical slices" and getting each "slice" to work properly before going on the next "slice" – greatly reducing the time required for integration. Also the "self-managing" teams tend to have higher levels of engagement for each Team Member – increasing overall productivity and encouraging everyone on the Project Team to step up when the going gets tough. The continuous release process reduces the risk of finding large (i.e. potentially catastrophic) technical problems late the development of the Product – effectively reducing the "Cost of Change" later in the Project Life Cycle.

Without delving into all the layers of detail associated with the "Agile" Product Development Process, suffice it to say that the Scrum Framework is designed around the creation of work items (i.e. User Stories, which are based on Story Points – the effort required to complete a User Story) which can be developed and tested "end-to-end" within a concerted effort (i.e. Sprint). Sprints are typically performed by several small Scrum Teams assigned to work through a sub-set of the Story Points within set timeframes (i.e. the standard Sprint cadence which is typically established in terms of days or weeks). Continuous re-evaluation of Scrum Team performance (per Story Point) is assessed and factored into determining more accurate estimates of future work. Backlog of remaining scope is re-assessed and any additional new Product Requirements or Project Scope (resulting from user testing or issues encountered) are added to the Backlog. A Backlog is comprised of Product Backlog Items (PBIs). Each PBI is typically a single User Story. There are two types of "Backlogs" - the Product Backlog which consists of all PBIs identified for the entire Product, and the Sprint Backlog which is all the PBIs selected by the Scrum Team for the next Sprint. When the Backlog is exhausted relative to that User Story, it is declared "done". User Stories can be aggregated to comprise an "Epic" (high level functional capability), and when enough "Epics" are completed to deliver the "business value" required by the organization, the overall Product Development Process is complete.

Note that each User Story is a deliverable Product. It is verified for end-to-end operational capability; thus, each version of the Product is (theoretically) able to perform as a separate stand-alone Product, initially for performing limited functions, but eventually with ability to handle more and more requisite Product performance functions, as Sprints are completed. This is a key aspect of the "Agile" PDP. You can release a functional Product at several Project Development junctures. What this means is that if your Project Team can produce an offering that satisfies the basic Product "Functionality" Requirements, firm commitment dates for release of the Product can be established. The end-Product might not have 100% of the capability requested (or be totally free of quality or reliability issues), but it will be functional and can satisfy the most importance Product release criteria.

Note also that although deterministic time durations for work completion are initially estimated, the "Agile" Team's ability to gauge remaining work typically improves over time (based on the after-the-fact realization of Scrum Team performance), enabling determination of more refined performance commitments, factoring in past results, and expected improvements. For schedule-critical Projects, some Product Requirements may be sacrificed to enable schedule adherence. For example, "In software development there a rule, borne out by decades of research, that 80 percent of the value in any piece of software is in 20 percent of the features." [*SCRUM* (Crown Business, 2014), pg. 11-12]. Thus, those last "bonus" Product Requirements are sometimes considered less important than meeting a Product launch date.

A shortfall of the "Agile" PDP is that even though it is designed to produce results quicker than other more conventional processes (i.e. "Waterfall" or "Iterative"), the lack of predictive Project Schedules and/or Product Requirements from the beginning can be problematic to making long-term commitments to Project customers and key stakeholders (e.g. Executives, Stockholders, Boards of Directors, etc.). This process is also considered better suited for small Project Teams, since it focusses on employee empowerment, accountability, and transparency. "Agile" PDPs, thus, take a mature organization and skilled workforce to enable its full potential to be exploited.

To recap, the "Agile" PDP is arguably the most flexible process for developing an inherently complex Product – to the degree that many customer/user Product Requirements are too difficult to determine until the System Solution is successfully tried and evaluated. This is especially true of effort which can be effectively performed by a homogeneous set of Project Resources (e.g. different levels of Software Development Personnel with the same basic capability) enabling flexible re-allocation of resources.

Since the "Agile" PDP schedule is based on understanding the amount of work that Scrum Teams can perform within a fixed Sprint timeframe (e.g. a one to four week cycle) you must typically begin work and gain experience about Project Team performance prior to establishing a Project Schedule baseline/commitment. Further, if the Product is one which must satisfy a myriad of customer types (and given that user involvement is an inherent part of the process), any number of diverse detailed Product Requirements can emerge throughout the Project Life Cycle. Thus, the original "Balanced" Project Plan is a bit illusive, but can usually be contained (to a degree) by Project Scope and Product Requirements trade-offs (i.e. deferring or eliminating lower priority activities). In addition, analytics from past learning can be applied to future estimates, when available. Past performance data on similar types of Projects (using a similar Project Team make-up) can provide valuable insights, as well. This is the ultimate example of "progressive elaboration".

Thus, the "Agile" approach can prove difficult for executives to genuinely accept – especially those who are familiar (and comfortable) with "Waterfall" PDPs where commitments are established very early in the PLC. But the notion of obtaining commitments later (i.e. after the Project is kicked off) is overcome by the recognition of successes achieved within significantly shorter timeframes than expected if using other than the "Agile" methodology. The fact remains, however, that the more Product Requirements known up front, the more successful the

ACHIEVING EPIC BUSINESS RESULTS

Project Team will be in executing the Project – it usually depends on how much up-front time is available, and how much time and uncertainty is involved in pre-determining those requirements.

Hybrid Product Development Process

A "Hybrid" PDP is comprised of two (or all) of the above Product Development Process types co-mingled within a single Project. An example is a Project that includes both hardware and software (and/or firmware) development and integration. The Project Team might employ the "Agile" PDP for the software (and/or firmware) development portion of the Project and employ a more predictive "Waterfall" or Incremental "Iterative" processes for the hardware development, while using a combination of the two processes during System Integration and Test activities. This usually takes good, complimentary Project Management Systems, and if performed well, can produce superior results compared to when employing a single Product Development Process approach for all activities; for multiple "Best Practices" are employed where appropriate, versus force-fitting a single PDP approach which can compromise (or sub-optimize) portions of the development effort. Figure 42 is a graphic that depicts an example "Hybrid" Product Development Process schedule.

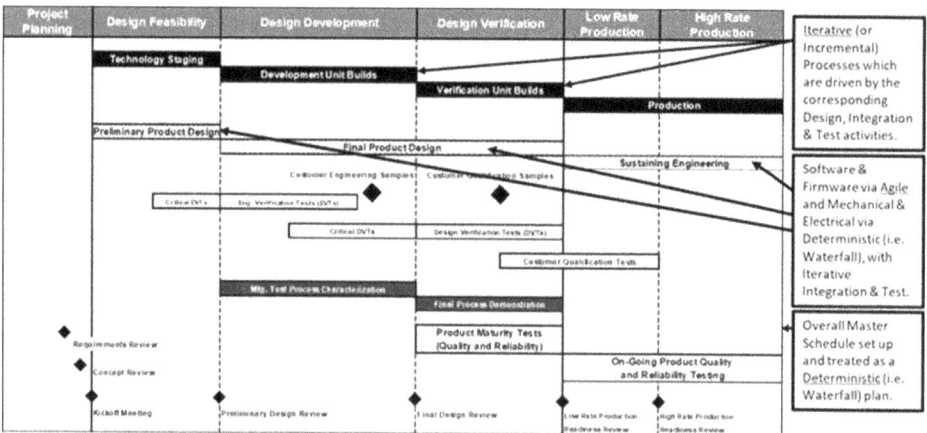

Figure 42. Example Hybrid Product Development Process Flow

GENERAL COMPARISON OF PDPS

Figure 43 is a table that shows a comparison of the various PDPs. PDP differences are most pronounced relative to: (1) Requirements (Project and Product); (2) Organizational Risk/Change Tolerance; (3) Development Team Composition; and (4) Strategic Project Management (Organizational Tenets which apply to their use). We have previously discussed the first three but should elaborate a bit on the latter. It should be clear from the content of this book that there is more to Project Management and Project Team "performance" than just assigning personnel and expecting them to be successful – there are many Organizational Responsibilities and assets which matter as well. My belief is that great organizations know this and are most likely great because they use this knowledge to its fullest extent.

Project Characteristics	Product Development Process Type			
	Waterfall (Deterministic)	Iterative (Incremental)	Agile (Adaptive)	Hybrid (Combo of PDPs)
Project Requirements	Determined up-front prior to Project Kick-Off, and consistent with Organizational Risk Tolerances	Driven by Priorities (Market Dynamics), Competitive Positioning, and Customer Preferences	Driven by Priorities, between Project and Product Requirements Constraints and Customer/Sponsor Preferences	Typically based on most stringent PDP
Product Requirements	Determined up-front prior to Project Kick-Off with Changes if necessary to re-Balance Plan	Majority determined up-front prior to Project Kick-Off, with expected Changes toward Project End-Date due to Priorities (Market Dynamics)	Solidified by end of Project, especially if Delivery Schedule Adherence is Driver (Focus is on the Highest Value Items on a continuous basis)	Typically based on most stringent PDP
Change Tolerance	Very Low	Moderate to High	Very High	Moderate to Very High
Development Team Composition	Functional or Cross-Functional	Functional or Cross-Functional	"T-Shaped" Skill Sets -- where ALL Team Members share an Interchangeable Breadth of required Skills, and some with Deep Expertise where needed	Functional or Cross-Functional
Types of Projects	General, Aerospace and Defense, Automotive, Construction, High and Low Complexity	Consumer Electronics, Production and Test Equipment	Software or Firmware Development, Education, Health Care, & Information Technology	Complex Systems comprising significant Hardware & Software Integration

Figure 43. PDP Comparison Chart

Is Your Organization Managing Projects Strategically?

Take the test, or at least see how your organization stacks up. An inventory of the key Strategic Project Management concepts espoused by this book can be kept, Chapter by Chapter. There is no established reference of good or bad, but you can see where your organization currently is, and use this tool to monitor progress. Each question starts with the phrase: To what extent does your organization......

31. recognize the importance of **PDPs (Product Development Processes)** to **Project Success?**

1	2	3	4	5
O	O	O	O	O
Never	Rarely	Sometimes	Most of the Time	Always

32. systematically manage **Project and Product Requirements** and control their changes?

1	2	3	4	5
O	O	O	O	O
Never	Rarely	Sometimes	Most of the Time	Always

33. understand and establish the **Best PDP Methodologies** for the various **Project Types?**

1	2	3	4	5
O	O	O	O	O
Never	Rarely	Sometimes	Most of the Time	Always

34. comprehend the key differences between **PDP Types** and their **Applicability to Projects?**

1	2	3	4	5
O	O	O	O	O
Never	Rarely	Sometimes	Most of the Time	Always

35. understand how **Strategic Project Management Principles** influence **Product Development?**

1	2	3	4	5
O	O	O	O	O
Never	Rarely	Sometimes	Most of the Time	Always

CHAPTER 8

IT's *EMPLOYING BEST PRACTICES*

Over the course of the last four decades, I have been involved in the development of numerous Products and Services, working in many different capacities, in various organizations, and spanning several industries. The most striking Lesson Learned from this experience is that you cannot employ "Best Practices" indiscriminately. One size does not fit all!

The term "Best Practices" seems to have fallen out of vogue, but I like it, nonetheless. Some like "Good Practices" better for it leaves the door open for further improvement, but I believe it is okay for "Best Practices" to "morph" over time. The term is defined as "Methods or techniques that have consistently shown results superior to those achieved with other means and are used as benchmarks." (*Wikipedia*, n. d.). "Best Practice" thus connotes a level of goodness that, if employed, will provide the user(s) with the best chance of success. It also implies that there are other "practices" that are available which are not "Best" for the intended needs – I call these "Less-than Best Practices" and "Better-than Best Practices". All these categories are addressed within this chapter.

The questions that we should ask ourselves are:

- Do we (as leaders) ensure that "Best Practices" are employed by the Project Team Leaders or do we leave it up to them to decide?

- Do we know how to determine "Best Practices" that should be employed on our various Projects?

- Do we endeavor to continually improve and adjust "Best Practices" as new and improved Tools & Techniques are made available?

This chapter provides insights into how to determine and maintain "Best Practices". I believe that application of "Best Practices" needs to be directed via Organizational Governance as part of the Strategic Project Management process. This position naturally supports the establishment of Project/Program Management Offices (PMOs).

Before delving into the specifics of "Best Practices", let me explain the approach taken and how I arrived at my conclusions.

Several years ago, I was approached to provide a four-hour Saturday morning PMI® chapter training session that would give PMs insight about the specific differences between Project Management roles in various industries – particularly Consumer Products and Aerospace and Defense industries. Based on my background and experience, the Training Coordinator thought I would be a good person to pursue for this topic. I had a few months to prepare and thought it would be a fun opportunity, so I accepted.

Long story short, I really got into this Project. I looked at the various categories of Tools & Techniques (e.g. for Project Scheduling, Cost and Schedule Control, Risk Management, etc.) and correlated them with "causes of unsuccessful project execution", for those "causes" are the reasons that the Tools & Techniques were developed in the first place. Then I took a crack at developing all the attributes necessary to define any type of Project you could possibly dream up and tried to put together an "expert system" that would determine the appropriate "Best Practices" for different Project types. Things started getting a little "out-of-hand", so I stopped, put together an informative training session, and decided to write my first book to both document this content and provide it for others to consider.

This chapter summarizes my findings about "Best Practices", and the logic behind how organizations can become more competitive and successful if they pro-actively determine those "practices" that make most sense for them to effectively govern their various Projects.

CAUSES OF UNSUCCESSFUL PROJECT EXECUTION

I have experienced more issues on Projects than I would like to admit. I have also seen, second hand, many other issues. So, I decided to capture these insights. I created the Figure 44 "fish-bone" diagram, then reviewed it with several other people I know and respect in the field of Project Management. This output evolved over several months of interviews and debates. I believe that it contains the breadth of issues one could encounter when managing a Project. You could argue about which general category to put some of the "causes" in, but I placed them in the categories I thought were most appropriate. The bottom line is, I wanted to make sure that I listed all the potential "causes of unsuccessful project execution" so that I could then identify all categories of Tools & Techniques developed over time to address them pro-actively.

I am not going to address all the details associated with the below chart in this text but do in my *Project Risk Management: A Practical Implementation Approach* book, in case you are interested in learning more about how I define them.

Leadership | Communications | Management Controls | Plans

Poor/No Training/Dev.
Team Dis-function
Organization
Experience Persona
PM Mismatch
Thoroughness Capabilities

Unclear Priorities
Poor Decisions
Untimely Inaccurate
Status
Incomplete
Unclear Direction
Incomplete
Poor Escalation

Poor Risk Mgmt.
Inadequate Cost/Sch. Cntl.
Poor Rqmts. Cntl.
Compliance (i.e., QA)
Verification Gap(s)
Poor Metrics
Poor Supplier Mgmt.
Poor Trade-offs

Perf. Margin   Cost
Poor Bases of Estimates
Sch.
Scope Omissions
Poor Assumptions
Inadequate Contingencies

Unsuccessful Execution

Competitive Threat(s)
Company Health
Team Physical Proximity Issues
Unrealistic Expectations
Strategy Chg
Cancelation
Market Chg

Insufficient Funding
Inadequate Facilities
Availability
Personnel Gaps
Capability Capacity
Insufficient Time

PM   Technical
Inadequate Productivity Tools
Problem Solving
ERP   Other IT
Inadequate Infrastructure
Financial   CRM
Inadequate Training

Specialized
Market Mismatch
Niche   Consumer
Aerospace   Other
Industry Mismatch
Commercial
Process Gap(s)
Non-adherence

Business/External Factors | Resources | Tools | Development Processes

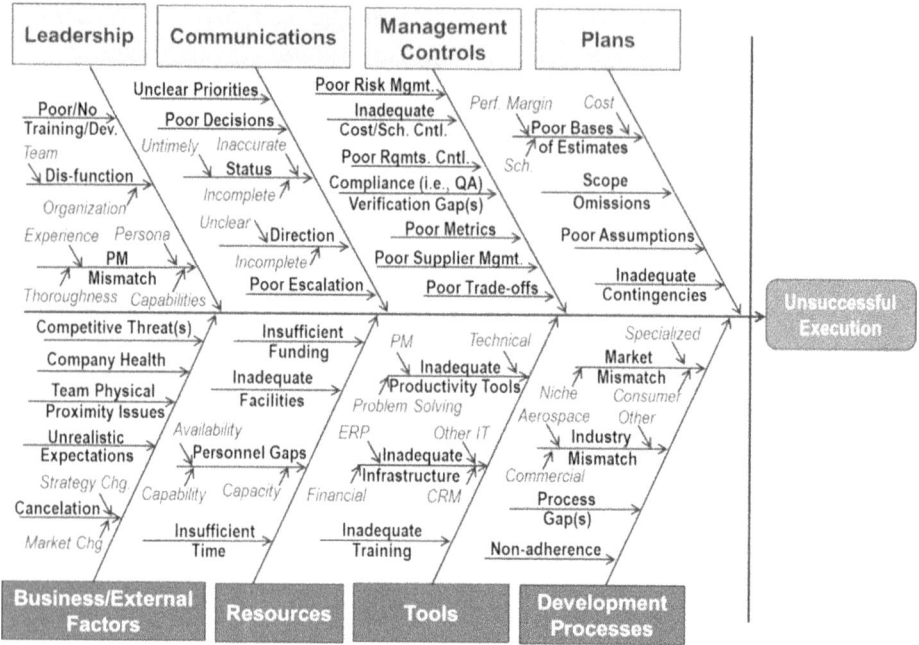

Figure 44. Causes of Unsuccessful Project Execution. Project Risk Management (PMI, 2016. p. 46)

One of the main messages from this "fish-bone" diagram is that the Project Manager and Team are not the only culprits responsible for unsuccessful Project execution issues; the organization has a major role in this as well – a very big roll. To drive this point home, I decided to segregate the "causes" into two major categories:

A.   those which are more heavily influenced by the PMs and their Project Teams; and

B.   those which are more heavily influenced by the Organization and External Factors.

The former is represented by the top halve of the "fish-bone" diagram (i.e. Plans, Management Controls, Communications and Leadership), and the latter is by the bottom halve (i.e. Development Processes, Tools, Resources and Business/Environment Factors). This is not to imply exact divisions of responsibilities, but it is a general partitioning that is reasonable from my experiences.

Causes More Heavily Influenced by PMs and their Teams

Arguably some of the most significant Project issues arise from deficiencies in Planning, Management Controls, Communications and Leadership. Most can be partially addressed via Organizational Governance (i.e. establishment of consistent processes, templates, rating criteria, metrics, databases, etc.). The below sub-sections discuss key responsibilities within these activities and some ideas for facilitating a more Strategic Project Management approach to determining the "Best Practices" to implement.

Project Planning. This topic has been discussed at length in Chapter 3 (Planning). The key from a Strategic Project Management stand-point is for the organization to facilitate Project planning through establishment of appropriate procedures, processes, training and data collection systems for improved (i.e. more accurate) future Project Schedule, Cost, and Scope of Work estimates. Arguably, the most significant Organizational Governance item is putting the necessary methods and tools in place – those which efficiently and effectively record, save, and retrieve actual past Project data for use as future Project BOEs (Bases of Estimates), and do so with attention to how the data is organized and the data fidelity that is most practical.

Project Management Controls. Most of the Project Management Tools & Techniques apply to "Management Controls". These are discussed in more detail within the next major section of this chapter. The key here (from a Strategic Project Management stand-point) is that there tends to be a fair amount of overlap between the different Project "Executing" and "Monitoring & Controlling" processes, and thus, their coordination and complementary design should be pre-established (i.e. not left to chance). Figure 45 a very good graphic which shows the major processes as espoused by PMI®. "Monitoring & Controlling" exists from day-one to the very end of the Project Life Cycle. Thus, organizational expectations governing internal Project review content, cadence and "goodness" criteria should get priority.

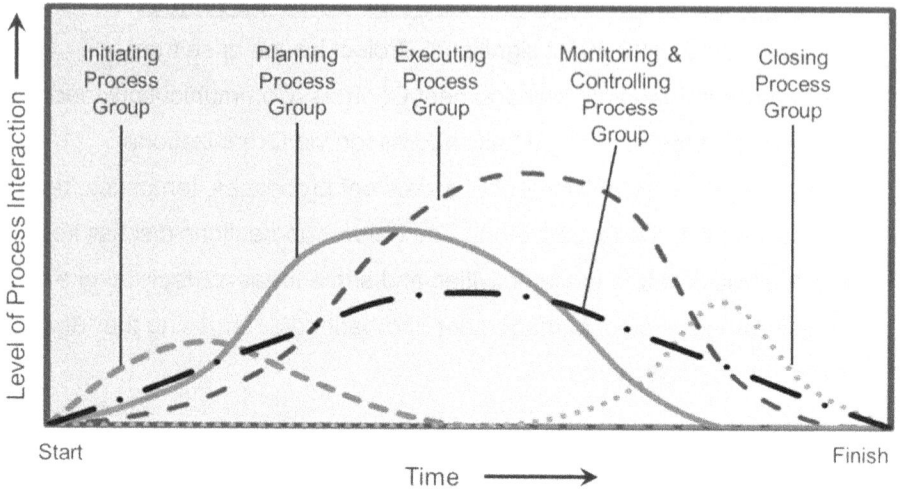

Figure 45. Management and Controls Activities Over the Project Life Cycle.
PMBOK® Guide – Fifth Edition (PMI, 2013b, p. 51)

The specific activities within the "Management Controls" arena are essentially all designed around managing Project Risks. As such, Figure 46 demonstrates the periodic Plan, Do, Check, Act process that typically takes place as the inherent Risk Management Control aspect of the Project Management Control process. The implication here is that a cadence is established to check pre-determined performance metrics and act accordingly.

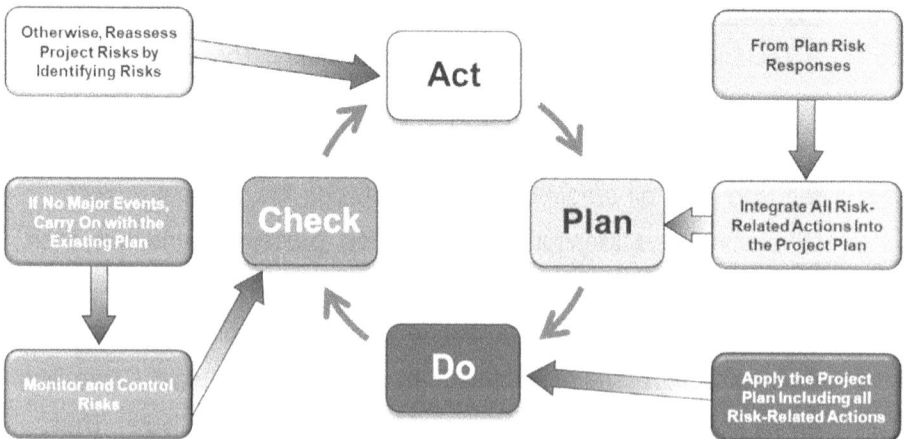

Figure 46. Re-curing Plan, Do, Check, Act Process of Project Management.
Practice Standard for Project Risk Management (PMI, 2009, p. 104)

<u>Project Communications</u>. "Communication" is one of the most important aspects of Project Management and more generally, Leadership. Aside from the basics, we discuss the communication of "priorities" and the "escalation" processes in detail within Chapter 2 (Managing Expectations). Within that chapter we also discuss the use of a RACI (Responsible, Accountable, Consult, Inform) Matrix and how it can facilitate communications and effective decision-making. Another important element of Project Management "Communication" is status reporting, which is discussed in Chapter 6: Maintaining a Balanced Plan. All aspects of Project Management "Communication" can benefit from the establishment of organizational processes and overt expectations to those leading the various Projects.

<u>Project Leadership</u>. "Leadership" is one the most important over-arching aspects of Strategic Project Management and is discussed in more detail within Chapter 10: Team Leadership. The key notation I would like to add here is the importance of training and personnel development. As an executive I commiserated often about how much money to expend on training. We typically want to ensure that key personnel are adequately trained, but at the same time, since training is discretionary (i.e. funds that typically come out of organizations' profits), when operating costs are tightly controlled, we tend to minimize the discretionary spending allowances, which includes the activities associated with personnel development. Organizations should (and often do) self-reflect on this, keeping in mind that the Tools & Techniques we employ to improve overall performance typically require a degree of training to ensure their effective use. Thus, from a Strategic Project Management stand-point, we should:

- select Project Management tools well – for effective, "user-friendly" tools are typically best to employ, provided they do not "break the bank";
- minimize the proliferation of different Management Tools that perform the same function; and

- provide the necessary training to ensure appropriate use of the various Project Management Tools & Techniques.

Causes More Heavily Influenced by Organization

Project Managers and Teams do carry a heavy burden relative to ensuring that their Projects are successful, but they are usually not in control of all the contributing factors that can jeopardize their Projects' success. Organizational Management (outside of the Project Team) plays a significant role as well, for some issues that can plague Project Team performance are more appropriately under their (i.e. management's) control – i.e. "Product Development Processes" employed, "Tools" used, "Resources" and other "Business/External Factors". Most of these should be aptly addressed via Organizational Governance. The below sub-sections discuss the responsibilities within these activities and some ideas to consider that can facilitate a more Strategic Project Management approach to determining "Best Practices".

Product Development Processes. We discuss this topic in detail within Chapter 7. Frequently, individuals on the Project Team and/or within the organization have knowledge about the "Best Practices" to use in establishing Project Scope of Work and the ultimate Project Plan. It is usually beneficial that Project Team Members have this direct knowledge, but it is not necessarily required. Suffice it to say that Product Development Processes (or Product-Oriented Processes, or Product Life Cycle Processes, as some refer to them as) are typically not re-invented over and over for development of similar types of Products or Services within organizations. These processes are usually retained, used, and adjusted/refined as an element of Organization Governance, sometimes via specific published Organizational Procedures and/or Work Instructions – a "good practice" to employ relative to Strategic Project Management. More on this, as well, in Chapter 9 (Lessons Learned).

Tools. We touched on this topic in the above Project Leadership category, especially with respect to personnel development for the effective use of Project Management Tools & Techniques. This category includes "Tools" for both productivity improvements (e.g. Project Management, technical design aids, etc.) and Organizational Information Systems (i.e. infrastructure "Tools" for managing Human Resources, company finances, planning and purchasing of materials, quality control, contracting and sub-contracting, etc.). The key is to not just provide the "Tools", but to ensure that all employees who use them are adequately trained, as well.

Resources. Unless in a Projectized Organization (see chart provided in Chapter 2: Managing Expectations), most Project Resources are typically "owned" by (or directly report to) someone other than the Project Manager. In Matrix Organizations the PM's Project Resource needs are, for the most part, under the control of other managers and/or groups. There is typically a Sponsor (or Sponsoring Organization) of the Project, who provides the funds and negotiates/sets the other key Project Requirements. The Human Resources are typically the hardest to control (in terms of the level of capability, amount, and availability). Thus, Project Management resource allocation is a critical Strategic Project Management responsibility within organizations' ranks. Project-to-Project priorities and needs must be understood by the Functional Managers, and Project Resource alignment optimization can be challenging at times. Portfolio Management processes help, especially with respect to determination of the resource pool (types and quantity) to satisfy inherently dynamic demands within the organization over time.

Business/Environmental Factors. This category is basically a "catch-all" for those External Factors, outside the direct control of the Project Teams, that could exist, and if so, can directly impact Project Team performance. The most troubling of these to Project Team Members are "unrealistic expectations". This topic is addressed in Chapter 2 (Managing Expectations), but it bears repeating that Organizational Management should not impose unfair and/or unwarranted expectations on Project Teams. Doing so is the antithesis of Strategic Project Management, for it creates a "no-Win" situation for the Project Team(s), and this is simply not fair, nor healthy for the organization's workforce. I believe that this becomes a more prevalent issue in organizations that:

1) are struggling to compete within the industry(s) engaged in;

2) have a very politically charged culture in their management ranks;

3) do not have the where-with-all and/or energy within the ranks to figure out how to determine necessary changes to improve Project performance; and/or

4) do not necessarily value the entirety of the employee-base.

PM TOOLS AND TECHNIQUES THAT ADDRESS "CAUSES"

The primary reason we see new Tools & Techniques emerge is that people have learned from their mistakes and developed new methods to help prevent the recurrence of past Project execution issues which, if gone unchecked, can potentially jeopardize future Projects (and business) as well. Many of the most advanced and effective Project Management Tools & Techniques were originated by the government to better manage highly visible Strategic Programs. EVM (Earned Value Management) has been around since the 1960's when it was referred to as C/SCSC (Cost/Schedule Control Systems Criteria) – and I started using this tool in the late 1980's. I first used an IMS (Integrated Master Schedule) program in the early 1980's – processing "punch-card" decks into huge "mainframe computers". I also used Monte Carlo Modelling & Simulation for SRA (Schedule Risk Analysis) in the early 1990's. All these usages were during my Aerospace and Defense days. Some of these tools were required by contract, and they were effective (I am sure) in giving our customers the objective data they sought to calibrate how well we were performing. Being a learning "sponge" in those days, I was able to use these tools well to help plan, negotiate and manage my contracts/Projects. Then as I changed jobs and industries, I found out that these advanced Tools & Techniques were not always necessary or beneficial for the development of every type of Product and Service, especially from a cost-effectiveness stand-point. This realization and experience provided me with the knowledge to formulate a frame-work for determining which Tools, Techniques and PM Competencies to apply for various Project types, based on Project Profile information (more on this to be addressed later in the chapter).

Figure 47 provides a graphic of the connection between "causes of unsuccessful project execution" and the general Tools, Techniques and PM Competencies that have evolved over time. As will be discussed shortly, there are various options available within each category of tool, and they all tend to have their place as "Best Practices" for certain types of Projects. The reason I include PM Competencies is that I have also concluded that PM Competencies can (at times) essentially make up for the use of Tools & Techniques that are considered "Less-than Best Practices".

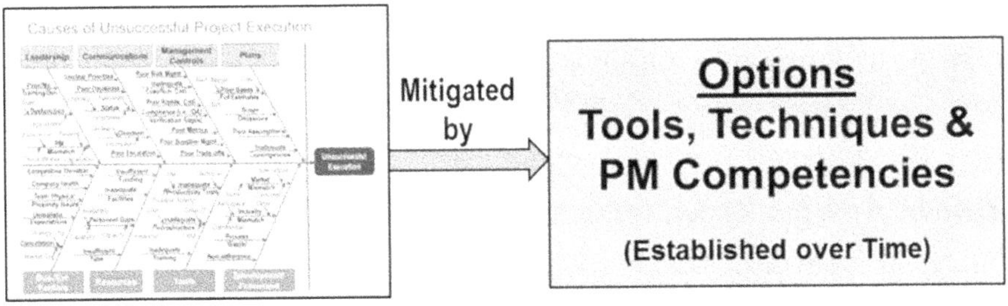

Figure 47. Tools & Techniques vs. Causes of Unsuccessful Execution. From *Project Risk Management (PMI, 2016, p. 198)*

The general categories of Tools & Techniques are listed in Figure 48. Within each of these categories are specific cost-effectiveness options to choose from. Since they are "general-purpose" options, there are typically several choices that are potentially applicable to any type of Project. Each will be briefly addressed in the subsequent sub-sections. A more detailed treatment of this information can be found in my book on *Project Risk Management: A Practical Implementation Approach*.

	Project Management Tools and Techniques
1	Risk Management
2	Cost, Schedule, Performance Estimating
3	Scheduling
4	Cost and Schedule Management
5	Quality Assurance
6	Requirements Management
7	Communications Management
8	Human Resource Management
9	Supplier Management

Figure 48. PM Tools & Techniques Categories. From Project Risk Management (PMI, 2016, p. 142)

Risk Management Tools & Techniques

Several of the more popular Project Risk Management Tools & Techniques are discussed in Chapter 4: Managing Risks. The Figure 49 chart shows various options to consider for employment on a Project. This is basically a "Bubble Chart" that is intended to show different Tools & Techniques within a range of increasing Complexity/Cost (on the X-axis) versus a range of increasing Effectiveness (on the Y-axis). These are all "relative" measures, and the "bubbles" are intended to encompass a "cost-effectiveness" area, to represent the rough complexity/cost variability against the relative variability in effectiveness – this area attempts to account for the variability in "user" skill levels. The conclusions I draw from this information are:

- Relative to management of Individual Project Task Risks – "Formal Risk Planning" using a Risk Register and Risk Matrix is a very good option for most Project types, whereby Project Team performance is highly scrutinized.

- Relative to management of Overall Project Risks – the combination of WBS (Work Breakdown Structure) and Expert Judgment with Modelling & Simulation can be very beneficial, but it takes some training and the right tools. I have found that for Overall Schedule Risk, good SRA (Schedule Risk Analysis) tools using statistical processing can be very beneficial, especially if they become more "user-friendly" (i.e. are designed to be easily used by people with various levels of experience and do so without entailing significant Organizational Support costs). I suspect that these will become more available over time.

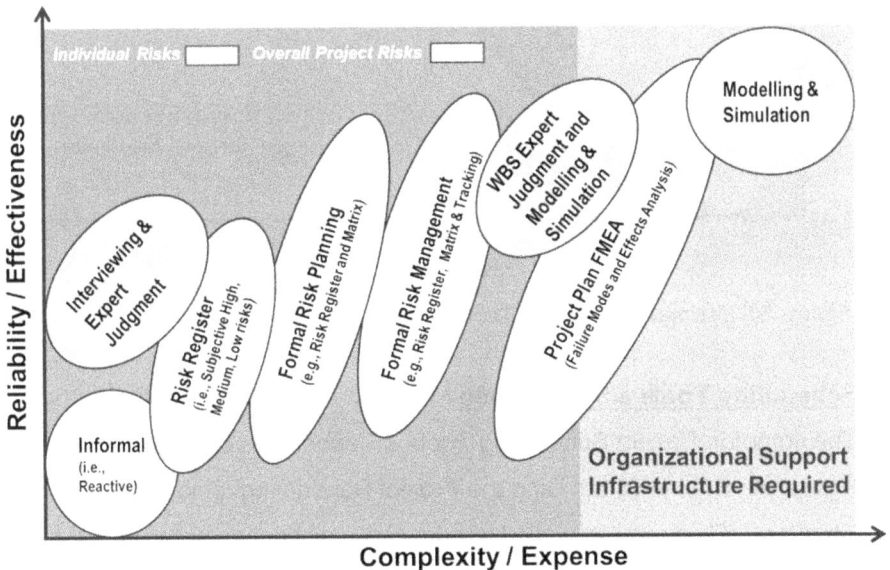

*Figure 49. **Risk Management Tools & Techniques.** Project Risk Management (PMI, 2016, p. 96)*

Cost, Schedule, and Performance Estimating

Estimating is discussed in detail within Chapter 3 (Planning). The only new information on Figure 50 is the advent of Modelling & Simulation to

193

hone estimates (if used in conjunction with Overall Project Risk Management). "Lean" processes can certainly help as well. "Lean" is not an estimating process per se but is a methodology one can employ to remove waste from Project activities and enable greater efficiency in producing accurate estimates. Thus, employment of "Lean" processes is typically a "good practice", but usually takes governance oversight and support to implement consistently.

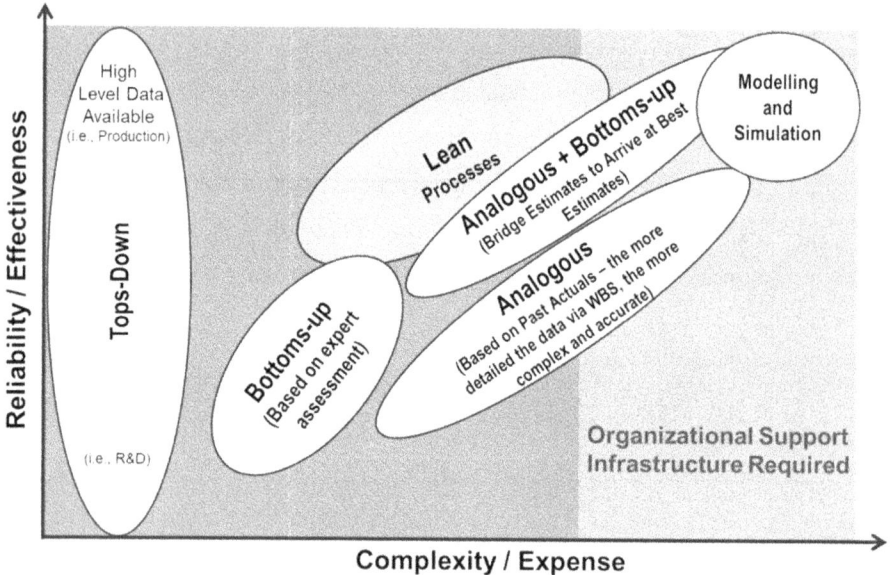

Figure 50. Estimating Tools & Techniques. Project Risk Management (PMI, 2016, p. 143)

Scheduling Tools & Techniques

The common Project Scheduling Tools & Techniques are depicted in the Figure 51 "Bubble Chart", and the Project Scheduling topic is covered in Chapter 3 (Planning) as well. Here I make a distinction between full-blown IMS and what I refer to as IMS Lite (my usual preference). Technically I consider IMS as not only the process of sequencing schedule tasks/activities defined by their durations and inter-dependencies (what I consider IMS Lite), but also including Project Resources and/or the ability to roll up "sub-Schedules" into a Master Schedule. Adding Project Resources is not real difficult, but it can be a bit cumbersome to maintain.

And "roll-ups" are generally difficult to set up and maintain due to the logistics involved and tendencies of inputters to deviate from established standards, so the process is more complicated – yet there is (I believe) an incremental benefit to be derived from doing so, if done in a "Lean" and well-coordinated way.

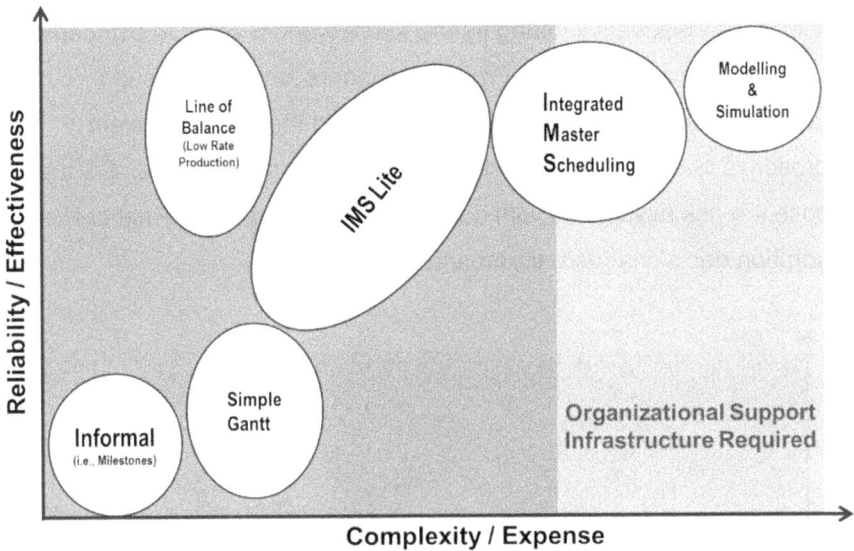

Figure 51. Scheduling Tools & Techniques. Project Risk Management (PMI, 2016, p. 147)

Cost and Schedule Management

Cost and Schedule Management is addressed in detail via a "notional" example in Chapter 5 (Cost of Change). Examples of the first 3 Tools & Techniques in the corresponding Figure 52 "Bubble Chart" (from left to right) are compared in that discussion. Typically, if EVM (Earned Value Management) or ES (Earned Schedule – a more recently recognized "trending" schedule tracking alternative) is not employed, then the "Actual+Plan vs. Time" approach is the default, unless the organization does not track Project Costs (or Effort) at all. I believe that it is safe to say that most organizations use the "Actual+Plan vs. Time" metric, but the simpler EVM or ES techniques could provide valuable Early Warning Indications, if considered. People tend to avoid using EVM. If you do and have not yet gone through the Chapter 5 (Cost of Change) discussion, please do so – it might cause you to re-consider that stance. ES measures "time spent" on tasks versus "time planned" and basically extrapolates actual performance (i.e. "time spent" vs. "time planned") to predict/estimate future potential Project Schedule/Delivery results. The primary reason for tracking ES metrics is to gain insight into the risks caused by subsequently changing the future work or effort to compensate for past performance issues. Project Managers know they need to establish Project Schedule recovery plans, and the most prevalent approach is to condense (i.e. add risk to) future task durations. ES metrics expose the risk associated with doing so – in part, to make Project Risk absorption decisions more transparent.

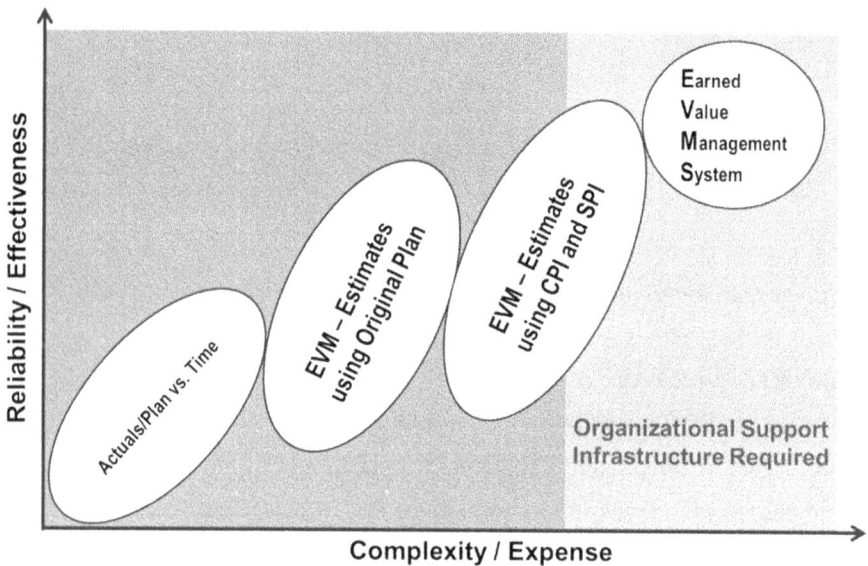

Figure 52. Cost and Schedule Control Tools & Techniques. *Project Risk Management (PMI, 2016, p. 152)*

Quality Assurance

There are many Six Sigma Tools available to facilitate managing Product and Process quality – and I do not intend to dive into any of them here. Even when we (or our organizations) decide on being reactive versus proactive (sometimes for good reasons) we should have a fair understanding of the Tools & Techniques available to us to solve for those immediate needs. We do not necessarily need to be Six Sigma Black Belts to be effective at Quality Control, but it does help to have access to people who are well-informed and knowledgeable of available tools to consider – for handling both pending and materialized issues. Although I was previously trained as a Six Sigma Black Belt Champion (basically, as a person assigned to manage and work with Six Sigma Black Belts to determine the most appropriate Tools & Techniques to apply for solving difficult Product and/or Process issues) I would need a re-fresher to effectively use some of the more sophisticated Tools & Techniques today.

The Figure 53 Quality Control "Bubble Chart" is not very complex. The entire Six Sigma suite of tools may be appropriate for some industries and organizations which require that level of precision to be competitive, but most do not – yet we all should be equipped with knowledge of the more popular and cost-effective options to satisfy our needs. This latter set of Tools & Techniques is what I refer to as Six Sigma Lite, and the specific options usually differ for the various industries, markets and organizations. Strategic Project Management calls for the identification of key Quality Control Tools & Techniques that apply to the organization's work and ensure that those who need to understand and effectively use them are properly trained to do so. I have seen a general migration away from providing work-related training (to improve productivity), and toward providing more mandatory employee training (e.g. Employee Harassment, Employee Safety, Time Reporting, Safe-guarding Information, etc.). I believe that this is somewhat because training is typically managed and controlled from within the Human Resources function, and that group gives priority to general personnel training needs relative to compliance with laws and regulations. Do not get me wrong, I am not suggesting that those training sessions are not needed, but I believe that additional "productivity improvement" training needs should be met as well. Fortunately for me, when I first started working at large corporations, "productivity improvement" tool training was required, so I was trained on many of the more common "productivity improvement" and "problem-solving" Tools & Techniques – and feel that that training was well worth-while for both me (professionally) and the organization.

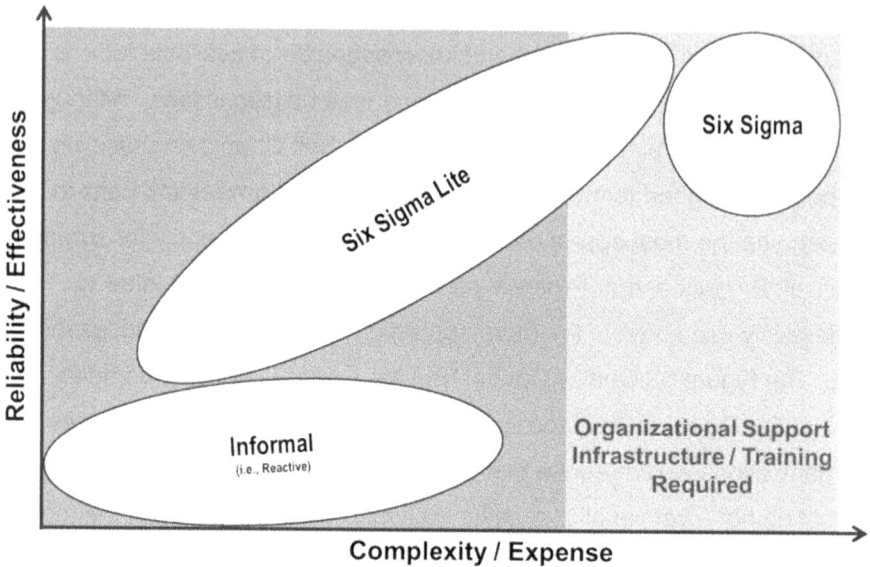

Figure 53. *Quality Control Tools & Techniques.* Project Risk Management (PMI, 2016, p. 156)

An example of the types of tools that could make up a Six Sigma Lite "tool-chest" is provided in Figure 54. Some are within the DMAIC (Define, Measure, Analyze, Improve, Control) grouping and others are within the DMADV (Define, Measure, Analyze, Design, Verify) grouping. Because there is so much variability in what an organization can necessitate, the Six Sigma Lite category has a broad cost-effectiveness "footprint". The relatively broad "footprint" of the Informal/Reactive option shown in Figure 53 is because use of this methodology can be costly, especially given the "Cost of Change" (per Chapter 5) and the negative ramifications that are endemic of using this approach as a primary option can lead to significant consequential costs.

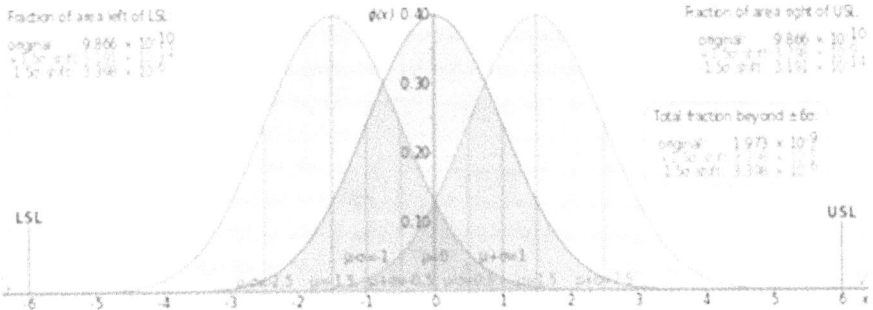

* Some **DMAIC** and **DMADV** Methods:

▪ Fish-bone Cause and Effects Diagrams	▪ Regression Analysis
▪ Control Charts	▪ Root Cause Analysis (e.g., 8D)
▪ Design of Experiments (DOE)	▪ Histograms
▪ Failure Modes and Effects Analysis (FMEA)	▪ Scatter Diagrams
▪ Pareto Charts and Analysis	▪ Analysis of Variance
▪ Business Process Mapping	▪ Gauge Repeatability and Reproducibility

Figure 54. Specific Quality Assurance Tools & Techniques. Project Risk Management (PMI, 2016, p. 157)

Lean Six Sigma is gaining traction as well – which is basically a more holistic approach to minimizing waste while at the same time accelerating "problem-solving" and process improvements.

Requirements Management

I found that Project Requirements Management, Communication and Human Resource Management interact so much that the best way to display the general Tools & Techniques associated with each was to put all three on a single chart, as shown in Figure 55. We discuss Requirements at length in Chapter 1, so I will not reiterate too much here. The only note regarding Requirements (Project and Product) that I would like to state is that since they can change often over the course of the Project Life Cycle, appropriate Change Control processes should be in place to ensure that the "Cost of Change" (refer to Chapter 5) is kept to a minimum – a key tenet of Strategic Project Management.

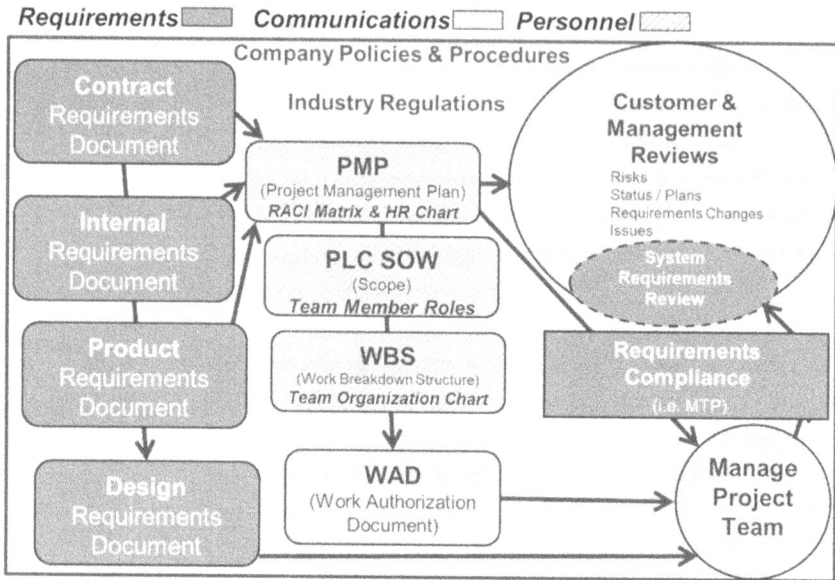

Figure 55. Requirements, Communications, Resources Tools & Techniques.
Project Risk Management (PMI, 2016, p. 159)

Communications Management

When researchers prioritize the most important skills and attributes of good Project Managers (and Organizational Leaders in general), the ability to effectively communicate is typically high on that list [(T.T. Barry, 2012) and (C. Skordo, 2012)]. Arguably, "upward" communication is the most visible (and career shaping) process – e.g. Project Status Updates, Phase Reviews, ad hoc Information Briefings, or Customer Briefings, for example. Preparing for these reviews and engaging in "conflict resolution" (if necessary) is also important, especially the peer communications with Function Managers, key Project Team Leads and SMEs (Subject Matter Experts). The "downward" communications to staff, suppliers and internal support personnel might be less visible to the rest of the organization but is nonetheless very important as well. Some of the key Tools & Techniques are provided in Figure 55, but this is just the "tip of the ice-berg". Below are some of the suggestions I have both received over the course of my career and have doled out to others, specifically those in Program or Project Management roles.

- Do not worry about over-communicating

- Avoid making rash decisions and communicating too hastily

- Avoid taking the credit for the positive Project Team accomplishments – give the credit to appropriate Project Team Members

- Take the blame and personally deliver the message regarding negative news – do not blame a Team Member or others

- Be doubly cautious regarding leaving recorded messages, especially negative messages

- Wait and cool down (i.e. let your heart-beat get back to normal) before rebutting on a "heated" topic

- Be objective and do not stretch the truth

- Reports need to be current, accurate and complete

- Direction needs to be unambiguous and clear

- Follow good escalation practices (see Chapter 2: Managing Expectations)

- Document new agreements and/or changes

- Make information easy to understand – graphics versus words when possible

- Always try to be calm and polite – display composure

- Remember, you are always "on stage", whether you think people are watching or not

Human Resource Management

Managing People can be both very rewarding and very challenging. A few practices that I find helpful are provided in Figure 55. These basically center around being organized (i.e. How do we get work done?). Some of the key work items are listed below.

- Organize the Project. I never really enjoyed developing a Project Management Plan, but I knew it was necessary for properly communicating with all Project Stakeholders. Eventually, I got accustomed to preparing and delivering Project Kick-Off presentations. I would use an older version from a past Project as a template and embellish upon it so that future documents were better. I also learned to value the RACI Matrix, Requirements

Compliance Matrix, a Project Organization Chart, the WBS (Work Breakdown Structure), the Risk Register and Matrix, the IMS (Integrated Master Schedule), EVM (Earned Value Management), and the use of our various communication media (e.g. e-mails, work-flows, intranet, data repositories, etc.). I also found that keeping information updated, "configuration controlled" and securely safe-guarded was important as well.

- Manage Meetings. I find that it is well worth my time to prepare an agenda and ensure that all the necessary people attend my Project Meetings. This is beneficial to all involved. Add to this being prompt, you are basically treating all with respect (especially regarding their time and expertise) and exhibiting common courtesy.

- Make Decisions. I always go back to the "Cost of Change" curve (Chapter 5: Cost of Change) when I think of efficient and effective decision-making. Important decisions usually necessitate interacting with others. It is imperative to have all the facts, generate and analyze the solution alternatives, and have a recommendation. But it is also equally important to know who all the necessary Project Stakeholders are (maybe, via a RACI Tool at times) – so that you (as an R [Recommender]) do not leave out any key individuals (especially the C's [Contributors] that R's are obligated to get inputs from).

- Deal with Conflicts. Conflicts are likely to surface both within the Project Team and outside the team and will have to be addressed and remedied whenever or wherever they arise. Having (or obtaining) all the relevant "objective facts" and exhibiting integrity, calmness and open-mindedness helps with arriving at amicable resolutions.

- Influence Actions. Project Managers must be good "influencers", especially in Matrix Organizations – for most Team Members are "owned" by Functional Managers. That said, influencing the Project Team Members is not necessarily the most important duty – influencing the Functional Managers (who assign the Project Team Members) and the Executive Team (who make the important decisions) are arguably the most impactful influential duties. "Inspiring" Project Team Members (versus influencing them) is the more appropriate descriptor when it comes to managing the Project Team.

- <u>Mentor Others</u>. Project Managers are in a great position to mentor others. Ideally, the PM is more of a "generalist" and a good communicator – which helps in keeping everything on an even keel. Being compassionate and empathetic also helps.

- <u>Involve Others when needed</u>. When I was young, I knew everything – or at least I thought that I did. Now, as I have aged and matured a bit, I realize that I do not know everything and tend to better understand what I do not know, and how (or from whom) to get the answers I need. I discovered that if I respected the positions (and Subject Matter Expertise) of others throughout the organization, I got much better cooperation and help from them when I needed it most.

Supply Base Management Tools & Techniques

The Figure 56 graphic is a very simplified look at Supplier Management from a Project Management stand-point. The most strategic activities are those shown at the start of the process flow. "Make versus Buy" decisions are typically sorted out at the Organizational Management level and might not be beneficial for many of the Project endeavors but are considered most beneficial for the organization as a whole. Project Sourcing Strategies can be extremely important to stakeholders, thus creating an upfront "strategy" approved by all the stakeholders is a "good practice". Some examples of key strategic decisions are listed below.

- Are there specific suppliers with complementary capabilities (e.g. CMs (Contract Manufacturers) with a deep customer base and ample/flexible capacity, or with specific competitive technology strength, or with a strong cost and/or quality capability, etc.) who should be considered, more as "partners"?

- Are there certain suppliers that are best for Product Development and others that are best for production of Products or deployment of Services? Do we need to compromise by having only one?

- How many suppliers are needed for "sourcing" different types of materials or services (e.g. Sole-Sources, Dual-Sources, Multiple Sources) to the benefit of our organization (e.g. for lower costs, for lower risk, for technical strength, etc.)?

- Does geography matter relative to cutting down on logistical costs (e.g. enabling "leaner" operations)?

- Are there certain out-sourced items which should be competitively sourced via an RFI (Request for Information), followed by an RFP (Request for Proposal) or RFQ (Request for Quote)?

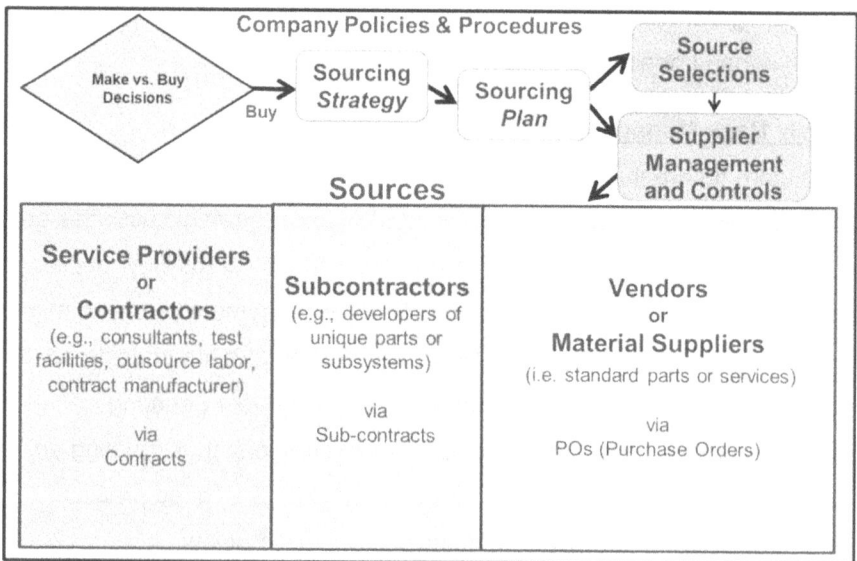

Figure 56. Supplier Management Tools & Techniques. *Project Risk Management (PMI, 2016, p. 167)*

Sourcing can make or break Projects. Our Project Sourcing plans should therefore consider several pieces of important information. Some of these considerations are listed below.

- How much management should be applied to each key source?

- How "financially viable" are the sources?

- How hard is it to interact with the sources relative to the contracting process, terms, and transparency?

- What are their quality certifications and credentials?

- Any historical performance (e.g. meeting delivery commitments, meeting quality expectations, etc.) to consider?

- How much priority will our organization receive vis-à-vis their other customers?

HOW "BEST PRACTICES" ARE DETERMINED

How do we know whether our Project Management "practices" are indeed the most appropriate for our type (or types) of Product Development activities? This is the question I once asked myself and it motivated me to probe deeper. My general conclusion is that we evolve our "practices" (i.e. the Tools & Techniques we employ) to correct for past mistakes or issues, and we can typically benefit from the introduction of new Tools & Techniques designed to facilitate improved Project performance. These new Tools & Techniques offerings are not likely developed by chance. Start-up companies endeavor to solve problems with innovated offerings (i.e. technologies and/or ideas), and to establish a business from their commercialization. The first chart in a presentation to potential investors is typically a definition of the "problem" being addressed. The "offering" is normally positioned as the optimal "solution" to that "problem", especially relative to the deficiencies associated with other "offerings" that are currently available. So, while people are attempting to make our lives easier via technology and innovation, we can look at the current offerings and determine whether we are employing those which make the most sense for what we are trying to accomplish. We sometimes do this in a more indirect manner – via "trial and error". I propose a very practical approach, by elaborating upon the work described earlier (and detailed in my other book on *Project Risk Management*) – figuring out (for ourselves) if we are using the "right" Tools & Techniques from those which are already available (like those presented in the previous section). The other part of this process (as is discussed in more detail within Chapter 9: Lessons Learned) is being willing to continually evaluate Project Management "practices" through honest retrospective assessments. This is a key aspect of Strategic Project Management which should not be ignored.

The Process for Determining "Best Practices"

We have discussed the various Tools & Techniques, not just the categories, but also the "options" within those categories. The next step is to determine the most appropriate "options" to utilize for our specific Project types and needs. Figure 57 depicts the inherent process that takes place, whether overtly recognized or not.

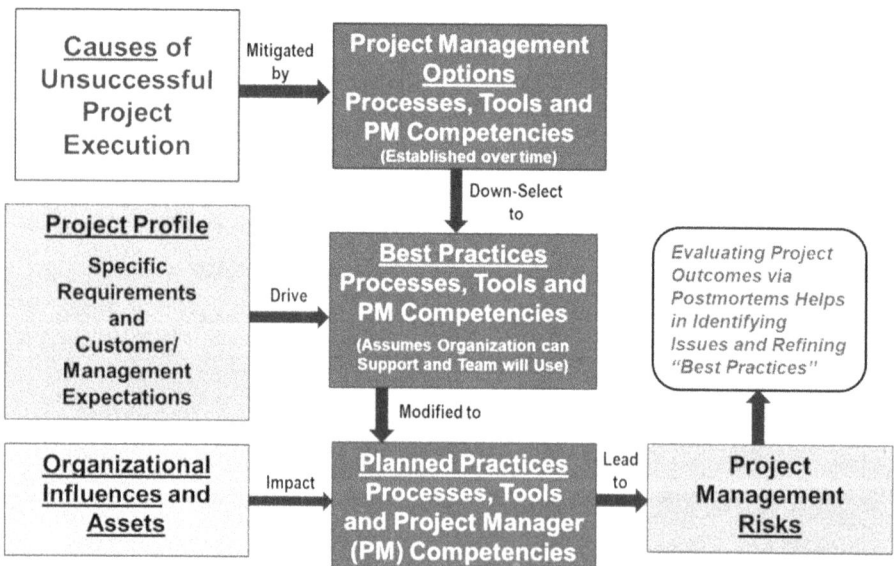

Figure 57. The Process for Selecting Tools & Techniques to Employ. Project Risk Management (PMI, 2016, p. 198)

Starting at the top, we see that "causes of unsuccessful project execution" have led to the currently available solutions (or "options" to consider). The process for down-selecting is driven primarily by our Project type – referred to here as the Project Profile (more on this in the next section). In an ideal world there is an optimal set of "Best Practices" which apply to our Project. The problem is, we do not tend to select the "Best Practices" due to several reasons. Let us investigate what some of these reasons are.

- We just do not know which "practices" are "best" to use

- We do not have the support or Organizational Resources to effectively utilize the obvious "Best Practices"

- Our Project Team Leaders tend to use those which they are most familiar with, which are not necessarily the "best options"

As a result of this selection process we either use "Less-than Best Practices" overtly or without really knowing/realizing that we are doing so. This leads to risks that we are either not aware of or choose to ignore. I believe it is typically the former reason. Nonetheless, if we measure our Project performance results after-the-fact (via Lessons Learned assessments or Postmortems/Retrospectives) we can potentially determine why we fell short, and then implement the necessary Corrective Actions to rectify the underlying systemic issues. Again, in an ideal world we do this over time and eventually settle upon the use of the "Best Practices" we should have been employing from the start. More on the realities associated with Postmortems (Chapter 9: Lessons Learned) that can derail us from reaping the benefits from this very sensible process. If we can conform to the ideal "Bests Practices" we are truly implementing Strategic Project Management principles to their fullest.

Project Profile Influences on Tools & Techniques to Use

What are the differentiating factors between Project types? If we know them, we can attempt to determine the "Best Practices" that we should be using to manage them more effectively. For example, if we are under contract to deliver an advanced Product by a certain date to avoid financial penalties and/or enhance future business, should we be using informal Project Scheduling methodologies or those which are the most effective? The answer is obviously the latter; thus, this Project Profile attribute should drive us to use the more effective Project Scheduling Tools & Techniques to improve our chances of being successful. Further, there are several other "factors" to consider as well, so if we look at all these "factors" holistically, we should be able to determine the appropriate suite of Tools & Techniques to utilize. Given the logic behind this approach, I have attempted to determine the various differentiating Project Profile attributes, as depicted in the two sets of characteristics shown in Figures 58 and 59 – those which are more Strategic (or Business related) and those which are more Tactical (or Project Plan related), respectively.

Customer Expectations (all that apply):
- ❏ High-Quality end Product
- ❏ Low-Cost end Product
- ❏ On-Time Product Launch
- ❏ Within Budget (if paid by Customer)
- ❏ None of the Above

Number of Customers (pick 1):
- O One
- O Few
- O Numerous
- O Indeterminate

Sales Channels (all that apply):
- ❏ Direct
- ❏ Thru Middleman or Middlemen

Project Initiation (pick 1):
- O RFI/RFQ Proposal
- O Mktg Strategy/Roadmap
- O Functional Organization (e.g., Engineering)
- O Project Manager

Business Case Justification (pick 1):
- O Customer Derived
- O Internal Market Evaluation
- O Both

Sales Contract Type (pick 1):
- O Contract – Firm Fixed Price (FFP)
- O Contract – Cost Type / Time and Material
- O Commitment or Internal Contract
- O Purchase Order (PO)

Market Type (all that apply):
- ❏ Specialized (e.g., Government, Department of Defense (DoD))
- ❏ Original Equipment Manufacture (OEM)
- ❏ Niche
- ❏ Consumer
- ❏ Commodity

Competitive Landscape (pick 1):
- O Sole Source
- O Preferred or Directed
- O Few Known Competitors
- O Many Competitors
- O Open Competition

Priorities (all that apply):
- ❏ Technical Performance
- ❏ Project Cost
- ❏ Product Cost
- ❏ Schedule
- ❏ None of the Above

Market Span (pick 1):
- O Localized
- O Different and Diverse Locales
- O World-Wide

Primary Company Point of Contact (POC) (pick 1):
- O Project Manager, per Customer
- O Project Manager, per Internal Process
- O Product Line Manager
- O Business Development Manager
- O Marketing and/or Sales Representative

Figure 58. Project Profile Strategic Business Attributes. Project Risk Management (PMI, 2016, p. 233)

Size–Project Cost (pick 1):
O   Very Large (>US$20M)
O   Large (>US$5M)
O   Medium (>US$1M)
O   Small (>US$100K)
O   Very Small (<US$100K)

Scope (pick 1):
O   Firm-cannot change
O   Firm-can Trade-off
O   Interim-with TBDs
O   Best Efforts

Product Cost (pick 1):
O   Firm Limit
O   Limit with tolerance band
O   non-committed but studied
O   non-committed Estimate

Schedule (Project Duration) (pick 1):
O   Negotiated with Reserve
O   Negotiated Aggressive
O   Fixed Required Date-Aggressive
O   Fixed Required Date-Comfortable
O   Best Efforts

Type–Complexity and Risk (pick 1):
O   Highly Complex and Risky
O   Derivative or Some Risk
O   Production or Low Risk
O   Level of Effort (LOE)-No Risk

Product Requirements Source (all that apply):
❏   Customer Provided
❏   Negotiated with Customer
❏   Internal Market Evaluation

Project Cost Flexibility (pick 1):
O   Firm-cannot change
O   Firm-can Trade-off
O   Interim with Bogies
O   Best Efforts

Requirements Stability (pick 1):
O   Firm-cannot change
O   Firm-can Trade-off
O   Somewhat Open-Ended (i.e., some TBDs)
O   Loose (i.e., Best Efforts)

Quality (all that apply):
❏   Per Contract
❏   Best-in-Class
❏   Per Industry Requirements
❏   Per Internal Requirements

Documentation (all that appy):
❏   Contractual Data
❏   Tech Data Package (Design)
❏   Validation Test and Failure Reports
❏   Manufacturing Instructions
❏   Collateral (e.g., Manuals, Specs, etc.)

Reliability (all that apply):
❏   Per Contract
❏   Best-in-Class
❏   Per Industry Requirements
❏   Per Internal Requirements

Safety (all that apply):
❏   Per Contract
❏   Best-in-Class
❏   Per Industry Requirements
❏   Per Internal Requirements

Other Design Considerations (pick 1):
O   Yes (e.g., maintainability, accessories, etc.)
O   None or TBD

Figure 59. Project Profile Tactical Project Plan Attributes. Project Risk
Management (PMI, 2016, p. 233)

BEST PRACTICES CAN BE CHALLENGING TO DETERMINE

Using the Project Profile information (as shown in Figures 58 and 59) to
determine "Best Practices" to employ should enable you to get close, but
only time can really tell. Project dynamics (e.g. Team Member
capabilities, Supplier capabilities, estimation accuracy, "unknown risks",
the Product Development Process, etc.) matter as well. Therefore, I
conclude that the Postmortem process (refer to Chapter 9: Lessons
Learned) is an essential "Best Practice" for any organization truly
motivated to continually improve its competitive position. This is where
Strategic Project Management can make a huge impact.

I tend to put Lessons Learned into two primary categories:

A. those which relate to the Product Development Process and Scope of Work; and

B. those which relate to Strategic Project Management.

The former tends to be easier for us to work out, for those Lessons Learned typically relate to the "technical" approach, and issues are somewhat expected and usually not so "personally" indicting. The latter, on the other hand, tends to be much more difficult to effectively address. We address both in Chapter 9 (Lessons Learned). Here, however, I want to address the "elephant in the room" which Organizational Managers tend to want to ignore, or at least address in a less overt way. The bottom line is that managers do not like exposing management-related issues – and from my experiences, those tend to be the issues that, if resolved, can provide the most benefit to the organization. But you cannot resolve what you do not choose to evaluate. I will admit that I encountered this issue early in my career, and at the time was too naïve and idealistic to know better.

As a new, idealistic, and energetic Project Manager I tended to be dogmatic about following process guidelines and ensuring that we addressed ALL issues with good systemic Corrective Actions. One of my "not so successful" Projects was fraught with technical and Organizational Management issues. As a Project Team we did all we could to be good "team players" by accepting far too much performance risk – and thus, we were constantly in "fire-fighting" mode. I was relatively new to the organization and wanted to address several issues which I felt needed to be resolved. I thought that the Project Postmortem process was just the vehicle to do so. Fortunately, I pre-reviewed the results of my team's analysis with the key Organizational Stakeholders prior to delivering my findings to the Executive Team. Nobody took issue with any of the "technical" Lessons Learned and their corresponding systemic Corrective Action Plans. The management issues were another story. I was pushed to drop several items and "spin" others to keep the managers off the "hot seat" – it was too embarrassing for them to be exposed. Even those which I managed to gain agreement to keep in the report eventually came back and bit me (and for a while I basically became a new "persona non-grata" within that part of the organization). The Project Team was just expected to take all the blame for every problem, whether it was their fault or not. And the Organizational Leaders seemed content to keep the "real" issues from being raised and effectively resolved. I eventually worked to resolve several of the issues behind the scenes.

Recently, I developed a Survey-Based Project Assessment Tool to facilitate the Project Postmortem process. It includes an evaluation of management-related issues in a more acceptable way – one set of results is provided in the Appendix of my **Project Risk Management** book. I tend to focus on the systemic Corrective Actions and present the underlying data at a higher level to keep it from becoming too personal or sensitive.

Less-than Best Practices

Using "Less-than Best Practices" typically adds risk to Project execution. This can be overcome at times by the competency of the Project Manager. The issue this can cause (relative to Strategic Project Management) is that various Project Teams can end up using different Tools & Techniques, and usually do so based on what the Team Leaders have grown accustom to using in the past – not necessarily the "Best Practices". This takes the organization off the hook (relative to establishing consistent Governance Guidelines) but can cause confusion, inconsistency, inefficiencies, and issues, as noted by some of the situations described below.

- If left to their own devices, Project Teams will usually establish different rating criteria and definitions (e.g. the meaning of Red, Yellow and Green). This can cause confusion due to potential inconsistencies between the Projects that are reviewed. As a result, these evaluation criteria need to be constantly re-stated at every meeting, and managers need to re-calibrate per Project. This is not a productive or appropriate process.

- When we leave it up to Project Teams to determine the Tools & Techniques to use, the organization typically sees a proliferation of different tools. This, in turn leads to greater training needs, more tool maintenance expenses, and could lead to substandard usage of tools by Team Members moving between Projects.

- Without even realizing it, an organization can be fostering the use of "Less-than Best Practices" when freedom for selecting Tools & Techniques is given to the various Project Teams.

- Status reporting that varies between Projects (i.e. lack of status update content control) leaves the door open for omitting "Project-Critical" information (e.g. Resource shortages, Requirements changes, etc.) – which could lead to detrimental future issues.

- Surprises due to issues which were either purposely or inadvertently overlooked due to lack of status update content control typically lead to higher "Costs of Change".

Better-than Best Practices

I put "Better-than Best Practices" in two general "buckets":

A. those which typically carry a high cost; and

B. those which are relatively inexpensive to implement, and generally good to embrace.

These "Better-than Bests Practices" can improve probability of successful Project execution, but some are complex and relatively expensive to employ. They also typically require Organizational Management sponsorship, and some require specialized support personnel and infrastructure.

Some "Better-than Best Practices" which tend to be costly are:

- Six Sigma Quality Control. Most organizations use some of the Six Sigma Tools & Techniques, but do not tend to have teams of Green Belt and Black Belt certified practitioners. The training is rigorous, time-consuming, and costly. Knowing how to effectively use ALL the various Six Sigma Tools & Techniques is good, but not necessary for most Projects or organizations.

- Project Plan FMEA (Failure Modes and Effects Analysis). This type of Risk Management methodology is costly and time-consuming. I have used this method once – for managing risks on a very complex Missile Development Program. It can greatly facilitate the Project Risk Management process if done well but is not practical for planning most Projects.

- EVMS (Earned Value Management System). Rigorous EVMS, using the various Earned Value performance measurement techniques (e.g. Milestone Method, Units Complete, quantitative Percent Complete, etc.) and conducting rigorous Variance Analyses can be time-consuming and costly. This method typically requires the "right" Financial Infrastructure and support staff to facilitate it. Simpler EVM techniques (e.g. Earned Schedule, using only Integrated Master Schedule time data) can be effective as well (refer to Chapter 5: Cost of Change), and may enable this "practice" to become more prevalent, for its Early Warning Metrics may be well worth the expense.

- Overall Risk Assessment using Modelling & Simulation. Current SRA (Schedule Risk Analysis) Modelling & Simulation Tools are Costly and require a certain level of "skill" to use – for they must integrate with an IMS tool which typically necessitates support staff to facilitate. This is the only valid/objective Overall Project Risk Assessment methodology to employ on Project Schedules, so it is a "Best Practice" for most "schedule-critical" Project applications and tends to be over-looked. New "user-friendly" Integrated IMS/SRA tools will undoubtedly become available, and when they do this will no longer be a seldom-used "Better-than Best Practice".

- IMS (Integrated Master Schedule) Tool. Current IMS tools are affordable but do require a certain level of "skill" to use. Roll-ups (i.e. integrating several lower-level schedules into an overall Project Master Schedule) are typically difficult to coordinate, costly, and generally require support staff to effectively create and maintain. IMS Lite is a good alternative for it is not as costly – and is considered a "Best Practice" for many Project applications but tends to be over-looked at times due to perceived tool complexity.

Some "Better-than Best Practices" which tend to be less costly but typically require Organizational Sponsorship are:

- Project Team Co-location. Team Co-location is ideal from a communication and collaboration standpoint. In today's world, with the proliferation of Internet, Intranet and Social Media Application Programs, the workforce can accommodate geographically dispersed Project Teams better, but when possible, co-location is still optimal.

- Lean Manufacturing. Organizations around the world have been practicing Lean Manufacturing to take waste out of the logistical and operational processes and enable lower Product costs. I saw the benefit of this methodology first-hand when in the Consumer Electronics industry. It took time, and an organizational attitude of "continuous improvement" – and in the end it led to "world-class" Product cost and quality.

- Lean Practices. Extending Lean "practices" to other (i.e. non-manufacturing) processes is naturally considered a beneficial endeavor – the idea is to take waste out of all the processes we can. This usually takes organizational commitment/sponsorship and the use of good Tools & Techniques. The ideal, from my standpoint, would be to have ready access to real-time top-level Project status information (e.g. Portfolio Dashboards with user drill-down capability) and to be able to conduct periodic Project

Reviews using data and information that is automatically provided through the normal course of activities engaged in by Project Teams (i.e. no need for development of briefing slide decks for Project updates, yet all the relevant data, metrics, and information is readily available within the IT [Information Technology] system).

- Organizational Development and Training. Organizational Leaders tend to struggle with determining the right amount of training to offer employees. Generally, training is good, but can be over-done if not effectively monitored – and since training funds are discretionary there is a desire to minimize training if possible. Training employees in how to effectively utilize essential Project Management Tools & Techniques can be well-worthwhile, however.

GOVERNANCE VIA ESTABLISHMENT OF A PMO

The last section identified several likely issues resulting from permitting Project Leaders to determine all their own Project Management Practices to employ. For this reason alone, organizations should consider the establishment of one or more PMO. There are other well-founded reasons as well. My top 10 reasons for establishing a PMO, including a couple "cautions" to consider when selecting the PMO Manager, are provided below.

- Assigning the Right PMs on Projects. PMs, by nature, are not a homogeneous group, for there are many potential career paths to that type of role. As such, there should be different levels of PMs – a topic which is further elaborated upon in Chapter 10 (Team Leadership). PM assignments should be carefully made in accordance with Project needs and PM competencies.

- Establishing Standards and Consistent Guidelines. A PMO Manager should be actively involved in evaluating PM "Best Practices" and establishing procedures and guidelines for all within the organization to embrace and adhere to.

- <u>Ensure Adherence to Established Procedures, Guidelines and Personnel Conduct Expectations</u>. Left to their own devices, PMs will establish their own Project performance metrics and ratings, as well as determine the type of information they deem important or unimportant. Even if we are provided guidelines to adhere to, we do not necessarily follow them unless we are held accountable to do so. PMO Managers provide that consistent oversight, not only for PM responsibilities, but personnel conduct as well.

- <u>Champion Process Improvements and Consistent Training throughout Organization</u>. The PMO Manager should be process-oriented (i.e. always looking for ways to manage Projects more efficiently and effectively) as well as one of the best Organizational Training resources.

- <u>Establish a PM Support Structure</u>. Provide a capable support staff for administrative help, use of Tools & Techniques, general communications, and assistance with difficult situations and decision-making pursuits.

- <u>Establishes a Solid Escalation Path which Advocates for the Project Teams</u>. The PMO Manager should be the first line of PM escalation, and the person who ensures conformance to appropriate escalation protocols. This individual should also be the "go-to" person for resolution of difficult conflicts affecting Project Teams and/or Functional Groups that affect Project Team performance.

- <u>Mentoring of PMs and Career Development Counselling</u>. It is difficult to advise others about how to effectively mentor or counsel their subordinates if you have not "been there and done that" yourself. PMO Managers should have been good, accomplished Program or Project Managers themselves, and if so, should be skilled at mentoring and counselling others.

- <u>Foster Productive Cross-Learning from within the Group</u>. At my PMO Staff meetings I would not allow PMs to discuss their specific Project status or performance. These meetings were established to discuss higher level concepts, like how to improve the entire group by sharing and discussing Lessons Learned and/or proposed group process improvement initiatives. This had side benefits, like the comparing/contrasting of differing approaches.

- <u>Be Careful about having a PM Run a PMO without having any prior Functional Management Experience</u>. This was my hardest job transition, and I failed miserably at my first attempt because I was more inclined to be the "Super-PM" for ALL the Projects instead of the PMO Functional Manager. A PMO Manager is foremost a Functional Manager and should not be expected to be the PM of all the Projects within the PMO.

- <u>Portfolio Management "Go-To" Person</u>. Portfolio Management is the "connective tissue" between Organizational Strategic Planning and Project Planning. The PMO Manager is (or should be) a vital part of that "connective tissue".

In conclusion, I have arrived at the following position regarding PMOs: that establishment of a PMO should be considered an organizational "Best Practice" – at least for those large Matrix Organizations endeavoring to practice and excel at Strategic Project Management. That said, a decision to establish a full-time PMO Management position will obviously have to consider several other factors, e.g.: the number of Program and/or Project Managers; the importance of Project Team consistency; the importance of Project execution, and budgetary constraints/considerations.

Is Your Organization Managing Projects Strategically?

Take the test, or at least see how your organization stacks up. An inventory of the key Strategic Project Management concepts espoused by this book can be kept, Chapter by Chapter. There is no established reference of good or bad, but you can see where your organization currently is, and use this tool to monitor progress. Each question starts with the phrase: To what extent does your organization......

36. recognize **Causes of Unsuccessful Project Execution** due to **Management's Influences?**

1	2	3	4	5
O	O	O	O	O
Never	Rarely	Sometimes	Most of the Time	Always

37. endeavor to ensure the use of **PM Tools & Techniques** that are **"Best Practices"?**

1	2	3	4	5
O	O	O	O	O
Never	Rarely	Sometimes	Most of the Time	Always

38. require Teams to conduct **Postmortems** to refine **Project Management "Best Practices"?**

1	2	3	4	5
O	O	O	O	O
Never	Rarely	Sometimes	Most of the Time	Always

39. endeavor to implement **Better-than Best Practices** (e.g. **Lean processes** and **Training)?**

1	2	3	4	5
O	O	O	O	O
Never	Rarely	Sometimes	Most of the Time	Always

40. recognize the **Benefits** of **PMOs (Project/Program Management Offices)** and use them?

1	2	3	4	5
O	O	O	O	O
Never	Rarely	Sometimes	Most of the Time	Always

CHAPTER 9

It's *LESSONS LEARNED*

As a child I learned that it was not wise to keep making the same mistake over and over again. We realize that it is in our own best interests and benefit to learn from our mistakes and ensure that we do not repeat them. A study of more than 150 New Products concluded that "the knowledge gained from failures [is] often instrumental in achieving subsequent successes... In the simplest terms, failure is the ultimate teacher." (*Research Policy,* 1985).

As an executive I saw that the organizations I worked for were adept at learning from "technical" and Product Development issues but were less inclined to publicize and/or overtly address issues that were due to organizational or management deficiencies. However, there is usually a tipping point (due to the accumulation of crises) whereby the latter can no longer be ignored, and "action" is necessary to effectively address the underlying issues. This topic was touched on in Chapter 8 (Best Practices) and I will not embellish much further here. My bottom-line assumption is that those interested in reaping the benefits from truly practicing Strategic Project Management are more interested in, and open to, the holistic aspect of retrospective Lessons Learned due to any underlying cause. By implementing appropriate systemic Corrective Action changes on a continuous basis our organizations continually improve and become more competitive. This is a basic tenet of Strategic Project Management.

TECHNICAL LESSONS LEARNED

The general topic of "technical" Lessons Learned is quite broad. These are the lessons we learn during Product Development and subsequently (i.e. after Products are Launched/Sold, and/or Services are Launched/Deployed). Many organizations establish processes to resolve these types of issues immediately to prevent subsequent re-occurrence. The Figure 60 flow diagram is an example PDLC (Product Development Life Cycle) which depicts the activities associated with "technical" issue discovery and Corrective Action. The center box represents the PDP (Product Development Process) that we follow to get to the desired initial end-result – i.e. a fully compliant Product and/or Service offering which is launched into the marketplace and/or to the Project Sponsor and does so within the competitive market constraints (e.g. Time-to-Market schedule, expected Quality performance, expected Product Cost, etc.). This flow implies a direct connection between all post-launch issues and the PDP of current and future Product offerings. This is particularly the case for organizations which conduct similar Product Development Projects on a regular/recurring basis. Some organizations break the Product Planning and execution/delivery activities into distinct and separable processes, as listed below:

- Project Initiation – associated with a Strategic Initiative, Product Roadmap, Business Case and/or Charter.

- Technology Staging – Organizational and/or supplier R&D (Research and Development) which might be identified as part of the Product Roadmap or a Strategic Business Objective.

- Project Planning – the traditional Project Life Cycle process of establishing a Baseline Project Plan (refer to Chapter 3: Planning).

- PDP (Product Development Process) – the Scope of Work associated with delivering a fully compliant Product and/or Service offering to the Marketplace (or Sponsor). Reference Chapter 7 (Product Development Process).

- Build & Ship and/or Deployment Process – the Production/Deployment processes.

- Sustaining Process – the process associated with post-Launch issue management (e.g. addressing Product Scrap, Yield, Quality, Reliability, Repeatability, etc.).

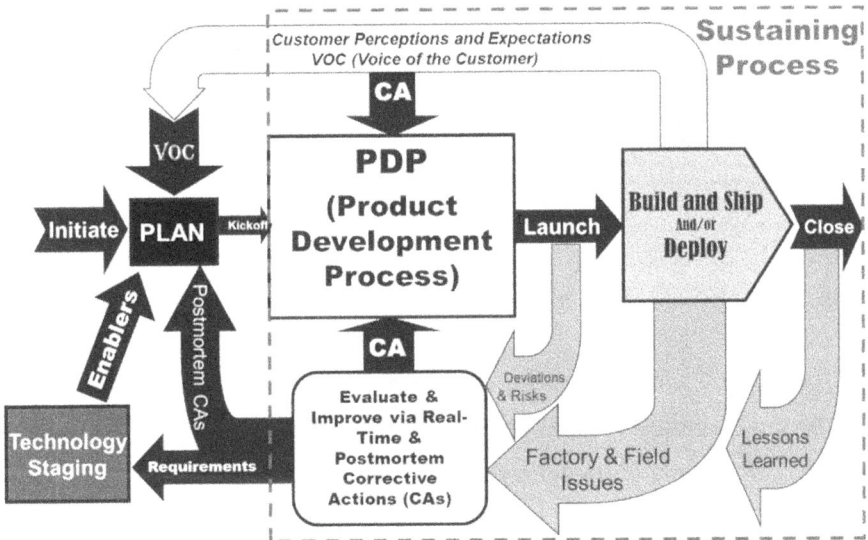

Figure 60. Example PDLC (Product Development Life Cycle) Activities. From Project Risk Management (PMI, 2016, p. 205)

For clarity, I believe it is important to make a distinction between the "PDLC (Product Development Life Cycle)" and the traditional "PLC (Product Life Cycle)". Some organizations call the PDLC process that I am referring to as the PLC, instead. The traditional PLC is depicted in Figure 61. This more traditional PLC process begins at the initial Product Launch to market and is associated with Product Sales over time (from Introduction to Retirement), whereas the PDLC includes all the other activities leading up to Product launch, and the subsequent retrospective activities for Product sustainment.

Many organizations establish feedback processes and separate organizational groups that directly address the causes behind post-launch issues, with the intent to make expedient changes wherever possible / practical – a very good Strategic Project Management practice.

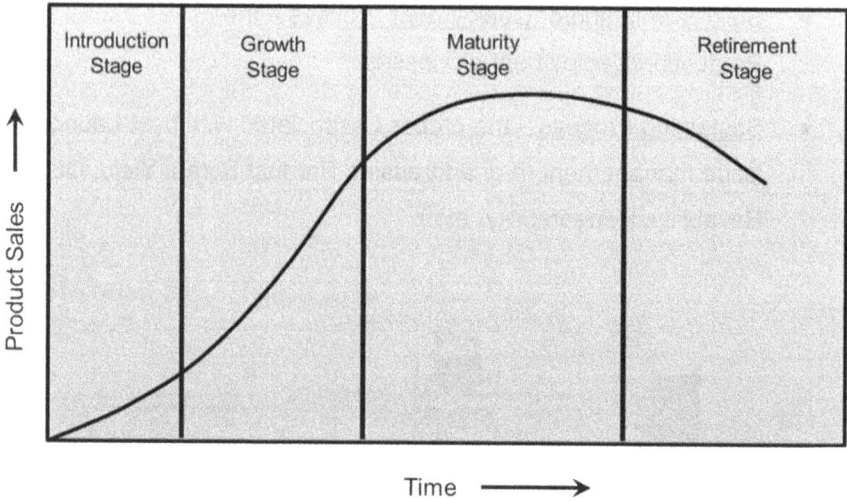

Figure 61. Generic PLC (Product Life Cycle). Project Risk Management (PMI, 2016, p. 12)

The PDLC Flow includes several exception paths (depicted in Figure 60 by the Feedback Arrows). Some of the more common categories, or types of "technical" issues are provided below.

- Design Rule issues (e.g. Process Steps, Threshold Limits, Materials, etc.)

- Test Failure causes (e.g. Product Usage, Environmental Robustness, Validation, etc.)

- Parts Specifications issues (e.g. Tolerances, Information on Drawings, Product Performance over its life and in the various non-operational and operational environments, etc.)

- Software Bugs (e.g. Code issues, Exception Path problems, Logic Conflicts, etc.)

- Compatibility issues (e.g. Integrating with older or newer systems, etc.)

- Scope Omissions (e.g. Development Steps omitted inadvertently or not originally deemed necessary, etc.)

- Regulatory Compliance issues (e.g. Safety, Federal Communication's Commission, American Disability Act, etc.)
- Fit-Check issues (e.g. Piece Part Dimensional Tolerances, Process Distributions, Binning Criteria, etc.)
- Tooling & Test Equipment Repeatability and Reliability issues (e.g. Functional and Physical inconsistencies, Product Wear, etc.)
- Contamination issues (e.g. Air-Particle Size and Count distributions, Out-Gassing, etc.)
- Use-Case issues (e.g. unexpected Consumer Use Behaviors, untested Data Paths, etc.)
- Assembly issues (e.g. Procedural Instructions issues, Operator error, wrong Parts, bad Parts, etc.)
- Design Margin issues (e.g. Failures at extreme conditions, long-term Usage Wear, etc.)
- Shipping & Handling issues (e.g. Shock, Vibration, Altitude induced Problems, etc.)
- Packaging issues (e.g. lack of Protection, Instructions errors, omitted Parts, etc.)
- Latent Defect issues (e.g. poor Soldering, Contamination, poor Assembly, etc.)
- Long-term Reliability issues (e.g. Temperature/Humidity exposure, Storage Life, etc.)
- Documentation issues and Mistakes (e.g. Manual typos, Ambiguity, Clarity issues, etc.)
- Benchmark Testing issues (e.g. comparative Performance, Speed, Capability, etc.)
- Integration issues (e.g. Form, Fit, Function surprises found at system level, etc.)
- Out-of-box Audit failures (e.g. Final Performance Test Coverage, visible Damages, etc.)

When we run into "technical" issues like those listed above, a pro-active organization typically takes actions to collect all the facts, determine the "root cause", evaluate alternative remedial actions and implement the agreed to Corrective Action(s). In the heat of the battle, the Project Team may be in more of a "fire-fighting" mode, and the immediate Corrective Actions are typically after-the-fact "workarounds". This may be a good temporary fix but is not where the Project Team should stop. Can the issue arise again? Should we implement a systemic change that can prevent future occurrences? These are the Strategic Project Management questions and actions to consider. Setting up and enforcing retrospective analyses to arrive at <u>systemic</u> process improvements is another "good practice" to employ, as will be elaborated upon below.

PRODUCT DEVELOPMENT PROCESS LESSONS LEARNED

The detailed Project SOW (Scope of Work) typically adheres to an established PDP (Product Development Process), the topic of Chapter 7, or a new PDP established to ensure that the resultant Product and/or Service offering(s) meet customer expectations. Technical Lessons Learned from technical issues (listed above) are normally important influencers to the PDP, thus there is a direct connection between them. Some common PDP Lessons Learned that typically necessitate systemic Corrective Actions are listed below.

- Scope Omissions (e.g. Development Process steps omitted inadvertently or not originally considered, etc.)
    - Omitted Requirements Verification or Validation
    - Invalid Assumption (e.g. PM wrongly assumed it would be okay with the Sponsor for the Project Team to drop or change a Product Requirement, etc.)
    - Estimation Error (e.g. inadvertently omitted past "Analogous" data during estimation process)
    - Poor Estimate (e.g. assumed a more capable Project Resource for an important task completion on time and within budget, underestimated risk/complexity, etc.)

- Process non-Adherence (e.g. Team Members purposely or inadvertently skipping Process Steps)
    - Test Articles with different Form, Fit, Function characteristics used for different Validation Tests (can cause a false sense of security regarding production Product/Process readiness and customer usage)
    - Test coverage and/or time reductions to make up Schedule and/or Cost issues

- o Test omitted for lack of appreciation for the specific test due to a "knowledge gap"
- Unofficially added a Product Requirement without considering repercussions (e.g. no follow-up validation, trying to "do the right thing" by being a good "Team Player", etc.)

- Test Plan issues leading to erroneous conclusions, e.g.:
  - o Sample Size too small to be considered "statistically significant" or valid to draw conclusions from
  - o Use of an Out-dated Test Method (e.g. not appropriate and/or not adjusted for newer technology)
  - o Use of Out-of-Calibration Equipment
  - o The Assumed Qualification-by-Similarity was inappropriate
  - o Decision to not have to perform necessary Regression Tests

- Test Facility and/or set-up issue
  - o Wrong or worn-out Test Fixtures
  - o Faulty Chamber (e.g. not sealed properly for Test, inappropriately influenced by surrounding activity and/or environmental conditions, etc.)

- Compatibility Testing lacking appropriate coverage
  - o All past Systems not tested for compatibility to save on Project Time and/or Budget
  - o Past Systems not available or not considered
  - o Test Scripts not thorough enough

I have seen all the above types of issues and am sure that there are many others. This is where good, experienced SMEs (Subject Matter Experts) can be worth their weight in gold. As seen from this list, there can exist issues which are embarrassing to divulge but are nonetheless communicated to ensure Lessons are Learned and appropriately acted upon. These issues also tend to be very visible and are difficult to cover up. Identifying them is important, but strategically it may be more important to come up with good systemic Corrective Actions to prevent their reoccurrence – a topic that is addressed later in this chapter.

PROJECT MANAGEMENT PROCESS LESSONS LEARNED

Technical, PDP (Product Development Process) and Project Management process issues are all likely to impact Project Team performance and are thus included in the Figure 44 Fishbone "Cause and Effect" Diagram shown in Chapter 8 (Best Practices). The Technical and PDP issues have been discussed in the previous two sections. Here we discuss the Project Management process issues, specifically. These processes are typically established at the start of the Project and several are performed throughout the Project Life Cycle. The general process for determining the specific "practices" to employ is discussed in detail within Chapter 8 (Best Practices) and is depicted in the Figure 62 Flow Diagram. The postmortem (or retrospective) assessment feedback process is shown as well. Basically, the Project Profile and Organizational Influences lead to decisions made on PM Tools, Techniques and Competencies. The Project Management Tools & Techniques are typically identified in the Project Management Plan documentation, and ultimate Project Team performance (when assessed) can give the organization invaluable insights, which in turn, should lead to the establishment of systemic process improvements. This last step closes the loop to true Strategic Project Management and future Project Team performance Improvements should be duly realized.

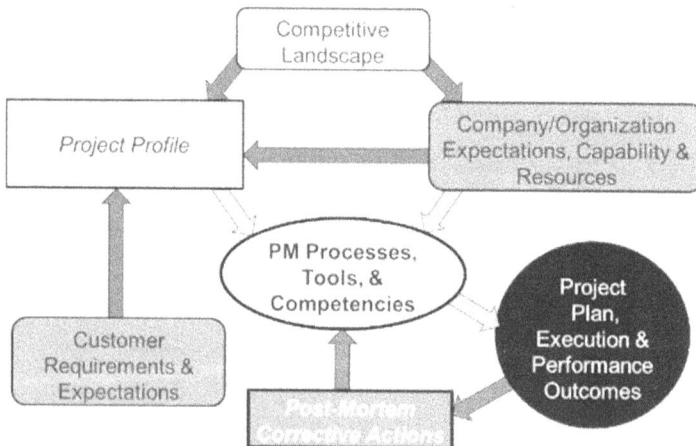

Figure 62. Project Management Assessment Process. Project Risk Management (PMI, 2016, p. 210)

The most actionable Project Management issues (excluding those addressed in the prior two sections) are categorized (per the Fishbone Diagram categories) and listed below.

- Management Controls

    o Risk Management – Is this a complex/risky Project that is heavily scrutinized? If so, does the Project Team understand Risk Severities and Overall Project Risks?

    o Cost/Schedule Controls – Is Project Schedule and/or Cost critical? Is the Project Team using tried and proven Early Warning KPIs (Key Performance Indicators)?

    o Requirements and Change Management – Are requirements and change control important to the Project? Are processes in place to limit the "Cost of Change"?

    o Supplier Management – Is the Project Team critically dependent on Out-side Sources to succeed? If so, are the Management Controls sufficient?

- Communications

    o Priorities – Are Project Priorities understood and differentiated so that Project Team can make good trade-off decisions? Do all Stakeholders understand and agree?

    o Decision Making – Do all Project Team Members and key Stakeholders understand their decision-making authority and role in decision-making?

    o Status Reporting – Are Project Status Updates current, accurate and complete? Do they enable appropriate Stakeholder visibility and expedient change decisions?

    o Team Direction – Are directions to Project Team Members unambiguous and clear?

- o Escalation – Are Escalation Protocols understood and adhered to?

- Leadership

  - o PM Competencies – Are the PM and other Project Team Leaders appropriately capable, experienced and thorough/diligent or do any need training/oversight?

  - o Team and Organizational Dynamics – Are there any dysfunctionality issues between Project Team Members or other Stakeholders which can impact performance?

  - o Training and Development – Are all Project Team Members appropriately trained and/or mentored to adequately perform their functional duties?

- Productivity Tools

  - o PM Tools & Techniques – Are all Project Team Members appropriately trained and/or mentored in the use of critical Project Management Tools & Techniques?

  - o Technical Tools & Techniques – Are all Project Team Members provided the requisite "technical" Productivity Tools necessary to successfully perform their jobs?

  - o Problem-Solving Tools & Techniques – Are all Project Team Members provided the Problem-Solving Tools and Training necessary to successfully perform their jobs?

  - o Infrastructure (Enterprise Resource Planning) – Are all Project Team Members provided access to the Infrastructure Tools necessary to successfully perform their jobs?

  - o Training – Are all Project Team Members trained in the use of all Productivity Tools necessary to successfully perform their jobs?

- Resources

  - <u>Human Resources</u> – Are all necessary Project Human Resources available when needed to perform Project Scope, and does there exist the necessary capability (i.e. expertise) and capacity (i.e. quantity)?

  - <u>Funding</u> – Are there sufficient funds available to meet planned (i.e. estimated) Project performance needs, with adequate Project Reserves to cover Project Budget risks?

  - <u>Time</u> – Is there sufficient time available to meet planned (i.e. estimated) Project performance needs, with adequate "buffer" to cover Project Schedule risks?

  - <u>Facilities</u> – Are there sufficient Facilities, Supplies and Equipment available to meet planned (i.e. estimated) Project performance needs, with adequate back-up sources to cover Project Scope risks?

The **LESSONS LEARNED POSTMORTEM PROCESS**

I am a firm believer that Project Postmortems (or Retrospectives) provide a path for "doing more with less". The more we learn from past mistakes to prevent their re-occurrence, the less time and energy we will expend to prevent repeating them. I also realize that there needs to be a high level of professional maturity within the organization to perform these on a regular basis and to avoid negatively impacting workforce morale in any way. It is much easier to self-reflect on a personal level than on an organizational level. But self-reflection has proven to be of benefit if performed to enable "constructive" change – "self-reflection allows for an increased awareness of problematic performance traits and the ability to develop solutions on how to adjust those aspects of your leadership style." (Executive Velocity, 2013).

"Process" does matter. In this chapter we look at the various Postmortem initiation processes, the general Postmortem process steps, and some options and cautions to consider for performing them in a productive way. Before diving into these topics, I want to first address an issue with Lessons Learned Postmortems that I feel particularly strong about – regarding post-analysis Corrective Actions. As individuals, we do not change by simply listing the Lessons Learned in a file and re-visiting them now and again. We should pro-actively take steps to change in a more permanent and natural way. As an organization, I believe that this is true as well. We should not simply record the Lessons Learned in an archive directory or folder for future Project Teams to retrieve and consider. We should instill "systemic changes" in our organizational activities (e.g. Policies, Procedures, Work Instructions, etc.) that can prevent or mitigate their future occurrence in a more permanent and natural way. Thus, "systemic change" should be pursued in every case. The Project Team experiencing the issue in real-time will typically develop and implement "workarounds" to get the Project back on track, but if these "workarounds" are not accompanied by "systemic change", we are not really improving as an organization. And this is what we should want as part of our Strategic Project Management methodology.

Initiation and Conduct of Postmortems

There are several potential reasons why Project Postmortems are initiated:

- Established as Project Process Requirement. They are required via organizationally directed Governance (i.e. a PLC Process Requirement). I advise organizations to establish Project Postmortems as a firm requirement that the Project Team leads must complete before they can work on another Project – meaning that they must document and present the findings and Corrective Action plans to the Executive Team.

- Special Edict per Contract or Request. These are special requests made by the Project Sponsor(s) (e.g. Organizational Management and/or Customer). This might be prompted by an unexpected number of issues encountered, or a special contract condition tied to final payment. In addition, a less extensive assessment might be requested at times to address and document a specific "technical" issue (i.e. perform a "root cause" analysis) to ensure that the issue was appropriately addressed before subsequent Project deliverables are accepted.

- Determine Improvement Initiatives. These may surface due to an elevated level of Crisis Management intervention (e.g. to address and resolve a major organizational crisis impacting business success). In some cases, this could entail the retrospective assessment of several Projects where there appeared to be an epidemic of similar performance by various teams over time (like the example presented in Appendix D of my book on **Project Risk Management**).

General Postmortem Process

Whether a Project Postmortem process is standardized or not, there is a typical process flow that they should follow. An example Postmortem process flow is briefly described below.

1) Establish a Process and Schedule. If not already established, the Project Team leader(s) should establish a specific process and completion timeline.

2) Assemble Assessment Team. Typically, the Project Manager and Team leaders participate in this process, provided they are all available. Other key stakeholders (i.e. key Functional Managers, Suppliers, etc.) may need to be involved as well.

3) Collect the Facts and Objective Data. The Project Team usually strives to collect facts relative to their performance (compared to the plan) and issues discovered throughout the Project Life Cycle, including the remedial action plans which ensued. Wherever possible, the Project Team should site specific examples relative to issue discovery, impact and remedy.

4) Analysis of the Information. This includes:

  a.   the identification of all issues encountered;

  b.   the Project impact resulting from the issues;

  c.   any collateral damage inflicted upon other Projects as a result;

  d.   the "root causes" behind these issues; and

  e.   the results associated with the "workarounds" and/or Corrective Actions employed to rectify and/or address the resultant impacts.

5) Determination of Alternative Systemic Change Options. Determine the potential approaches which, if implemented, would prevent, or mitigate re-occurrence of the issues. These approaches should focus on "systemic" ways in which all Projects could effectively address the general "root causes" (and test this theory against situation(s) experienced to confirm effectiveness).

6) Determination of Systemic Corrective Actions and Owners. The Project Team should determine the most cost-effective systemic Corrective Actions to implement, identify the owners, and establish implementation plans.

7) Follow-up on Implementation and Assessment of Effectiveness. Upon approval of the Corrective Action plans, the Management Team should follow-up on implementation progress and keep track of effectiveness, especially with those incurring high costs (i.e. to Project Schedule and/or Budget). The PMO Manager is a good candidate to consider for managing and controlling this activity.

Postmortem Process Cautions

Some general cautions relative to the processes used to conduct productive Project Postmortems are provided below.

- Ensure that ALL Relevant Facts are Brought Forward. Some of the facts are obvious (e.g. Project Costs, Schedule and issues documented in Project Status Updates and Project Phase

Reviews), but others may not be as obvious (e.g. Requirement Changes, Scope Changes, Resource Conflicts/Dynamics, and Risk Management items). Some relevant contributors to Project success, or lack-thereof, could be overtly or inadvertently left out – in either case this is an opportunity lost.

- Assess BOTH Good and Poor Performance. The tendency it to focus on issues, but it is also wise to look at successes to ensure that their "causes" are accounted for as well. Specifically, you do not want to resolve an issue and inadvertently cause a different problem in an area or activity where the Project Teams were always performing well.

- Was "Root Cause" Actually Determined? Sometimes the "root cause" of an issue can be illusive and if not careful, your Project Team could end up fixing a "symptom" without resolving the underlying "root cause". 8D's and 5 Whys are good Tools & Techniques to use to prevent this.

- Are the Corrective Actions "Systemic"? "Workarounds" are not typically "systemic" Corrective Actions by nature, thus, a Lesson Learned corrective action should not rely on the availability of a "workaround". Systemic changes typically relate to a more generally applied Process, Procedure, Work Instruction, etc.

- Are the Corrective Actions Truly Effective? It is always a good idea to play back the events that led to an issue to determine if the proposed systemic Corrective Action(s) would indeed solve the problem. Further, if a systemic Corrective Action has a hefty "price-tag" associated with its implementation the owner should establish a process for re-visiting how it works on future Projects.

- Ensure that the Process is Not a "Witch Hunt". One of the most important "cautions" is resisting assignment of blame to a group or individual for an issue. This requires a degree of organizational (as well as personal) maturity. If employees discover that blame and/or punitive actions result from Postmortem evaluations, there will be a tendency to either avoid being honest about issues and/or a resulting morale issue to deal with as an organization.

POSTMORTEM PROCESS OPTIONS

There are at least a couple general approaches to conducting a Project Postmortem. I have conducted them in the very deliberate way described above, as well as via the use of a well-designed and executed Questionnaire (or Survey).

In response to a request by my boss (the CEO who I worked for), I developed a survey-based Project Assessment tool to evaluate why the other division was having so many problems with Project performance on Development Contracts. This organization was accustomed to developing Products using internal funds, but as the organization grew it started bidding on government RFPs (Request for Proposals) and received several Development Contracts. It turns out that the rigidity of <u>Contract</u> Research and Development and the less-forgiving customer expectations were not appropriately accounted for when determining the Tools & Techniques to manage these Projects. I had a suspicion as to what the problem areas were but was not naïve enough to "open up a can of worms" by proclaiming my thoughts – for being the General Manager of the other division, my criticisms could be considered "politically" motivated and I did not want that. Instead, I decided to build a questionnaire around the Fishbone Diagram on "Causes of Unsuccessful Project Execution" shown in Figure 44 of Chapter 8 (Best Practices). After constructing the questionnaire, I requested that all the PMs in that division provide a survey input for every contract they managed over the past several years. This survey asked for responses to questions in the following categories:

- Relevant Project Administrative Information
- Relevant Project Profile Information
- PM Tools & Techniques Used

- General Project Outcomes
- Project performance Assessment (per Fishbone Diagram)

I tabulated the results and provided my observations from the inputs – note that these were not my inputs, just my observations. Then the Division Leaders and I formulated Corrective Action plans. Within a couple months the actions were completed and within a year the Project Teams were all performing noticeable (by Internal Management and Customer Sponsors) better. A "sanitized" version of the above information is provided in the Appendix D of my *Project Risk Management* book.

I have since used the questionnaire described above as an assessment tool successfully for evaluating several other Projects within General Groupings, as well as Individual Projects alone (requesting multiple Stakeholder inputs per Project). I was previously advised by other executives that this Survey Methodology was not advisable and would not work, yet it worked out well on several uses – and the decision process behind its design was to capture the Project Management Lessons Learned in a relatively "safe" way. The rationale behind why this approach works well is provided below.

The Ideal Postmortem Approach

The characteristics that I believe are representative of an ideal Project Management assessment and/or Postmortem process are:

Efficiency Goals:

- Minimal Complexity – Easy and Straight-Forward
- Minimal Expense
- Minimal Amount of Time
- Minimal Effort – Gets Team Promptly to Next Assignment

Effectiveness Goals:

- Maximum Use of Data that is Factual and Relevant
- Maximum Objectivity (versus Subjectivity)

- All Potential Areas of Concern are Assessed
- Assessments of Both Positive and Negative Performance
- Eases "Which Hunt" Concerns by Participants
- Results in Valid Systemic Corrective Actions
- Consistent Evaluations Across Organization

Comparison of Traditional versus Survey Approaches

Figure 63 provides a comparison of the two Postmortem assessment approaches side-by-side, as assessed relative to the above stated goals. This table is not intended to rate the differences, per se, but it does lead to some logical conclusions. Below are the key take-aways.

- It is difficult to construct a Survey Instrument to aid in Postmortem evaluations of Technical issues, for there are far too many potential "causes" of "technical" issues, and it would be very cumbersome to use a survey. Thus, the "Traditional Approach" would be the recommended method for that type of Postmortem.

- General Project Management performance assessments should address all the potential issues (i.e. Causes of Unsuccessful Project Execution), and these can be included in a survey. Further, these potential issues should be assessed from both positive and negative perspectives in as safe a way as possible/practical, thus the "survey instrument" is the recommended method for doing so. And this should be completed immediately after Project completion, to capture the data when relatively fresh in the minds of the Project Team Leaders.

- Product Development Process Lessons Learned could be determined by either assessment method. Given the need to perform these types of assessments (and "technical" issue assessments) immediately after issues surface, a Project Postmortem process could be (and probably should be) obsolete after the Project is concluded, for systemic Corrective Actions should have already been implemented.

Ideal Process	Typical Team Approach	Survey Approach
Easy and Straight-Forward to Implement	◆ Must develop a Process if Standard does not already exist. ◆ Complexity can vary -- is Process dependent. ◆ Very good for **Technical** and **PDP** Lessons Learned assessments.	◆ Must develop a Standard Survey if one does not already exist. ◆ Typically takes a capable Administrator. ◆ Very good for **Management Process** Lessons Learned assessments.
Minimal Expense	◆ Expensive is Process dependent. ◆ Typically requires many hours of effort and meetings with several participants. ◆ Dependent on how many in-process real-time Lesson Learned analyses were performed throughout PLC.	◆ Survey development can take significant effort. ◆ Expense is based on participants and their time to answer questions. ◆ Assessment can be completed by smaller team.
Minimal Amount of Time to Obtain Results	◆ Usually takes several Meetings between key Stakeholders. ◆ Several Reviews of Findings, Conclusions, Corrective Actions. ◆ Time can drag on if Team is multiplexing.	◆ Survey Analytics can be Standardized and assessed by small Team. ◆ Several Reviews of Findings, Conclusions, Corrective Actions. ◆ Post survey Meetings can drag on if Process is new.
Minimizes Effort (Gets Team Promptly to Next Assignment)	◆ Dependent on number of iterations required. ◆ Effort can be compromised if Team is in demand next Assignment.	◆ After team inputs to survey they can move on to next assignment. ◆ May require Interview if data is confusing. ◆ Administrator skill-level matters.
Maximizes use of Data that is Factual and Relevant	◆ Obvious Data is provided. ◆ Potentially embarrassing Data may not be forthcoming. ◆ Sometimes Data is contentious and "the most influential negotiator wins."	◆ Much of the Data is based on subjective inputs. ◆ More Respondents participate when Anonymity is secured. ◆ In general Inputs are more truthful.
Is Objective (vs. Subjective)	◆ Can be very objective if ALL facts are surfaced ◆ Sometimes discretion is used to avoid embarrassment and fear of being blamed.	Some data is provided, but most inputs regarding processes and management perceptions are subjective. Helps if administrator is impartial.
Ensures ALL Areas of Concern are Assessed	◆ Allows for "Cherry-Picking" of Data and thus, skewed Results.	◆ Good if designed to require that ALL aspects of the Project are assessed.
Eases "Witch Hunt" Concern (i.e. Assignment of Blame)	◆ Difficult to ease this concern. ◆ Team is tempted to "Spin" the more subjective Personal Management Issues.	◆ Respondents can be protected via Anonymity (not so for PM of a single-Project survey) - but multi-Project surveys can resolve this.
Assesses Both Positive and Negative Performance	◆ Focus is typically on Issues (negatives) relative to Technical and PDP Lessons Learned.	◆ Obtains Inputs for all potential Project Team Performance concerns. ◆ Typically less focused on Technical and PDP Lessons Learned.
Results in Valid Systemic Corrective Actions	◆ Yes, for Technical and PDP related Issues. ◆ Not necessarily for Management Process related Issues.	◆ Most appropriately addresses the germane high-level Management Process Issues and their resolution. ◆ Depends on Organizational maturity.
Ensures Consistent Evaluations Across Organization	◆ Most postmortems vary based on Team preferences. ◆ Most consistent for assessment of Technical and PDP Issues.	◆ Provides for consistency and multi-Project assessments of Management Processes.

Figure 63. Comparison of Postmortem Process Types and their Applicability

Is Your Organization Managing Projects Strategically?

Take the test, or at least see how your organization stacks up. An inventory of the key Strategic Project Management concepts espoused by this book can be kept, Chapter by Chapter. There is no established reference of good or bad, but you can see where your organization currently is, and use this tool to monitor progress. Each question starts with the phrase: To what extent does your organization......

41. direct use of an **Established Process** for assessing **Technical Lessons Learned** in **Real Time?**

1	2	3	4	5
O	O	O	O	O
Never	Rarely	Sometimes	Most of the Time	Always

42. capture and include all **Product Life Cycle-Related Issues** in its **Lessons Learned Process?**

1	2	3	4	5
O	O	O	O	O
Never	Rarely	Sometimes	Most of the Time	Always

43. strive to pursue appropriate **Systemic Corrective Actions** to **Prevent Issue Re-Occurrence?**

1	2	3	4	5
O	O	O	O	O
Never	Rarely	Sometimes	Most of the Time	Always

44. assess **Strategic Project Management-Related Causes of Unsuccessful Project Execution?**

1	2	3	4	5
O	O	O	O	O
Never	Rarely	Sometimes	Most of the Time	Always

45. establish **Lessons Learned Processes** to address **ALL Improvement Needs** appropriately?

1	2	3	4	5
O	O	O	O	O
Never	Rarely	Sometimes	Most of the Time	Always

CHAPTER 10

It's *TEAM LEADERSHIP*

We have discussed several important Strategic Project Management topics throughout this book, and peripherally touched on Team Leadership. There seems to be no end to the number of Leadership "Silver Bullet" processes that are espoused, so I do not intend to add to them here. There are some generally accepted Leadership Attributes that I believe are valid, and thus included them in my book on **Project Risk Management**, so I will briefly reiterate these since they are entirely relevant to the topic of Strategic Project Management. From my experience, however, the most relevant Strategic Project Management aspect of leadership is Organizational Governance associated with Project Management Resource development, Organizational Structure, support services and Project assignment considerations. In Chapter 8 (Best Practice) the PMO (Project/Program Management Office) structure (which I wholeheartedly support) is addressed in detail, including the need for support staff and training/development, so I will not repeat that in this chapter. My focus in this chapter is on the assignment of Project Management Resources.

I have also established several "Rules of Thumb" that I believe are relevant and potentially helpful to those who hire Project Managers (i.e. what you should look for in a prospective Project Manager), and those aspiring to either become a Project Manager or move up the Project Management ranks.

PROJECT MANAGERS ARE NOT ALL EQUAL

In some organizations there seems to exist a misconception that if you are identified as a Project or Program Manager you should be able to manage any Project. I am not speculating but saying this based on experience. Without exception, every large organization that I have worked at was (at one point in time) organized with a pool of Project Managers (within a PMO or dispersed throughout the various Business Units) who were (or at least seemed to be) assigned almost indiscriminately. Now in actuality, I believe that those assignment decisions did involve a discussion of candidate competencies, but the assessment seemed to be based purely on general perceptions by the decision-makers involved and did (at times) lead to poor assignment choices. I am a firm believer that Project Management classifications (or levels) are important and essential for large organizations which conduct a mix of simultaneous Projects at any specific point in time. I also believe in the establishment of PMOs to ensure a degree of consistency in management practices, as well.

Figure 64 is a general comparison of five progressive levels of Project Management Competencies. These levels are based primarily on PM knowledge and experience and point to the types of Projects that they could be assigned to. Also provided is a recognition of the amount of relative management oversight that each level would warrant. A chart like this serves several purposes, such as:

A. provides minimum requirements for various PM assignments;

B. specifies the amount of oversight and mentoring expected;

C. provides "career path" expectations; and

D. facilitates resource alignment (i.e. should help determine the number of individuals in each category to support the various organizational needs).

Level	Category	PM Knowledge	PM Experience	Project Types	Oversight Needed
1	Unexperienced	Aware of Role, Accountability, Function	No Relevant Experience	Simple, Low Risk, Non-Strategic	Significant Oversight/Mentoring
2	Familiar	Comprehends Basic PM Concepts	Can Apply Basic Management Principles	Medium Complexity/ Risk, Non-Strategic	Regular Oversight/ Mentoring
3	Proficient	Knowledgable of PM Techniques	Relatively Proficient	Medium Complexity/Risk, Strategic	Periodic Oversight/ Mentoring
4	Advanced	Understands Advanced PM Techniques	Significant Experience/ Proficiency	Complex, High Risk, Strategic	Minimal Oversight
5	Mastery	Expert in Advanced PM Techniques	Significant Experience & Breadth	Large Strategic Complex Projects or Business Unit	Can Oversee/ Mentor Others

Figure 64. Sample Project Manager Classification Table. Project Risk Management (PMI, 2016, p. 172)

This above categorization also suggests the minimum requirements for a PMO Manager position (i.e. Level 5) – which could vary depending on Project types within that PMO. In general, as noted in Chapter 8 (Best Practices) a PMO Manager should also possess some experience in Functional Management as well, for this type of job is a Functional Management position, and the people who are hired for this position clearly should have a high level PM capability, but should not be acting as (or expected to be acting as) the "Super PM" over ALL the Projects.

TOP 10 LEADERSHIP ATTRIBUTES

Years ago, I embarked on a study to find out what Leadership Attributes were considered most important by the researchers on the subject [(Scordo, C., 2012) and (Barry, T. T., 2012)], and to contrast them with the attributes I thought were most important to be an effective Project Manager. The below listing emerged. This list is in order of perceived importance (from top to bottom) and several of the attributes tend to over-lap, but I support these findings and included this information in my prior book on **Project Risk Management**. Thought I would simply re-iterate the list here, for my coverage of the various aspects of Strategic Project Management would not be complete, otherwise.

- Vision and Ability to Inspire

ACHIEVING EPIC BUSINESS RESULTS

- Communication Skills
- Integrity
- Enthusiasm and "Can Do" Attitude
- Empathy and Compassion
- Competence
- Ability to Delegate
- Composure
- Team-Building Skills
- Problem-Solving Skills

MY TOP 10 PROJECT MANAGEMENT "RULES OF THUMB"

Over the course of my career I have recognized several Project/Program Management "Rules of Thumb" that I embrace and have espoused to those who work for me. Below is a summary. I believe that they fully support the intent of Strategic Project Management and when applied appropriately enable Achievement of Epic Business Results.

Set Aggressive Targets

Working to Aggressive Targets to meet Project commitments can be extremely powerful if the Management Team can cope with the concept and not become tempted to "use it as a club".

"Parkinson's Law" Supports Setting Aggressive Targets. Parkinson's Law states that "effort expands to meet the time allotted". What this means is; if you set a future "target date" to complete a specific task, you are unlikely (due to basic human behavior) to complete the task any earlier. Thus, odds are that you either meet the date or exceed it. This certainly applies to "target budgets" as well.

Organizational Recognition of Aggressive Targets versus Commitments. The problem associated with working to aggressive targets is that it tends to drive managers crazy – "Did we leave something on the table?". The desire to be successful tends to get the best of us at times, and as a result, indirectly causes us (the people doing the work) to be more conservative in establishing commitments. Why put an overly aggressive target on the table if it is only going to come back to bite us as a firm commitment? You (the people doing the work) might do this once, but that is a Lesson Learned that typically leaves a lasting impression. If an organization finds itself behind its competition, the managers should consider honestly self-assessing how they subvert themselves by putting the workforce in a potential "no-win" situation. Again, working to aggressive targets to meet commitments can be extremely powerful if organizational behavior can be controlled and enable it.

Here is an idea to consider. Why not get strategic? Use Integrated Master Schedules with Schedule Risk Analysis tools to establish commitments with reasonable "percent confidence" (refer to Chapter 4: Managing Risks). Use the nominal CP (Critical Path) task durations as the "targets". Nobody should object to that. Given the relatively low "percent confidence" (% Confidence) of those estimates on risky Projects (something that most people do not realize), the Project Team is not likely to meet them, but it will essentially ensure a much better chance that the commitments (set at higher % Confidence) will be made. Skeptics might push back because of the "optics" of having "Buffer" in the schedule (i.e. the time difference between a high % Confidence [>50%] and the nominal CP [<20%]), so start by setting a commitment date deadline and work the nominal schedule back by identifying the key Individual Project Task Risks and proactively attempt to mitigate them. Keep doing this until you have an acceptable/achievable % Confidence in meeting the requested deadline. As a result you end up with a good, "balanced" Project Plan that all Project Stakeholders should be okay with.

Be an Effective Problem-Solver

In Chapter 5 (Cost of Change) we discuss the logic behind the fact that expedient decision-making on Corrective Action Plans or Workarounds enable us to minimize Project Costs (e.g. Actual Costs, Schedule, Quality, etc.). To get to these decisions, we must be able to efficiently and effectively problem-solve. This does not mean that PMs need to know everything, but they should know who to consult with who does, and how to manage the effort.

> <u>Know the Tools & Techniques</u>. It behooves us to use the "best" Tools & Techniques available to tackle important Project issues as they surface. To know if your Project Team is using the "right" methodology to solve a problem, there should be at least one person within the organization who understands the most beneficial options to choose from, and if you cannot fine one you might want to consider hiring an SME to consult. Sometimes we know this from experience. Other times we must evaluate options and decide. Bottom-line, if you do not know the "right" approach, find someone who does (or should) – do not "wing it".

> <u>Frame the Problem</u>. Sometimes the problem-solving methodology or approach is obvious if we have the right data and facts at our disposal. The Problem Statement is important to get right.

> <u>Do not Over-Analyze to Seek the "Perfect" Solution</u>. When we are in "the heat of battle" we do not always have the time and resources to determine the "optimal" path forward. Be prudent – with a decision that is rational and justifiable. We cannot be perfect all the time, but we can be prudent, and should be.

Negotiate Diligently and with Integrity

After taking my first "Negotiations" Training class it finally dawned on me that my job as a PM was an endless series of negotiations. The most important take-away from that training, however, was that "information is king", and that I needed to do my homework on everything that was potentially debatable. Facts are our "friends", and we should understand all that we can before taking a stance and defending a position.

> <u>Challenge Plans and Estimates</u>. PMs should put themselves in the Project Sponsor's shoes and challenge estimates from others as the

Sponsor would. This accomplishes three goals: (1) helps with understanding the inputs better; (2) validates whether the estimates are rational and well supported; and (3) enables you to be better prepared to appropriately communicate the recommended plan to others for approval.

Respect Functional Subject Matter Expertise. There is a tendency for us to sometimes discount the value of others who are Organizational Experts in certain areas that we are very knowledgeable about ourselves. I was a System Engineer, and thus liked to show off how much I knew until I found myself having to be involved in too many of the details, and I had to realize that my role was PM, not System Engineering Lead. I found that I was much better off if I respected the expertise of all others who I worked with. This takes work off my plate, makes me more likeable, and I found that people who are appreciated tend to do a better job.

Gain Buy-in. Buy-in does not necessarily mean consensus – a consensus is good, but is not always achievable, especially if dissenting Stakeholders are held to success criteria that conflict with one another – a situation that can become common-place in Matrix Organizations. One of the primary jobs of the PM is to ensure that the Project Objectives are met, and that trade-off decisions are aligned with Project Priorities and Stakeholders expectations. There will be times when someone is unsatisfied, but regardless, it is up to the PM to get everyone "on-board" to support the final decision.

Understand All the Facts. I found that doing my "homework" was never fun, but I learned to appreciate it when I was promoted into my first major PM role. The contract negotiation process included first negotiating my Project Team's position with the internal Executive Team, then developing an acceptable "customer negotiation strategy", and finally negotiating my company's position with the customer. During this experience I was introduced to "bridging" Bottom-up estimates with "Analogous" estimates to get the plan approved

Internally – basically developing two complementary assessments. As a result, I also had a more defendable BOE (Basis of Estimate) to negotiate with the customer.

Re-Balance the Plan when Necessary. The worst situation as a PM is the one where you steadily show that the Project is "on-track", and eventually must divulge that Project Deliverables are jeopardized due to the realization of an issue that spawned from a major Risk Item that was absorbed to accommodate a late Product Requirement change. This is more common than one might think, and it is due to absorbing too much risk while not realizing or appropriately recognizing it. Most instances I have witnessed arose due to lack of Risk Management Governance guidelines (refer to Chapter 4: Managing Risks), yet the PM and Team are the usual targets of blame. I cannot overstate enough the importance of establishing Risk Tolerance Thresholds which prompt an appropriate Project Re-Balancing (refer to Chapter 6: Maintaining a Balanced Plan) as early as possible to mitigate the "Cost of Change" (Chapter 5) and improve both Project Team performance and morale.

Pre-review with Key Stakeholders. I found out the hard way that pre-reviews with my internal Stakeholders was always worthwhile, and that it is never acceptable to surprise your own Management in a public forum. It is never comfortable providing a recommendation to the external customer (at a major review) that is not even supported by your own management. Fortunately, I survived this experience, but I have seen others who were less fortunate than me.

Do not Lie. I have known people who overtly lied to get their way when negotiating – they thought it was fair and justified. I have always had a personal Integrity issue with this. A good negotiator once informed me that he was effective because he had Integrity, and everyone knew it. He would not lie. He would also be very careful on what he did or did not divulge, however. That was some of the best advice I ever received.

Take Away Everyone's Excuses

After giving a brief Program update as the Spotlight Speaker (warming up the crowd for the featured Keynote Speaker) at an NMA (National Management Association) meeting many years ago, I took a couple questions at the end, and had to take one from the person at the head table in front of me – the President of our division. He asked me if I could summarize my job in a single sentence. After thinking (and sweating) for a moment, I answered "I continually strive to take away everyone's excuses". Fortunately, he liked my answer. The fact is, I still like that answer, and believe it is important to address here.

Evaluate what can Prevent Performance Achievement. This is basically one of the first steps in Project Risk Management – i.e. Risk Identification and Assessment. If your Project Team performs Risk Management well, you can bolster chances of success. Some refer to this as "performing a premortem" (i.e. a managerial strategy in which a project team imagines that a project or organization has failed, and then works backwards to determine what potentially could lead to the failure of the project or organization. [Wikipedia, 2018])

Make Assumptions to take Away Individual Risks. I found that as a PM, I could break down barriers to success by accepting documented assumptions from estimators. This is particularly effective when considering trade-off options. For example, I once asked a Project Lead to tell me what was driving a future task completion date so much. I was told that he added some time to resolve the usual "completion definition" issues from the group he was dependent on. I got the two Leads together to decide up-front "what constituted completion" of that predecessor task. He then agreed to take that extra issue-resolution time out of his estimate by documenting the assumption that I would ensure that the agreed-to definition was adhered to. So, it was essentially on me, as PM, to eliminate that risk – and I did it with pleasure.

<u>Make Changes Early – Reduce the Cost of Change</u>. Sometimes, if you have a risk that is almost a certainty (i.e. very high likelihood) yet has a relatively low impact to the Project if it materializes, you can make a change early to avoid the likely "Cost of Change" later. For example, if you are counting on a very busy test facility to be available when needed, but the owner will not commit to that open-ended requirement, you might be able to provide a financial incentive to gain the commitment. Thus, you absorbed a relatively small added Project Cost but prevented a schedule delay. This is akin to establishing an insurance policy by paying a premium.

<u>Make Justifiable Decisions that Hold up to Due-Diligence Scrutinization</u>. One of the nerve-racking meetings I ever took part in was one that re-enforced this decision-making concept in a major way. I was a PM of a large, strategically important Advanced Development Program administered by the US Army. Out of the blue, months into the contract, I was called by an executive at the company, asked a couple cryptic questions, then was requested to attend a meeting the next morning with the Division President and his staff to explain how I down-selected a subcontracted effort that was bid on by two competing companies who offered different technological solutions. Apparently, unbeknownst to me, the losing bidder announced publicly that they were considering suing the government (for purportedly having a perceived bias against their technology), and our Executive Team was concerned that we would be sued as well. My team's Subcontracts Administrator's boss assumed we were in trouble and "spooled up" the President and his staff. The evening before this meeting took place, I happened to receive a letter from the losing bidder stating that they appreciated the way our company handled the situation (i.e. the fair bidding and assessment process, as well as the out-briefing and adherence to contract Evaluation Criteria as directed by the Government Agency) and did not want us to read the news and get alarmed, for they had no intention of suing our firm. When I tried conveying this to the Subcontracts Manager, I did not get a return call

(no text messaging in those days), so after showing this letter to the Executive Team they were relieved, but also a bit concerned about the Subcontracts Manager's judgment. Bottom line, I understood my organization's potential exposure and took all the necessary actions to protect the company by following a squeaky-clean down-selection process, which was diligent and ultimately praised.

Team-Building through Selflessness

PMs who are good "team-builders" tend to be good organizers and communicators and are a bit selfless. I believe that selflessness is the most difficult trait to exhibit but is one that tends to attract people and engender loyalty. People who possess this trait have the innate ability to veer away from the natural tendencies driven by human nature and self-preservation. These individuals typically have a degree of self-confidence that is very noticeable, and they also tend to lead-by-example.

Different Teams need to be Managed Differently. I have discovered that as a PM I had to act like a "Player-Coach" and had to be the most versatile individual on the team. Player-Coaches are less common today in organized sports but are very common in local recreational leagues. As an avid sports enthusiast (and athlete-of-old) I tend to equate the dynamics of Business Teams to Sports Teams. I believe that this is what attracted me to Project Management. From playing team sports I recognized that since the make-up of every team is typically different, those teams that were most successful where usually led (or coached) by individuals who could objectively recognize strengths and weaknesses of other individuals and formulate a "game-plan" which comprehends the individuals' talents in a way that exploits their strengths and appropriately compensates for their weaknesses. As a "Player-Coach" you are actively involved, and if versatile enough, can find ways to morph the way you play in a way which enables the team to put its best foot forward most of the time. I believe the same is true for versatile PMs. You have to be more concerned about team performance than personal recognition.

One of the best experiences of my career came when I was assigned as one of the four Senior Directors picked to run one of the four highest priority "make-or-break" Product Development efforts in the company. To survive in our highly-competitive marketplace, the Executive Team decided to cancel all other Projects and focus the entire organization on the top four. The four of us had to negotiate for which Project to manage and for the key individuals that we wanted on our teams. I decided to let the other three "duke it out" and I would take what was left. My boss initially thought I was being passive-aggressive and disgruntle, but I assured him that I was not. I was assigned my Project (got the one nobody else wanted) and after the other three Project Managers chose their key Team Leads, I went to each of the Department Heads (i.e. Functional Managers) and asked them to identify the remaining individuals in their groups who they believed had the highest potential (i.e. had the most "fire in their belly") and to assign them to my team as Leads. I promised to mentor them and asked the managers to act as "back-stops". They agreed, thus these Functional Managers became, by default, part of my team as well. Bottom line, our team performed so well it was given a rare Performance Excellence Award, for we ended up launching a Product (which everyone considered the biggest potential Loser) that ended up becoming one of the most successful Strategic Products for our company. What a "Team-Building" experience!

Giving Credit and Taking Blame. Taking blame when things go wrong and giving the credit to others when things go well is truly selfless behavior. The human tendency is to deflect blame and take credit. It is obvious (at least to me) as to whom I would prefer to work for. And leaders who engender loyalty can usually get a lot more done than those who do not.

<u>Servant Leadership</u>. What can I do to help? PMs who ask this question and are sincere about it, are exhibiting Servant Leadership. This is what "Team-Building" is all about, and when you are willing to help Team Members succeed, they typically appreciate it and endeavor to show thanks through their performance.

Mentor and Train Team Members

I have seen PMs get incredibly frustrated with Team Members who were ill-prepared to perform their jobs at peak levels. Leaders, in general, would prefer all "A Players" on their teams. Unfortunately, this is rare and not practical in most large companies/organizations. This is where training and mentoring come into play.

<u>Be a Trainer</u>. When I was a Program Manager, I found myself constantly wanting to train Team Members on how to use Tools & Techniques which could improve our chances of success. In those days, even if a PMO existed, the PMs were either directed (per contract) to use certain Management Tools & Techniques and/or given the latitude to use the methodologies they chose (or were most comfortable with using) – not much Organizational Governance, per se. I typically opted for the most effective, thus the most complex tools. So, I would usually take it upon myself to train my Team Members and ensure that we were all well prepared and capable of using those Tools & Techniques. As head of a PMO, I would require certain PM Tools & Techniques to be employed by all the Project Teams and would normally have to administer the requisite training myself. This always proved to be worthwhile.

<u>Be a Mentor</u>. I tend to hire PMs that are coachable and are interested in mentoring others. This type of individual tends to have a good attitude (which I appreciate) and can make a good Promotional Prospect. Although I do believe that one can mentor in group environments, I tend to prefer doing so one-on-one behind closed doors. Mentoring, from my standpoint, makes Performance Reviews obsolete. To be effective, I believe it needs to be more of a mutually

agreed to journey, than an event. My experience is that mentoring takes patience, developing a good report with one another, establishing trust, being observant, being a good listener, and realizing that you cannot solve every issue right away.

Start with a Sense of Urgency

One of the most detrimental attitudes a PM can assume early in the Project Life Cycle is to think that there is plenty of time to make up for a slow start. It is not uncommon to see a spending chart that shows less is being spent than was planned at the onset of a Project. This could be due to several reasons, but the primary culprit that I have seen is slower than planned resource assignments to the Project by Functional Managers within the organization. Making up for lost ground early in the Project Life Cycle can become a never-ending ordeal and should be avoided. I am thus a firm believer that PMs should start their Projects with a "Sense of Urgency" to avoid getting behind, and instead, try to gain as much of a "cushion" as possible.

Do not get Behind due to Resource Issues. I spent the early part of my PM career working in a large Matrix Organization and discovered that I needed to spend at least 25% of my time coordinating and negotiating Resource Assignments at the start of every Project. This required developing a good report with the Functional Managers, setting up the Project's Cost Control Matrix to ensure organizational accountability, and never taking "no" for an answer (PMs should be selfish when it comes to resource allocation – and should never worry about these types of conflicts getting escalated). As a manager of Project Managers, I would always inspect the early "Spend-Rate" data. Getting behind does not look so bad until you construct a "catch-up" chart that shows a near-impossible ramp-up of resources to get back on track.

Coordinate the Staging Activities. Never take Project "Receivables" for granite. Receivables, in this context, are items or actions that other entities deliver to your Project, and which your Project is dependent upon to be successful. Some organizations establish "Technology Staging" or R&D (Research and Development) teams to work on Basic Technology which enables future, more competitive Products. These Deliverables, or under-lying Project Requirements that are expected to be fulfilled by others (people or entities outside the direct control of the PM needing them), are not necessarily managed as tightly as the more directly controlled Product development activities which they are slated to support or enable. As a customer of these inputs, it behooves you (as a PM) to actively coordinating their delivery.

Do not Forget the Supply Base. I have a basic tenet that I have learned to follow relative to out-sourced "Receivables" – you cannot micro-manage suppliers too much. This is a bit of an exaggeration, but it does connote an important message. I have observed a basic pattern throughout my career (one that I followed as well, until I was "burned" by it) – to assume that suppliers will always deliver as expected. The problem with this is that suppliers have their own internal priorities, and thus, cannot be as easily controlled as internal resources, without direct high-level intervention at times. Being proactive by insisting on interim milestones and some oversight latitude is a good way of keeping the "Cost of Change" down and minimizing the need for high-level intervention. Furthermore, you might be inclined to blame a supplier for a Project misstep or issue, but most executives frown upon this lack of accountability by a PM. So, do not learn this lesson the hard way – like I once did.

Cheerlead

This might sound a little odd, but it is completely warranted and advisable for PMs to "cheerlead". The Project Manager should act like a CEO of a Start-Up Company seeking funding. Having been in the Start-Up world for a few years I noticed that investors tend to base their decision to invest, in part, on the passion exhibited by the leader. They typically insist on hearing directly from the CEO or Founder and believe that this person's passion is sometimes more important than the Product idea itself.

ACHIEVING EPIC BUSINESS RESULTS

Have a Good Positive "can-do" Attitude. A positive "can-do" attitude can be infectious. I find that leaders who are passionate, helpful, and positive can more effectively encourage/influence Team Members and promote the type of "team dynamic" that improves overall Project performance.

Focus on Positives First when Bringing up Negatives. I found that, especially when performing Performance Reviews, it is best to start with Positive Feedback and eventually get to the negative. When you start with the negative first, the recipient of the news typically has a tougher time being receptive to anything else, so get the Positive Feedback out first to ensure that it is appropriately received.

Discourage Negativism – an Organizational Virus. I would rather hire someone with a great attitude and less capability than to hire the most capable person who has a bad attitude. Obviously, getting both a highly capable person with great attitude as well, is preferable, but in my book, attitude is given a very high priority. Negative attitudes tend to put people off, which leads to less cooperation and potential internal strife – all leading to poorer overall team performance.

Never Complain without Offering a Viable Solution. I do not usually have many steadfast rules, but this is one – do not complain without offering up a solution. It is easy to complain, and warranted at times, but it is not productive unless you know of a better viable solution.

Walk Around. I do not remember precisely when I first heard about MBWA (Management by Walking Around), but I do know that it sat well with me and I have tried to make a habit of it. Its effects became more pronounced when people working in my organization would say "we've missed having you come by". It is that "human touch" which can make a profound impact and difference within an organization if done well. You know when it is not being done well when you hear that it is being referred to as a "bed check". Inadvertent or not, it is always advisable to do this in the middle of the work-day so that people are not feeling like they are being checked-in on, especially towards the end of the work-day or later.

People Buy Things from People They Like. I once had a boss who ran the Sales & Marketing Organization at the company I was at – I was the Business and Technology Planning Manager under him for a while. When I eventually left the company, he wrote me a great letter of recommendation (unsolicited) and offered me this one simple piece of advice that he had lived by – he said, "If you remember anything from your time working for me, remember this one phrase: that people buy things from people they like!" Obviously, I never did forget it, and have decided to duly pass it on. Cheerleaders are typically likeable, and that attribute has its benefits.

Realize that You are Always "On Stage"

The advice I pass on to everyone who is "career-oriented" is: "Be aware that you are always on stage!" Whether we believe it or not, when we are in a leadership position (and PMs are, by definition, leaders) our actions and words are always being observed and scrutinized. One of my biggest pieces of "scar tissue" came from verbally chastising (over the phone) a key Team Member on a Project I ran. In the heat of anger, I left this person a scathing phone message, which he duly forwarded to the organization's entire phone list. This was a wake-up call, for sure. It seems like every time I have faltered it came back and bit me. Over the course of my career I have taken several pro-active steps to keep my composure in-check and assume that nothing I do is ever truly private – so I tend to act accordingly and tend to pass this on to others for their benefit – from my mistakes.

Lead by Example – it is Noticed. Leading by example can be difficult at times, but I have found that it has (on most occasions) served me well. We cannot be perfect, but we can certainly endeavor to be good examples.

PMs are Always Being Watched – for Several Reasons. Good PMs are usually great potential candidates for other leadership positions. Managers and executives tend to watch them closely and inquire about them as a result. In addition, there is a tendency for co-workers to (unfortunately) get a bit jealous of others who do well, and savor opportunities to advertise when they fall from grace, even if it is just a minor fall. So, try not to give anyone that "ammunition" or opportunity.

Be Fair and Equitable. Inequity (the inconsistent treatment, recognition, compensation, etc. of people) can damage Organizational Effectiveness. I have seen attempts to disguise it – some attempts that work for a very long time – then get exposed for all to see – and ultimately lead to poor morale, organizational dysfunction and "mass exodus". This is never good. Leaders who are overtly inequitable (or appear to be) are not trusted. The "perception" of inequity tends to have just as much of a negative impact.

Be Harder on Yourself than on Others. I have always been hard on myself and thought that gave me a right to be hard on others. I finally accepted the fact that each of us is "wired" differently, and just because I was okay with being held to a very high standard (for it motivated me) this tact is not necessarily a good thing for others. One of my biggest regrets is that I was too hard on my son. He was so gifted I could not accept anything less from him than taking full advantage of those gifts. I finally realized the negative impact this had on him and our relationship. I ultimately learned to be less demanding. I believe that, since then, this realization did wonders for our relationship. Further, I believe this directly translates to relationships we have as leaders of others in the workplace, as well.

Over-Communicate

Over-communicating does not mean doing so haphazardly. The only time I have seen over-communication criticized was when there should not have been any communication on a specific topic due to its inappropriateness (e.g. Security Classification, Competitively Sensitive

Nature, Personal Information, unfounded Rumor, etc.). Highly educated workforces tend to need the rationale behind decisions that affect their jobs, and PMs are obligated to communicate this type of information well, as an essential part of their job.

What is the Vision? Why are we doing what we are being directed to do? How does it get us to the desired end-state? Articulating the vision behind the organization's strategy and distilling it down to our current jobs can give added purpose to those commissioned to complete the work. I know that I worked harder and with a greater "sense of purpose" (and clarity) when I understood the rationale behind what I was being asked to do. This led to greater productivity and a higher level of performance. Thus, a key reason why this leadership attribute is considered one of the most (if not, the most) important to possess.

Clear and Concise. Communicating concisely (i.e. with as much brevity as possible) and clearly (i.e. with no ambiguity or chance of being mis-interpreted) is almost an art. This seems more natural for some people, than others. However, communication skills can be acquired and should be overtly worked on by those aspiring to be in leadership positions. This is considered a very high-priority requirement for PMs. By doing so you can avoid a myriad of issues, excessive rework, and unnecessary problems.

Current, Accurate and Complete Status. Those three words (Current, Accurate and Complete) were drilled into my head when I worked as a PM in the Aerospace and Defense industry. I grew to appreciate them, but I have unfortunately seen Project Status Updates that missed the mark on one or more of these tenets. In most cases, where the "Complete" was "Incomplete", there were no set standards (by Organizational Governance) as to what constituted "Complete" – which has led to my assertion that the Project Status Update content and Ratings Definitions (e.g. Red, Yellow, Green) should be precisely spelled out and communicated by Organizational Leaders. Use of

Standardized Templates should also be considered (refer to Chapter 4: Managing Risks, and Chapter 6: Maintaining a Balanced Plan). Advise on how to deal with "Currency" of information is also provided in Chapter 6.

Document Communications. I am a firm believer in documenting information and decisions. Some people call this "covering" yourself, but I tend to think that it is important to have a record for future reference, nonetheless. I am not a believer of having "secret" records, for whatever we document should be openly shared and given an opportunity to be scrutinized by those with vested interests. I am also an advocate of making key Project Assumptions and Project Priorities very visible (e.g. front and center at all key Project reviews) for assumptions take away risks, and if not correct or appropriately bought-into, can become detrimental issues. This last point gets back to the objective of making necessary Project changes as soon as possible, per Chapter 4: Cost of Change – for determining that our assumptions were not truly "bought-into" until late in the Project Life Cycle can potentially lead to unrecoverable ramifications.

Avoid Engaging in "Side Deals". To explain what I mean by "Side Deals", here is an actual example:

> I once took over a sizable organization and was bombarded by requests from all my new key Direct Reports to meet and discuss issues. At the very first session I listened to an issue and that person's recommended solution. He asked if I agreed, and I told him that I would respect the team's decision if all Stakeholders agreed. Shortly thereafter one of the other Stakeholders came barreling into my office, complaining about the decision I had just made, which was conveyed by the person I had just met with. Apparently, he expressed my agreement (leaving out "if all Stakeholders agreed") as firm direction to the rest of the organization, and this spooled up the person who was most negatively impacted and in adamant disagreement with the

recommendation. Apparently, this was the normal Mode of Operation prior to my arrival – a culture of "Side Deals". I then assemble all my Direct Reports and made it very clear that I do not engage in "Side Deals" and that decisions I make must come directly from me, and nobody is authorized to speak on my behalf.

The above Scenario can exist at any level, and within any organization. The bottom-line is that it is up to the leader to shape the culture, and to not allow this type of destructive activity to perpetuate the organization.

LEADERSHIP AND **STRATEGIC PROJECT MANAGEMENT**

Most people understand that leadership capabilities have a direct impact on Organizational (and Project) performance. The Strategic Project Management approach espoused in this book steps back and takes the broadest perspective relative to ensuring that subordinate activities and employees are given the best chance to succeed. All the top 10 recognized leadership attributes are exemplified in the various "Rules of Thumb" that are presented. One of the most important messages is that to improve organizational performance (and especially, Project Management performance) Organizational Leaders should set the standards and provide both the example and processes that work most effectively. Do so, and your holistic Strategic Project Management practices should provide All employees with the greatest chance of being successful – and as a result, not only will your organization prosper in ACHIEVING EPIC BUSINESS RESULTS, your employees will as well!

Bests of Fortunes to You All!

Is Your Organization Managing Projects Strategically?

Take the test, or at least see how your organization stacks up. An inventory of the key Strategic Project Management concepts espoused by this book can be kept, Chapter by Chapter. There is no established reference of good or bad, but you can see where your organization currently is, and use this tool to monitor progress. Each question starts with the phrase: To what extent does your organization......

46. differentiate **PMs** (i.e. Project and Program Managers) via the establishment of different **Competency/Capability Levels?**

1	2	3	4	5
O	O	O	O	O
Never	Rarely	Sometimes	Most of the Time	Always

47. hire **Leaders** who exhibit the **Attributes** espoused by the consolidated assessment lists noted in this Chapter?

1	2	3	4	5
O	O	O	O	O
Never	Rarely	Sometimes	Most of the Time	Always

48. assign **PMs** who exhibit the **Attributes** that are consistent with those of **Good Leaders?**

1	2	3	4	5
O	O	O	O	O
Never	Rarely	Sometimes	Most of the Time	Always

49. encourage **PMs** who follow most of the Project Management **"Rules of Thumbs"** noted in this Chapter?

1	2	3	4	5
O	O	O	O	O
Never	Rarely	Sometimes	Most of the Time	Always

50. enable **Strategic Project Management** via **Holistic Organizational Leadership** practices?

1	2	3	4	5
O	O	O	O	O
Never	Rarely	Sometimes	Most of the Time	Always

REFERENCES

Abdication. (2018). *Wikipedia, the free encyclopedia.* Available online at https://en.wikipedia.org/wiki/Abdication

Agile Software Development. (2018, April). *Wikipedia, the free encyclopedia.* Available online at https://en.wikipedia.org/wiki/Agile_software_development

Barry, T. T. (2012, May). **Top 10 leadership qualities of a project manager**. *Project Times.* Retrieved from http://www.projecttimes.com/articles/top-10-leadership-qualities-of-a-project-manager.html

Best Practice. (n. d.). *Wikipedia, the free encyclopedia.* Available online at https://en.wikipedia.org/wiki/Best_practice

Crown Business. (2014). ***SCRUM (The Art of Doing Twice the Work in Half the Time)***. New York: Jeff Sutherland and J. J. Sutherland.

DCMA (Defense Contractor Management Agency). (2012, October). **14-Point Metric (Earned Value Management System [EVMS] Program Analysis Pamphlet [PAP] DCMA-EA PAM 200.1)**

Delegation. (2018, March*). Wikipedia, the free encyclopedia.* Available online at **https://en.wikipedia.org/wiki/Delegation**

Earned Schedule. *PMBOK*® *Guide* – Sixth Edition (PMI, 2019, p.233)

Epic. (2019, August)**.** *Merriam-Webster.* Available online at https://www.merriam-webster.com/dictionary/epic

Executive Velocity. (2013, May). **3 Leadership Benefits of Self-Reflection**. Beth Miller

Harvard Business Review. (1993, July-August). ***Building a Learning Organization***. David A. Garvin

Manifesto for Agile Software Development. (2014, February). Available online at https://agilemanifesto.org

Parkinson's Law. (2015, June). Available at http://www.fluent-time-management.com/parkinsones-law.html

Premortem. (2018, April). *Wikipedia, the free encyclopedia.* Available online at https://en.wikipedia.org/wiki/Pre-mortem

Project Management Institute. (2009). ***Practice Standard for Project Risk Management***. Newtown Square, PA: Author.

Project Management Institute. (20013a). ***Practice Standard for Program Management*** – Third Edition. Newtown Square, PA: Author.

Project Management Institute. (20013b). *A Guide to the Project Management Body of Knowledge PMBOK® Guide)* – Fifth Edition. Newtown Square, PA: Author.

Project Management Institute. (2016, April). *Risk Management: A Practical Implementation Approach*. Newtown Square, PA: Michael M. Bissonette.

Project Management Institute. (2017). *A Guide to the Project Management Body of Knowledge PMBOK® Guide)* – Sixth Edition. Newtown Square, PA: Author.

Research Policy. (1985). The New Product Learning Cycle – Vol. 14, No. 6., pp. 299, 309. Modesto A. Maidique and Billie Jo Zirger.

Risk. (2015, June). *Wikipedia, the free encyclopedia.* Available online at http://en.wikipedia.org/wiki/Risk

Scordo, C. (2012, October). **10 Things that make a good Project Manager Great**. *Recruiter.com.* Retrieved from https://www.recruiter.com/i/10-things-that-make-a-good-project-manager-great/

Strategic Management. (2018, February). *Wikipedia, the free encyclopedia.* Available online at https://en.wikipedia.org/wiki/Strategic,management

Todd Smith (2018, March). **"You can't improve what you don't measure"**. Retrieved from http://www.littlethingsmatter.com/blog/2010/08/23/You-Cant-Improve-What-you-Dont-Measure/

What is Six Sigma? (2016). *iSixSigma®.* Available online at http://www.isixsigma.com/new-to-six-sigma/getting-started/what-six-sigma/

www.ingramcontent.com/pod-product-compliance
Lightning Source LLC
Chambersburg PA
CBHW060418100426
42812CB00030B/3225/J